STITCHING OUR
STORIES TOGETHER

Stitching Our Stories Together

JOURNEYS INTO INDIGENOUS SOCIAL WORK

**Carrière, J. &
Richardson, C.,** *eds.*

University of Regina Press

Printed and bound in Canada. The text of this book is printed on 100% post-consumer recycled paper with earth-friendly vegetable-based inks.

Cover art: "Medicine Bags" by Trevor Hopkin, University of Regina
    Photographic Services
Cover design: Duncan Campbell, University of Regina Press
Interior layout design: John van der Woude, JVDW Designs
Copyeditor: Kelly Laycock
Proofreader: Rachel Taylor

Library and Archives Canada Cataloguing in Publication

Title: Stitching our stories together : journeys into Indigenous social work /
    Carrière, J. & Richardson, C., eds.
Names: Carrière, Jeannine, editor | Richardson, Catherine Lynn, 1962- editor
Identifiers: Canadiana (print) 20240457854 | Canadiana (ebook) 20240457870 |
    ISBN 9781779400581 (hardcover) | ISBN 9781779400574 (softcover) | ISBN
    9781779400598 (EPUB) | ISBN 9781779400604 (PDF)
Subjects: LCSH: Social work with Indigenous peoples—Research—Canada. | LCSH:
    Social service—Research—Canada. | LCSH: Graduate students—Canada.
Classification: LCC E78.C2 S78 2025 | DDC 362.8497/071—dc23

10 9 8 7 6 5 4 3 2 1

University of Regina Press, University of Regina
Regina, Saskatchewan, Canada, S4S 0A2
TEL: (306) 585-4758 FAX: (306) 585-4699
WEB: www.uofrpress.ca

U OF R PRESS

We acknowledge the support of the Canada Council for the Arts for our publishing program. We acknowledge the financial support of the Government of Canada. / Nous reconnaissons l'appui financier du gouvernement du Canada. This publication was made possible with support from Creative Saskatchewan's Book Publishing Production Grant Program.

Contents

⋇⋇⋇⋇⋇⋇⋇⋇⋇⋇⋇⋇⋇⋇⋇⋇⋇

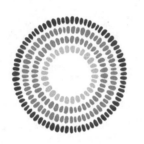

Acknowledgements

We dedicate this book to Indigenous gradudate students who may be contemplating, writing, defending, or struggling through their final stages of graduate work. We have been honoured to work with those who published in this book with us, and we applaud their contributions to their families and communities. We hope that the book inspires more Indigenous students who are dreaming about a graduate education and that you achieve this through your dedicated hard work and the support of those who love you. We have been on this journey ourselves, and we recognize its ongoing demands through many hills and valleys. We also dedicate this book to those who were denied the opportunity to pursue post-secondary education—the Missing and Murdered Women, Girls, and LGBTQ2S+ who were taken away too soon. We raise our hands to all Indigenous students who have overcome obstacles to come this far, and those in the process of overcoming. Education doesn't solve everything, but it can open spaces for new dreams and possibilities. All our relations!

Introduction

Catherine Richardson and Jeannine Carrière

⁂

This volume is entitled *Stitching Our Stories Together: A Collection of Indigenous Graduate Research Journeys*. Like many Indigenous writers and researchers before us, we have chosen to work with a metaphor that resonates culturally. As Métis, both editors—Sokhi Aski Esquao (Jeannine Carrière) and Kineweskwêw (Catherine Richardson)—have had relatives who were proficient with a cloth, needle, and thread. Some of their handiwork was created before Mr. Singer presented our communities with the classic black sewing machine with the whirring foot pedal. Those ancestral hands have brought into being jackets, winter coats, fur-lined moccasins, mitts, and whatever else was needed for warmth and survivance (Farrell Racette et al., 2021; Vizenor, 2008). My (Catherine's) grandmother Evelyn even made little dresses from flour sacks for her daughters when they were living on a trapline. Our ancestors even adorned dogs and horses in beautiful, intricately beaded vests.

Métis have stitched together blankets, quilts, fishing nets, and clothing as well as mended relationships and kept families on track. Jeannine has a story about one of her mothers. As an adoptee, she was blessed with two moms. She writes:

> Hmmm, well my adopted mother, who we eventually discovered was
> Métis, lined up her kids and grandkids to make quilts on a sort of "family

assembly line." She would ask everyone to do their part, ranging from choosing the fabrics that sort of matched (I *loved* that part), to putting them together in a pattern. She would get us all to help with the stitching, telling stories all the while. She also made braided rugs, with a similar process using her "lineup" of helpers. Even my dad was involved in that as he could braid tighter than anyone. Stitching was only one part of the process, but it was the part that held everything together.

There is another expression that relates to being with family, around the kitchen table—kiyokêwin (visiting) (Vowel & Swain, 2020). When we laugh together, we feel better, more grounded and connected to our loved ones. Related to the title, being in stitches refers to this kind of laughter and elation. The editors remember being overtaken by spontaneous and intense laughter, including after completing a successful four-day ceremonial gathering. The ceremony elicited a range of emotions, courage, compassion, and directed prayers for our people and for "Aski"—Mother Earth. In an experience of bliss, our group laughed their way home, often uncontrollably, elated with the joy of being in community and experiencing the blessings of ceremony.

In addition to stitches as laughter, stitches are also said to have preemptive value. The cautionary adage goes "a stitch in time saves nine," and points to the anticipatory act of avoiding future catastrophe. As editors, we believe this book serves that kind of function: by supporting and showcasing Indigenous research and newer Indigenous researchers, we are anticipating a future where Indigenous knowledge and methodologies take their place in the academies of higher learning and beyond, across these lands where Indigenous ways of being and knowing once composed the totality of local knowledges. This book may serve as inspiration for those Indigenous undergrads who are contemplating entering a post-graduate program and seeing some of the possibilities offered by Indigenous research.

Between its covers, this volume encompasses teaching and experience from Métis scholars emerging from areas known as Alberta, Saskatchewan, and Manitoba, and some with a current starting point in British Columbia. Knowledge is included from the Kwakwaka'wakw of the We Wai Kai

Nation of Cape Mudge and from the Tatanka Najin (Standing Buffalo Dakota Nation). Much of the writing for this introduction took place on the unceded lands of the ləkʷəŋən territories and the Kanien'kehá:ka in Tiohtià:ke/Montreal. Indigenous knowledge creation offers one way of pushing back against settler ideas, and myths around pan-Indigeneity, as we highlight our own nations, communities, and individual realities.

The authors have created space for sharing Two-Spirit and LGBTQ2S+ experiences. In this volume, mel lefebvre has dedicated attention to Two-Spirit experiences and the creation of spaces where various forms of artistic and cultural expression create safety and possibility for our dear Two-Spirit kin. In one of our earlier books, *Calling Our Families Home*, we conclude with a letter by Kiwetinohk Kisik (trish pal). In their chapter entitled "Li nom di noor ka pawaachikayt (Dreaming Bear Man)," from one of our earlier books, *Speaking the Wisdom of Our Time*, Alberta Beck encourages us to share what we have learned from Two-Spirit people. Alberta also nudges us to remember that making simple changes, such as acknowledging someone's chosen pronouns, is not difficult. Our reticence comes from deep-seated heteropatriarchy rather than a lack of flexible intelligence. We are all capable of re-learning and adapting to new contexts. The inclusion of hitherto excluded groups relates to the research position "Nothing about us without us" (Wolff & Hums, 2017). For decades academics have been writing about "Indigenous communities" while overlooking some community members who have been erased through non-dominant narratives and heteropatriarchal religions.

Trish, along with authors and thinkers such as Leanne Betasamosake Simpson, Sarah Hunt, Kim Tallbear, Alberta Beck, and Riel Dupuis-Rossi, reminds us that our gender nonbinary kin have been with us forever, alongside various forms of love relationships (Hunt & Holmes, 2015; Simpson, 2013; Wilbur & Keene, 2019). Much of that knowledge was attacked by the Church (or churches), which promoted patriarchy, forced cisnormativity, and even committed punitive violence against women and gender nonconforming folk. Religions, which tended to focus on social control, held a problematic view that oppressed people are easier to manipulate and control; Christianity in the Indigenous world has been one of the greatest re-socialization projects (Bradford & Horton, 2017; Foran, 2017). Many Indigi-folks today are reclaiming the Indigenous spiritual practices of their people (Kim-Craig, 2023). However, perhaps initially as an act of survival, many Indigenous people today continue to identify as Christian (Kim-Craig, 2023). Today, people have more choice in regard to their spiritual practices; some integrate aspects of many teachings in ways similar to the syncretic religions of South America, combining both Indigenous and Christian beliefs and rituals.

As this introduction was being created, twenty-five Indigenous delegates from various Indigenous nations were preparing for a meeting with the Pope, in Rome, to discuss the violent realities of "residential schools"[1] (Malone, 2021). Hopefully, there was acknowledgement of the harm that was done to Two-Spirit and gender nonconforming children, as well as cisgender children, by representatives of the Catholic church. We hope that this book is being launched into a time of great healing for Indigenous people, and that the words offered here may contribute to that momentum.

In the midst of ongoing colonizing practices in Canada, we look for signs of light. The Canadian government's appointment of Inuk Mary Simon as governor general of Canada is worthy of celebration, although it, sadly, follows on the heels of Nunavut member of Parliament Mumilaaq Qaqqaq's resignation in protest of racism in government (CBC Radio, 2021). In her exit speech, she writes "I have never felt safe!" and "outs" parliamentary security as racist in their harassment of her in parliamentary buildings (APTN News, 2021). Activist and educator Vikki Reynolds reminds us that we cannot move ahead as a country until we address these inequalities and injustices that continue to happen for Indigenous people on a daily basis. Vikki writes:

> We are all in a dirty bathtub (of social injustice) together. We can't have just relationships together until we address oppressions and inequalities. (Reynolds, personal communication, November 24, 2021)

---

1 Despite this euphemistic name, these institutions could more appropriately be referred to as prison camps for Indigenous children.

This is part of the commitment of Canadians who choose to engage with the Truth and Reconciliation Commission's Calls to Action. Of course, it is important to mention, for those who take the mutualizing metaphor of "reconciliation" seriously, Indigenous people are not the ones dirtying the water. We have nothing to apologize for to the settler community and our "push back" or reluctance to participate must be seen as an act of resistance, not violence or "reverse racism." We continue to struggle for cultural and personal survival.

However, Indigenous people do take on a large role of keeping the water clean and calling in/out those who would see it contaminated (Richardson, 2021). The Indigenous relationship to the lands and waters acknowledges our energetic connectedness to every aspect of the living world through the life force that we share. We acknowledge that we are related to all living beings, including the elements of water, air, fire, and earth, to our other-than-human kin (or more-than-human kin). These teachings of relationality have informed the water carriers and land defenders, acknowledging our responsibility for taking care of the land knowing that the land takes care of us. Teachings tell of prophecies serving as cautionary tales, reminding us to leave things as they are: don't pull uranium from the earth, waters aren't for sale. We know, in theory, to respect the Body of Mother Earth. Many of us try to do that, every day, in our earth walk—others not at all. We live in tension regarding human needs, desires, and the pressure we put on Mother Earth. We remind ourselves to turn to our teachings and relational ethics, and community conversations, about how best to mitigate the human footprint and live respectfully with the natural world. We are a part of nature, but we, as humans, have more power than any other species for destruction, as well as for thoughtful action. We have the potential to use our strong minds to align with the greatest good and act as stewards of our own lands, waters, and air. Moving forward sometimes means letting go of past actions that did not serve us, such as destructive means we learned from being part of a colonial society.

Canada is not a revolutionary country. It is a nation borne from British and French imperialism, with a program of intense erasure of Indigenous life and colonial violence that propped up a Euro-settler society on unceded Indigenous lands (Davis et al., 2017; Richardson, 2021). Indigenous youth, young scholars, bring a new energy and a clarity around their rights and identities resonant with the slogan "Respect existence or expect resistance." These words are a protective call asking, or demanding, that Indigenous people and our lands be treated with respect.

This book is an example of an Indigenous-centred activity. These authors are revolutionary in their own way. They are helping to keep Indigenous knowledges alive in the face of capitalism and heteropatriarchy, merging traditional ways of knowing with current technology to inspire Indigenous futures that reach across the globe (Lewis et al., 2018). This is a big responsibility. However, we must remember there is no direction for Indigenous scholars other than forward. When we try to sit in mainstream spaces, we are marginalized. When we try to sit in Indigenous spaces, we are accused of being elitist or exclusionary, leaving behind the people in community and traditional teachings. Sage, sweetgrass, and dream catchers can be bought in any mainstream "alternative" new age or crystal shop, some made in China. It's as if our knowledges have been rubber-stamped for universal usage, as if we have given away copyright and provided a user's manual to reproduce our teachings. One of the drawbacks of living in a worldview that decries personal ownership and possession is that others think that "unowned" items are there for the taking. This applies to Indigenous lands, cultural traditions, and even to children. Today in Canada, Indigenous people hold only 626,000 square kilometres or 6.3 percent of Canada's landmass (Spence, 2024). Obviously, this low percentage of land holding is problematic, hence the rise of the #landback movement. A Haudenosaunee speaker recently said, on a panel at Concordia University, that she would respect land acknowledgements if each one was accompanied by the return of one acre to the local Indigenous community (Rematriation and Kahnistensera's Stewardship of the Land, May 22, 2024). There are still many public conversations to be had about what a fair and just redistribution of lands, between settler and Indigenous communities, might look like. The speaker pointed out that Indigenous communities need more land for their future children.

In relation to the issue of ongoing disproportionate and questionable removals of our children, and despite decades of child welfare research recommending policy change:

In Canada, 53.8% of children in foster care are Indigenous, but account for only 7.7% of the child population according to Census 2021. This means 14,970 out of 28,665 foster children in private homes under the age of 15 are Indigenous. (Indigenous Services Canada, n.d.)

Of course, this continues to be unacceptable. Separating mothers from children constitutes a genocidal policy designed to disrupt Indigenous communities and nations (National Inquiry into Missing and Murdered Indigenous Women and Girls [NIMMIWG], 2019). These violent acts constitute an attack on Indigenous nations that are often undermined in their efforts to build infrastructure and "know how" in relation to offering their own culturally informed safety planning for children needing love and care (Carrière, 2005, 2007, 2008; Carrière & Richardson, 2013, 2017; Montgomery et al., 2016; Sinclair, 2019). These removals often take place in a social service context where preventative supports are not offered to Indigenous families. We are told there is no money for that while there appears to be endless funding for foster placements. There is debate within Indigenous communities whether the child (and youth) protection systems should be changed or eliminated altogether. There has been some positive change recently in British Columbia, Canada, where child protection responsibilities have been handed back to delegated Indigenous agencies. While positive, this is just the first step in a long road to decolonizing family services.

While Indigenous realities evolve in many different directions, one unfortunate "spin off" is the issue of the "Pretendian." Recently, the question of "who is Indigenous" and the problems associated with self-definition have arisen to the forefront across institutions. Universities have been struggling with this question in relation to hiring and many prominent researchers and professionals have been exposed for falsifying an Indigenous identity. Tensions arise when establishing the criteria for Indigeneity and certain vulnerable citizens, such as Indigenous adoptees or disenfranchised individuals, do not meet established criteria due to forced disconnection from family and kin (Carrière, 2005, 2007). While these individuals explore their ancestry, they are situated alongside a movement of non-Indigenous people making Indigenous identity claims and seeking to benefit from resources designated for Indigenous communities (Leroux, Campbell & Belcourt podcast, 2022). And, although there can be identity questions related to colonialism's disruptive processes, these folks' identity questing can be complicated in the current context of outrage over those who falsely claim Indigenous identity (Podcast Maria Campbell; Leroux, 2022). These dynamics cause so much pain and confusion that we have not yet implemented processes for gently exploring these issues, with community supports and Elders in place for the "emotional holding" that needs to happen. Processes of exclusion weigh heavily on Métis people after decades of exclusion from the Canadian Indigenous "body politic" (Richardson, 2016). In *Belonging Métis* I (Catherine) lay out the findings of my doctoral research, which present issues of Métis exclusion and the suffering it caused due to colonial erasure and attacks on people who are seen as "mixed race" or "not Indigenous enough" (2016).

From a social work and counselling perspective, our main concern has always been to promote a sense of inclusion and belonging as a path to survivance (Carrière & Richardson, 2017). As Indigenous people, we have lost so many of our kin. Good social work practice is about keeping people alive, cared for, and part of our community. However, this is not the majority experience for Indigenous people involved with child welfare. Sadly, the quality of intervention does not seem to be improving on a national scale, despite decades of solid research advising on Indigenous-centred practice (Blackstock, 2009; Carrière, 2008; Carrière & Richardson, 2017; Montgomery et al., 2016; Sinclair, 2019; Sinclair et al., 2009). Racism and social exclusion are not merely academic topics: we need to put our energy and creativity into making this society liveable for our Indigenous kin. Research and writing, when accomplished with heart, with sound analysis, and with a spirit of love and care, can make all the difference in the world.[2]

These are trying times indeed. Therefore, the young and new Indigenous scholars and authors deserve to be acknowledged for their accomplishments.

---

2 On a number of occasions I have been contacted by people telling me that my writing made a big difference for them, particularly writings on Métis identity and response-based practice.

These accomplishments often come at a great cost. Spiritual and emotional pain of all sorts can be part of working one's way through academia. Managing home life, love life, community life and responsibilities, and the grief from the ever-present losses can be enormous. Yet, they move forward, with movements of the pen, the keyboard, the paintbrush, the tattoo needle, with or without child care, mightily focused while multitasking. They face the tasks of writing proposals, applying for funding, seeking quiet working places, moving through the waves of failure and success. We hope that this book is one expression of their success and their multi-faceted brilliance.

This book is divided into three sections. The introductory section is composed of this Introduction and then Chapter One on the topic of Supervision by Dr. Jeannine Carrière and Catherine Richardson. Then we enter a section entitled Embedding Child Welfare Research into Indigenous Methodologies.

In Chapter Two, entitled "Researching Culturally Informed Approaches: Supporting Indigenous Youth Aging Out of Ministry Care," you will meet Robert Mahikwa whose thesis topic and experiences as an Indigenous-identifying graduate student reflect a shared journey towards cultural and ancestral reconnection, healing, and re-alignment. Robert holds a Bachelor of Social Work degree and a Master of Indigenous Social Work degree from the University of Victoria, which is located on the traditional and sacred lands of the ləkʷəŋən, W̱SÁNEĆ, Songhees, and Esquimalt peoples. Robert teaches sessionally in the School of Social Work at the University of Victoria, as well as Indigenous Studies in the Centre for Indigenous Education and Community Connections at Camosun College. Indigenous research methodologies, Indigenous social work, and Indigenous mentorship are key areas of interest in Robert's scholarly works.

In Chapter Three you will meet Shelley LaFrance. Shelley is Métis on her father's side with Cree and French ancestry from St. Boniface of the Red River Métis. Her Cree grandmothers came from Green Lake. Her chapter is entitled "A Métis Grandmother's Knowledge: Stories of Grandmother's Teachings and Métis Child Welfare in British Columbia." Shelley's chapter is informed by her social work practice as well as her research. Through a blended approach of storytelling and autoethnography, she explores responses to the question "How can the lived experiences and teachings of a Métis grandmother and Métis women enhance social work practices for social workers and community members, as well as organizations and agencies that serve Métis children and families?"

In Chapter Four, you will meet Tanille Johnston, whose Bakwam name is Laqwalaogwa. She is Ligwilda'xw from the We Wai Kai Nation belonging to the Cape Mudge Indian Band on Quadra Island, which is off the coast of Vancouver Island near Campbell River. Tanille has been a social worker for over ten years and completed a Master of Social Work with an Indigenous specialization in December 2019. Her thesis focused on defining Fatherhood in Kwakwaka'wakw communities to encourage social workers to engage more frequently, and respectfully, with Fathers. Her chapter is entitled "An Inquiry into the Stories of Indigenous Fathers and Their Paths into Fatherhood: A Narrative Analysis Conducted with Kwakwaka'wakw Fathers." Tanille believes that children, and communities, can benefit from the protective factors potentially offered by men, also in terms of child raising. Tanille has committed her energies to offering culturally conscious home studies for Indigenous families in rural and remote communities on Vancouver Island, with the hope that more nurturing, Indigenous homes will be opened up to care for children in the system.

Section Two is entitled Arts-Based Knowledges and Practices. Here in Chapter Five you will meet mel lefebvre, who presents their work here in lower case as a political stance, as a step towards decolonizing. mel is a Two-Spirit (2S) Red River Métis, nêhiyaw, French, Irish traditional tattoo practitioner. They are a mother, community worker, artist, and PhD student at Concordia University in Montreal. mel's master's research creation podcast centres storytelling by urban Indigiqueers, trans, Two-Spirit people, and Indigenous women on their life journeys, collective care, and self-care. mel's chapter is entitled "centring stories by urban indigiqueers/trans/two-spirit people and indigenous women on practices of decolonization, collective care, and self-care." mel is an instructor in First Peoples Studies at Concordia University.

Chapter Six is written by Shawna Bowler, a member of Tatanka Najin (Standing Buffalo Dakota Nation) and an urban Indigenous woman who comes from Red River Métis and European ancestry. She has spent her life living and working as a social worker within urban Winnipeg, on the ancestral lands of the Treaty One Territory and in the heartland of the Métis people, where the waters are sourced from Shoal Lake 40 First Nation. She has also worked in rural and northern Manitoba, the traditional territory of the Cree, Dakota, Dene, Ojibway, and Oji-Cree First Nations, and the Métis Nation. Much of her social work practice has been spent accompanying women who have experienced gender-based violence. Shawna's beadwork practice is part of her arts-based research and social work practice, as well as an expression of healing, self-care, and resistance. Shawna's chapter is entitled "Stitching Ourselves Back Together: Urban Indigenous Women's Experience of Reconnecting with Identity through Beadwork." Shawna's beautiful beadwork in the traditional Métis floral patterns is highlighted on the cover of this book.

Chapter Seven is comprised of an essay by Juliet Mackie. Juliet is a member of the Métis Nation of British Columbia with Cree, Gwich'in, and English ancestry from the Cowichan Valley on Vancouver Island. She is a painter and beadwork artist with maternal roots in Fort Chipewyan and Red River. Juliet moved to Tiohtià:ke/Montreal in 2015 to pursue postsecondary education. She holds a BFA in painting and is currently a PhD student in the Individualized Program at Concordia University. Juliet's multidisciplinary research explores portraiture as a means of strengthening identity for Indigenous women. Her chapter is entitled "Reconstituting Indigenous Identities through Portraiture and Storytelling: Reclaiming Representation for Indigenous Women and Two-Spirit People." This leads us into Section Three of the book, Indigenous Bodies and Meaning Making, and Victoria May's chapter, Chapter Eight, which can be described both as arts-based and body-centred.

Victoria May is a Red River Métis (St. Boniface) who grew up in Prince Albert, Saskatchewan. Victoria is the great-granddaughter of two of the Métis men who fought against Lii Canadas, Jean-Baptiste Delorme, and Joseph Vermette. In April 1885, Joseph Vermette gave his life fighting for the Métis way of life and for land during the Battle of Fish Creek: he is buried at Batoche. In her research, Victoria seeks to revitalize the Michif language through dance and oral acquisition. Her chapter is entitled "Dancing My Way Home: Cultural Reclamation through the Embodiment of the Michif Language." Here, Victoria describes a "story gathering" through the creation of a performance with dance and music, carrying on her family's tradition of fighting for the vitality of Métis culture.

In Chapter Nine, "Researching through miyo ohpikinâwasowin (Good Child-Rearing): A Framework for Knowledge Emergence and Transmission," Lindsay DuPré describes herself as a Métis scholar, community organizer, mom, and auntie, who was born and raised in Ontario on Haudenosaunee, Anishinaabe, and Wendat territories with her Métis family originally from Red River in Manitoba. Her chapter stems from her PhD study in which she positions her research objectives as influenced heavily by her desire to protect the integrity of knowledge systems for her son and generations after him. She describes children as knowledge producers and bases some of her learning from a research framework that includes four key principles of miyo ohpikinâwasowin (good child-rearing): attentiveness, care, play, and balance. Lindsay states that "bringing my family into knowledge spaces with me—either physically or by reference—is an intentional epistemological, axiological, and methodological choice. It is an exercise of relational accountability."

This leads us into N. Katie Webb's chapter on body awareness and body positivity. In Chapter Ten, Webb's chapter "Fat Bodies in Space: Explorations of an Alternative Narrative" awaits the reader, offering ways to valorize the Indigenous. Here, Webb presents expansive reformulations of size with a critique of the western bio-medical model's limited and decontextualized understanding of corporality and body. They identify as a Two-Spirit person of Indigenous and settler ancestry and a second-generation adoption survivor. Webb brings lived experience to this work, along with a commitment to social justice work and a drive to address systemic inequity and racism within health, education, and social sectors. In this highly engaging chapter, Webb challenges society's "fear of fat."

Finally, we end with the Conclusion followed by a poem from award-winning Métis poet katherena vermette.

REFERENCES

APTN News. (2021, June 15). *Powerful speech delivered by NDP MP Mumilaaq Qaqqaq | APTN News.* Youtube. https://www.youtube.com/watch?v= -vQnzQIQn48

Blackstock, C. (2009). The occasional evil of angels: Learning from the experiences of Aboriginal people and social work. *First Peoples Child & Family Review,* 4(1), 28–37.

Bradford, T., & Horton, C. (2017). *Mixed blessings: Indigenous encounters with Christianity in Canada.* Vancouver: UBC Press.

Carrière, J. (2005). Connectedness and health for First Nation adoptees. *Paediatrics & Child Health,* 10(9), 545–548. https://doi.org/10.1093/pch/10.9.545

Carrière, J. (2007). Promising practice for maintaining identities in First Nation adoption. *First Peoples Child & Family Review,* 3(1), 46–64. https://doi. org/10.7202/1069526ar

Carrière, J. (2008). Maintaining identities: The soul work of adoption and Aboriginal children. *Pimatisiwin: A Journal of Aboriginal and Indigenous Community Health,* 6(1), 61–80.

Carrière, J., & Richardson, C. (2013). Relationship is everything: Holistic approaches to Aboriginal child and youth mental health. *First Peoples Child & Family Review,* 7(2), 8–26. https://doi.org/10.7202/1068837ar

Carrière, J., & Richardson, C. (2017). *Calling our families home: Métis peoples' experiences with child welfare.* Vernon: JCharlton Publishing.

CBC Radio. (2021, June 16). Nunavut MP Mumilaaq Qaqqaq on leaving politics, and why she feels no pride in Canada. *As It Happens.* Retrieved from https://www.cbc.ca/radio/asithappens/as-it-happens-the-wednesday-edition-1.6067864/nunavut-mp-mumilaaq-qaqqaq-on-leaving-politics-and-why-she-feels-no-pride-in-canada-1.6068158

Davis, L., Hiller, C., James, C., Lloyd, K., Nasca, T., & Taylor, S. (2017). Complicated pathways: Settler Canadians learning to re/frame themselves and their relationships with Indigenous peoples. *Settler Colonial Studies,* 7(4), 398–414. https://doi.org/10.1080/2201473X.2016.1243086

Farrell Racette, S., Kurd, N., & Miner, D. (2021). *Christi Belcourt.* Fredericton: Goose Lane Editions.

Foran, T. P. (2017). *Defining Métis: Catholic missionaries and the idea of civilization in Northwestern Saskatchewan 1845–1898.* Winnipeg: University of Manitoba Press.

Hunt, S., & Holmes, C. (2015). Everyday decolonization: Living a decolonizing queer politics. *Journal of Lesbian Studies,* 19(2), 154–172. https://doi.org/10.108 0/10894160.2015.970975

Indigenous Services Canada. (n.d). Indigenous children in foster care. Retrieved April 27, 2024, from https://www.sac-isc.gc.ca/eng/1541187352297/1541187392851

Kim-Cragg, D. A. (2023). "We take hold of the white man's worship with one hand, but with the other hand we hold fast our fathers' worship": The beginning of Indigenous Methodist Christianity and its expression in the *Christian Guardian*, Upper Canada circa 1829. *Religions*, 14(2), 139. https://doi.org/10.3390/rel14020139

Leroux, C., & Belcourt, C. (2022). Podcast. Youtube.

Lewis, J. E., Arista, N., Pechawis, A., & Kite, S. (2018). Making kin with the machines. *Journal of Design and Science: MIT Media Lab*. https://doi.org/10.21428/bfafd97b

Malone, K. G. (2021, November 10). Indigenous delegates to have private meeting with Pope Francis during Vatican visit. *CBC News*. Retrieved November 29, 2021, from https://www.cbc.ca/news/canada/manitoba/indigenous-delegates-to-meet-pope-in-vatican-1.6245309

Montgomery, H. M., Badery, D., Fuchs, D., & Kikulwe, D. (2016). *Transforming child welfare: Interdisciplinary practices, field education, and research*. Regina: University of Regina Press.

Morriseau-Beck, D. (2020). Li nom di noor ka pawaachikayt (Dreaming Bear Man) – A Métis Two-Spirit journey. In C. Richardson & J. Carrière (Eds.), *Speaking the wisdom of our times*. Vernon: JCharlton Publishing.

National Inquiry into Missing and Murdered Indigenous Women and Girls (Canada). (2019). *Reclaiming power and place: The final report of the National Inquiry into Missing and Murdered Indigenous Women and Girls*. https://www.mmiwg-ffada.ca/final-report/

Richardson, C. (2016). *Belonging Métis*. Vernon: JCharlton Publishing.

Richardson, C. (2021). *Facing the mountain: Indigenous healing in the shadow of colonialism*. Vernon: JCharlton Publishing.

Simpson, L. B. (2013). *Islands of decolonial love: Stories & songs*. Winnipeg: ARP Books.

Sinclair, R. (2019). Aboriginal social work education in Canada: Decolonizing pedagogy for the seventh generation. *First Peoples Child & Family Review*, 14(1), 9–21. https://doi.org/10.7202/1069584ar

Sinclair, R., Hart, M. A., & Bruyere, G. (Eds.). (2009). *Wícihitowin: Aboriginal Social Work in Canada*. Winnipeg: Fernwood Publishing.

Spence, W. (2024). What percent of Canadian land is Indigenous? NCESC Geographic. Retrieved April 29, 2024, from https://www.ncesc.com/geographic-faq/what-percent-of-canadian-land-is-indigenous/

Vizenor, G. (Ed.). (2008). *Survivance: Narratives of Native presence*. Lincoln: University of Nebraska Press.

Vowel, C., & Swain, M. (2020). Back 2 the land: 2Land 2Furious. *Briarpatch: The land back issue*, 49(5), 20–23. https://briarpatchmagazine.com/articles/view/back-2-the-land-2land-2furious

Wilbur, M., & Keene, A. (Hosts). (2019, March 19). Decolonizing sex (No. 5) [Audio podcast episode]. In *All My Relations Podcast*. https://www.allmyrelationspodcast.com/podcast/episode/468a0a6b/ep-5-decolonizing-sex

Wolff, E. A., & Hums, M. (2017, September 5). "Nothing about without us"—Mantra for a movement. Huffpost. https://www.huffpost.com/entry/nothing-about-us-without-us-mantra-for-a-movement_b_59aea450e4b0c50640cd61cf

Supervision and Mentoring
Beyond the Destination

Jeannine Carrière and Catherine Richardson

ABSTRACT

This chapter outlines some of the important concepts that we have come across in our journeys as academic supervisors for graduate students. The chapter speaks to our pedagogies and ways of being as Métis scholars placed in a position of passing on what we have learned while navigating the western academy. We have learned much from our students and describe this learning, the humility, and the gifts we have received as witnesses to graduate student progress and completion of their academic journeys. This completion, however, was not their only destination. We acknowledge how their research has given further insights to a topic and has also made their families and communities proud. For many, the research process has also given them strength to address other life journeys. In this chapter, we explore the differences between mentoring and supervision through an Indigenous lens, and we hope to pay homage to all Indigenous graduate students who are pouring through obscure literature, speaking to their relatives, and second-guessing themselves every step of the way. Graduate education is not for everyone and remains as the road less travelled for some. We hold up our hands to those who have taken this road and those who are still dreaming about it. **Keywords:** *Indigenous, Métis, supervision, mentoring, knowledge-building, ceremony, epistemology, connectedness*

✸✸✸✸✸✸✸✸✸ ✸✸✸✸✸✸

> *Engaging in decolonizing Indigenous research means that we focus on strengthening our own knowledges, rather than focusing our energy and the entirety of our efforts on dismantling colonial knowledge systems. (Hart, 2009)*

What is the difference between graduate student *supervision* and *mentoring*? Are they one and the same or are they differently nuanced by dynamics such as power, pedagogy, and the degree to which the student is upheld? In terms of approaches to learning, we know that these two processes differ based on the cultural context, whether Indigenous or European, for example. How are these concepts defined and described through an Indigenous pedagogical perspective? These are questions we asked ourselves as we were conducting research for this chapter and as we reflected upon our experiences as graduate-student supervisors at the Universities of Victoria, Montreal, and Concordia. In those contexts, we have supervised both Indigenous and non-Indigenous students in both an Indigenous-focused and a mainstream social work program.

I (Jeannine) have experienced that, in student supervision, after some time it is difficult to establish who is the teacher and who is the learner as I find these relationships enriching and informative no matter which role I'm in. For me, this emphasizes the importance of a strong committee member to help separate the forest from the trees as I have often stated to graduate students. I have had the privilege of being a Master of Social Work "supervisor" for several years now. In the most recent ones, I have been mentoring and co-supervising PhD students in various post-secondary institutions. Most of the students I have worked with are Indigenous, and this gives me great honour and joy. In the back of my mind, I often remember the words of Māori educator Graham Smith as

Jeannine Carrière, circa 1980. Courtesy of the author.

he aimed to get 1,000 Indigenous graduate students "across the line" and into Aotearoa/New Zealand's professional world where more Māori educators are needed (personal communication, 2016). Here in Canada, and on Turtle Island, we also experience a serious lack of Indigenous teachers, at all levels, as well as Indigenous professionals to guide a national decolonization process in education and the social services. These needed changes have been spelled out in Canada's Calls to Action of the Truth and Reconciliation Commission (TRC, 2015).

In reflecting on my questions, I set out to seek external information to guide me, as any academic might. I was torn between the title of supervisor and the title of mentor and, as such, returned to my teachings that stem from my grounding and location as a Métis woman. These ancestral connections guide my academic work on many levels, which I will delve into later in this chapter. For now, I wish to begin with the concepts of mentoring and supervision and how these are defined in western academic literature.

McLaughlin (2010) stated that an "academic mentor not only establishes a working relationship with a student, shepherding the student through the doctoral process to completion and preparing him or her to become a successful professional after graduation, but long after the student moves on, becomes a lifelong colleague and source of guidance" (p. 872). This definition resonates with me as I have experienced that many graduate students have stayed in touch with me throughout the years: I have had the pleasure of seeing their development and watching them take their place in the world as Indigenous scholars who often go on to continue their studies and scholarship. An interesting observation by Brian Uzzi is that "mentors who generally have the best records and the best reputation tend to attract students who have the most talent coming into the program to begin with" (Uzzi, quoted in Allen, 2020) and that there is a special "sauce" of ingredients where current research doesn't provide a full recipe, but offers a few hints. "First, it's clear that the best mentors pass on something that goes far beyond subject-matter expertise" (Allen, 2020).

This last sentence had me intrigued when I read it as it reflects how I am drawn to graduate students who are both addressing a subject that lies in my realm of expertise and with whom I can envision the contributions they will make to their families, Nations, and communities. My contribution as an Indigenous advisor involves creating that special sauce that encourages students to study topics that excite them within methodological approaches that resonate culturally while they also evolve and grow as a relative and role model to others. Culinary references aside, the role I can play in lifting up graduate students is truly the essence of how we use terminology such as "all my relations" in the work we do as graduate student supervisors/mentors. As I have learned from my esteemed colleague Kundoqk, the current director in the School of Social Work at the University of Victoria, it is important for us to ask *so what?* in our academic work. So what do Indigenous scholars have to say about the processes of supervision and mentoring?

The Native American and Indigenous Scholars Collaborative (NAISC) propose that, "For Native American and Indigenous students, the dilemmas and stress of 'walking in 2 worlds' are best mediated by role models and, if possible, mentors who understand both worldviews as well as expectations of content" (NAISC, n.d.). Having been a graduate student for several turns around the sun, I understand the academic experience while being an Indigenous person. This experience can feel like a walk on foreign land, and the imposter syndrome can be real. One can feel doubly troubled studying on one's traditional territory with the knowledge that it is both unceded and unrecognized. Indigenous students are typically aware of the importance of one's relationship to land, to place, to Mother Earth. The calls for responsibility and accountability extend past those to our academic committee and institutional policies.

How many times do Indigenous graduate students *and* their supervisors ask themselves how they managed to get to graduate education and research? The authors in the NAISC project further propose that activities such as spending additional time with mentees outside of class, mentoring them to prepare professional presentations on their work, and linking them to leadership activities are important components to being a graduate student supervisor. To me this reflects the rationale for this book. The messages in graduate research often sit in place on a library shelf or in a computer file, while they should be shared with the world at large. Indigenous research is meant to bring benefit to the world, and to Indigenous people and communities, at the very least. However, Indigenous knowledge has the power to do so much more than that. It can change hearts and minds and offer hope to the world's disconnected and suffering. It can offer *a way back* to culture, holism, and well-being.

Cajete (2021) reflects that "much of modern education imposes a preconceived psychological pattern of the right and wrong ways to do things" (p. 136). Further, he states that, for most of his career as an educator, he has held biases, of which he is aware, but uses his position "to invite the sharing of experiences and expertise," and to support joint actions such as combining Indigenous and western knowledges to advance the future of a new generation of educators (p. 137). As a graduate student supervisor who is not without bias, I find this admission inspiring. Every exchange with a student is a means to explore those biases and an opportunity for learning and growth. I don't have to agree with a student's analysis of a topic, but it is my responsibility to encourage the exploration of various ways to discuss their topics and to ensure they are clear in their discussion in order to educate others far more important than myself. Another bias is my foregrounding or prioritizing of Indigenous students and research. This requires shared ethical commitment on the part of departments because it moves resources away from the mainstream to the margins, a movement that faces some ideological opposition. The fact is that Indigenous mentors are needed for creating the platform, the cultural safety, and the cultural embeddedness for Indigenous research to flourish. Epistemologically, one enters another world when doing Indigenous research—a world rich in ideas and poor in financial resources and mainstream support. This kind of mentoring goes beyond intellectual engagement and touches on the realms of the emotional, the physical, the spiritual, and the social. For example, sometimes it involves holding ceremonies and accompanying students through episodes of grief and loss. For the student, this kind of care and attention can make the difference between success and failure.

In a discussion on the importance of having a supervisor/mentor, Nelson and Youngbull (2015) begin their article with a description of this role in a graduate student's life:

> As a freshman, everything was new to me especially transitioning to campus and college life. I remember being nervous and shy meeting my mentor for the first time. We quickly found out that we both were what some call "Heinz 57" Natives—representing multiple tribal affiliations! And that kind of broke the ice for us. But it wasn't anything she said in particular that made me feel comfortable—it was how she presented herself. She made me feel important. I felt as though she truly cared about my well-being and was committed to helping me be successful in my academic endeavors…which was surprising to me because we had just met. Her role in my life has grown to encompass mentor, friend, colleague, and most importantly, sister. We've become part of each other's family. Our lives are entertwined and I am truly blessed to have her as a source of leadership, guidance, and inspiration. (2015, p. 90)

I am not proposing that as a student supervisor we should aim to bond into life-long sisterhood or become "adopted kin" with all our students.

However, what strikes me about this quote is the care that her supervisor/ mentor had for her and that we can "supervise" graduate work with compassion and a worldview that sustains "all my relations" as I was taught by my own graduate supervisors. These were the folks I learned from who demonstrated respect for me as a person and a researcher and made suggestions while being clear and kind. They would check in with me if it seemed I had disappeared and offered encouragement during the dark times of trying to complete a project that felt like it had no ending. They modelled that approach for me, which in turn I have attempted to pass on to graduate students, some of whom are featured in this book. In my opinion I feel it is important to bring our humanity to this role. It is also important to recognize that academic supervision and mentoring also entails making a contribution to the student's family and community. When I get tired, I remember that Indigenous graduate research is a communal effort for the betterment of our Nations.

In the chapter "Métis Methodology" in our book *Calling Our Families Home: Métis Peoples' Experiences with Child Welfare* (2017), we wrote that as Métis/Indigenous researchers, we acknowledge that we are both insiders and outsiders in our research but even though we may work at a university, we remain located as part of our Indigenous families and communities. The notion of epistemological separateness is not possible. This means that, in alignment with our values, all things are connected, which makes it difficult to be overly removed and separate from the topic and people in our research.

The positioning of insider/outsider reflects a major epistemological shift in the field of research. This "interpretive turn" depicted a movement contesting the notion that objectivity and researcher separation from the studied subject and the social world is possible (Howe, 1998). What things mean came to hold importance over mere facts and the search for one truth. Increased subjectivity became possible, as the researcher became more aware and transparent about the influence and inevitability of their "presence" in the research—of the impossibility of remaining completing outside and changes or knowledges that were being created. As such, researchers were offered ethical possibilities of declaring biases, positionality as relevant for research "validity," and subjectivity in the study. For example, if we are studying poverty, and we come from poverty, it is helpful to acknowledge that our personal life experience informs the conceptualization of the topic in ways that are enhancing and contextualizing. In qualitative research, we don't impose or project personal experience over those of research participants, and over the informing literature, but we discuss "relationships" and how these data sources (e.g., stories, experiences, testimonies, publications) all inform each other. As a Métis researcher, I walk the balance between over-identifying with the experience of Métis research participants whilst being informed by Métis cultural knowledge.

In supporting our students to identify a topic and resources, we recognize that students begin a journey both personally and professionally where they search to implement a method that resonates with their values related to research. They also learn to recognize when philosophical ideas are compatible and whey they are not, related to basic assumptions and epistemological positions. Indigenous students are aware that colonial violence was embedded in much of the research on Indigenous Peoples in the past and take active steps to redress this history and ensure that research is ethical and beneficial. Their personal location reminds them to conduct themselves in certain ways, knowing they often represent their family and community. Some students choose to include Elders for ceremonial and spiritual guidance within their methodology. Some may include traditional practices such as berry picking, weaving, or storytelling to reflect further on their topic or how their topic will be addressed in a method that is conducive to Indigenous research. We have offered to sit in ceremony with students and participated in rituals that supported the process of receiving inspiration and creating a research study that reflects their aspirations and the standards of the growing Indigenous academy.

In the research process, we strive to implement checks and balances to promote accuracy and the appropriate representation and interpretation of human experience in context. For example, many Indigenous researchers employ a form of storytelling as a methodology. In such a case, we might articulate our own role as researcher as well as identifying the kinds of stories and themes that are personal and those which contain shared aspects or meta-stories that relate more generally to being Indigenous. We would identify the situational logic of the study within the realm of the broader context. One can identify a meta-story or backdrop of a person's life experience in which a unique and personal life experience can be captured, serving as context to the larger study and as a "case study" or "data" in itself. We identify stories or accounts as co-constructions of the teller and interviewer rather than mere observations or pure representations. Practices of descriptive accuracy help promote solid and rich knowledge creation. Self-knowledge and reflexivity are crucial aspects of the research process and can be documented through mapping, journaling, artistic endeavours, and writing about self-location.

In her ground-breaking book *Decolonizing Methodologies: Research and Indigenous Peoples*, Māori scholar Linda Tuhiwai Smith writes that "self-determination in a research agenda becomes more than a political goal. It becomes a goal of social justice which is expressed through and across a wide range of psychological, social, cultural and economic terrains" (1999, p. 116). Similarly, we believe that Indigenous research must relate to the aspirations and growth of communities. We believe that Indigenous research can inform programming, policy, and the decolonizing movement that is making momentary and sporadic gains in Canada. As research supervisors, we often ask ourselves, and our students, how we can follow ethical pathways in research that accurately reflect cultural teachings and historical knowledges while creating new paths forward in contemporary society? How can our research contribute to cultural survival and knowledge making from an Indigenous perspective?

CULTURAL SURVIVAL IN RESEARCH—
WHO ARE WE IN THIS RESEARCH *AS* CEREMONY

I (Cathy) was born and raised on the Coast Salish territory of Snuneymexw on Vancouver Island. My ancestry is Métis/Cree, Gwich'in, English, and Scandinavian. My relatives held lot 162 in the St. Andrews parish of the Red River Settlement. My mother is from Fort Chipewyan and my father is from northern England. I give thanks to the Coast Salish ancestors, Elders, and people for the life I have enjoyed on this beautiful land. As part of the Métis diaspora, my family has found refuge and safety on Vancouver Island while many Métis faced intense racism and persecution on the prairies. This history led me to the topic of my PhD dissertation: How is it that we survived culturally while living "underground" (e.g., hiding culture and remaining silent about our Native ancestry), and what role did stories play in our cultural survival as Métis? My goal is that research should always be liberatory. I will explain my process of working through various research questions, choices, and tensions that arose in my research in "Becoming Métis: The Relationship between the Sense of Métis Self and Cultural Stories."

Firstly, Métis research can be informed by a wide range of Métis scholars (Adams, 1995, 1997; Carrière, 2005; Lavallée, 2009; Logan, 2001; Richardson, 2004); poets (Arnott, 1995; Menard, 2002; Scofield, 1999); and biographers (Campbell, 1973; Cariou, 2002), who are important sources that may inform Métis research providing themes and historical context related to being Métis.

In our own reading and writing, both of us have explored relationality and interconnectedness in relation to children, culture, and colonialism (Carrière, 2005, 2007; Carrière & Richardson, 2009; Richardson, 2003, 2005, 2008; Richardson & Nelson, 2007; Richardson & Seaborn, 2009). With a similar reflexivity, we ask: How will we know if we stray from an ethical position in representing Métis knowledge, old and new, and the sacred lives of people represented in our research? How can we be sure that what we are offered by research participants remains true to initial meaning and is not exploited or misrepresented? Indigenous research chair Michael Hart cites Shawn Wilson in reminding us that "you are answerable to all your relations when you are doing research" (Wilson, cited in Hart, 2009, p. 158).

Doing research requires a strategy for operating in a number of worlds (Richardson, 2004, p. 71). For a Métis researcher using a Métis research style, this involves weaving ideas and theories together from Indigenous writers as well as drawing from western or European sources that are attuned to the goals of Indigenous research. Ideas can transcend their cultural origins and have a "meeting place," even though the epistemological origins are worlds apart. This is another aspect of congruency—that Métis methodology may draw from both Indigenous and western knowledges to create a "third space" or Métis design in cases where the ideas are epistemological allies.

SOUPS, STEWS, SAUCES, AND OTHER METHODOLOGICAL CONCOCTIONS

At one point I remember being reminded that it's fine to have an epistemological stew, just not a soup. The ingredients must "go together" in a way that makes sense. Philosophical/epistemological principles, like influences from different worldviews, may hold some congruence and work together in a helpful way. When we throw just anything in the pot, some things (e.g., epistemological and ontological ideas and assumptions) don't go together very well and the result is not effective. In my doctoral research, I had to return to the drawing board a few times. I would do more reading and try to identify the worldview and belief systems underlying the particular methodological approach.

One of the pronounced assumptions is whether something appears in its "essence" (phenomenology) or whether live situations and identities are "constructed" through living. These approaches are typically antithetical—they do not go together because they constitute fundamental opposites. Today, I try to get students to identify assumptions and what they mean before using them to form the conceptual or theoretical grounding for their study.

ETHICAL POSITIONING

As researchers, we may draw inspiration from one another. For example, Vikki Reynolds, academic, therapist, and activist, drew from Cathy Richardson's Métis methodology to create her own methodology based on her topic—solidarity. She writes:

> Métis Response-Based therapist Cathy Richardson created a Métis methodology for her PhD dissertation (2004), which held her entire process

accountable to the cultural practices, traditions and ethics of her Métis culture. After consulting about my fears and concerns, Cathy inspired me when she suggested that what I needed was to create a Solidarity Approach that would help me hold all of my PhD process accountable to the ethics and practices of solidarity from my activist culture. (Reynolds, 2014, p. 133)

Vikki shares the ethic that we aspire to of remaining accountable to our community. She describes this decolonizing position from her perspective of showing solidarity while we would speak about cultural accountability:

The ethics of solidarity require that I do not replicate exploitation or abuses of power in my work or the inquiry of it. Solidarity requires that I begin all of my work from a decolonizing place, trying to hold myself accountable to my settler privilege on the unceded indigenous territories in which I live and work. I hold a decolonizing and anti-oppression frame for all of my activism and my paid and unpaid work. (Reynolds, 2014, pp. 132–133)

For me (Jeannine), social justice is an important aspect of research. As researchers, we implicate so many people in our study: participants, communities, ethics' board members, supervisors, and students, as well as those who hold the purse strings. We have a responsibility to do our best, to build relationships, to do no harm, and to create knowledge that is helpful for the community, and for humanity.

My life as a Métis woman and an adoptee has been complicated by both of these factors, however I choose to name them. Here is what my personal location looks like.

I was born prior to the Canadian adoption nightmare for Indigenous Peoples, called the Sixties Scoop, but share in many of the stories and experiences of those adoptees who felt "that learning about themselves as Indigenous people would involve reconnecting with their birth and cultural communities" (Carrière & Sinclair, 2009, p. 261). I am a Métis woman, adopted at birth in the Red River area of Manitoba. I was reconnected to my original family at the age of twelve, when I met one of my sisters for the first time, and life since then has never been the same. Throughout my life I have met a large extended family; I know through our genealogy that I am connected to the strong and courageous Métis Nation of Manitoba. This gives me great pride. My location extends to how motherhood has changed my life and how education has given me the confidence to assert who I am in the academy and beyond. But most of all, I am a Métis woman.

As Cathy has mentioned, part of the joy in working through a Métis methodology is the work that happens with graduate students. In this section I will attempt to point out some of the issues that have surfaced as part of the student/supervisor relationship. I will begin with describing this relationship as a parallel to an old Métis visiting routine that I am describing as a methodology.

VISITING AS MÉTIS SOCIAL WORK METHODOLOGY

Visiting is one of the oldest Métis interventions that we know of (in personal conversation with Bryan Fayant, Fishing Lake Métis Settlement, Alberta, 2010). According to Bryan—and I concur—years ago Métis people used visiting as a way to check up on each other to ensure that basic needs were being met and to find out if they needed any assistance. It was a way of eliciting knowledge and information about the human experience and how people were doing. As Métis people we're always ready to help our family and neighbours in our communities because we knew that "what goes around comes around." This is a teaching that has been in our circles since time immemorial. Métis visiting is similar to early interventions in social work that focused on ensuring neighbourhood social health: "The settlement workers, influenced by the radical social gospel movement and a social justice orientation, had a somewhat different approach to the provision of charity, and they focused on the social and economic conditions to assist their 'neighbours in need'" (Jennissen & Lundy, 2006). Métis visiting, however, is full of humour, teasing, music, dancing, sharing of food, and storytelling. The model of Métis student/supervisor relationship may not include jigging in my office, but certainly we engage in much chatting, storytelling, humour, and teasing in the spirit of gaining trust, sharing of ourselves, and working towards decisions that set the course for the research journey ahead. Métis-specific research tends to be scant, therefore I see my role in encouraging the Métis voice in graduate work as extremely important. There are several complexities that Métis students can face.

THE COMPLEXITIES AND CONFUSION AROUND DEFINITIONS OF MÉTIS PEOPLE IN CANADA

If students are attempting to identify an "authentic" Métis voice in their literature review, for example, they may encounter some frustrations and challenges. When choosing a topic related to the Métis experience in Canada, students are usually delving into unpaved territory that can be bumpy along the way. For example, as described by Evans et al. (2012),

> The lack of health research on and with Métis communities is as indisputable as it is troubling. T. Kue Young (2003) searched the Medline database for the period of 1992–2001 for articles related to Aboriginal health in Canada. Only two of the 254 articles identified provide data about Métis people. A search of the social science databases for the period of 1995–2005 garnered similar results: 96 articles addressing Aboriginal health of which only thirteen concerned the Métis (Young, 2003). Since Métis people comprise over 30 per cent of the total Aboriginal population in Canada, it is clear that there is a significant underrepresentation of Métis-related research in the literature. (Evans et al., 2012, p. 56)

Another problematic issue for students conducting Métis specific graduate research is the topic of identification for Métis peoples. Evans et al. (2012) describe this as "an unavoidable issue in Métis research" (p. 60). The term *Métis* can include many distinct Indigenous communities and histories. We recognize the definition set out by the Métis National Council, wherein "'Métis' means a person who self-identifies as Métis, is distinct from other Aboriginal peoples, is of historic Métis Nation ancestry and who is accepted by the Métis Nation" (Métis Nation of Ontario, n.d.). In working with graduate students, I have engaged in conversations of who the Métis in Canada are, recognizing that it is an evolving definition in many respects. There are some cautionary messages, however, that I feel are important.

While we work with this evolving definition, sources in the literature understand and utilize "Métis" differently, and in using these sources to inform our research, we may be unwittingly contributing to further obfuscation of who the Métis are and how they can be identified for the purposes of delivering services in the community. In their literature review on Métis health research, Kumar et al. (2012) identify the compounded effect of the homogenization of Métis people into the category of "Aboriginal" in very material terms: while status First Nations and Inuit have access to First Nations and Inuit Health Branch services and non-insured health benefits, these services and benefits are not available to Métis. In terms of health outcomes, for instance, while circulatory diseases are the leading cause of death among registered Indian women, cancers represent the predominant cause of mortality among Métis women. Métis also experience stress and marginalization in ways that are unique compared to First Nations individuals (2012, p. 26).

Texts such as those by Barkwell et al. (2006), Kimelman (1985), and Canada (2012), identified a general "confusion" over who the Métis are, which has contributed to less-than-appropriate services being delivered to our communities. Métis epistemologies are positioned in a number of ways since we are a group of complex and diverse peoples. To state that one methodology or method is "the" Métis-specific way of conducting research would be ludicrous. We are a people of many nations, although stating that we are "mixed blood" peoples simplifies our identity and puts us on dangerous ground. Being Métis is not as simple as stating we are mixed blood, and this can't be promoted as the generalized experience of being Métis in Canada. Although our rights to land, to self-governance, and to define our identity are becoming matters of public concern, the well-being and lives of Métis people and communities remain marginalized and invisible to mainstream and Indigenous leadership and under-researched in the academy. For example, there has never been a national study of Métis well-being and health, and as a consequence of this and other factors, there are no established "best practices" for working with Métis families, children, and communities. This oversight has created far-reaching difficulties and complexities for the Métis and has created some barriers and frustration for Métis students or other students wanting to engage in Métis-specific research.

These experiences can be captured in their writing under their methodology section, and I encourage all Indigenous graduate students to examine themselves and their ways of knowing carefully before entering into the analysis of data that we describe as "meaning making."

INDIGENOUS MEANING MAKING

For social work practice meaning making is the process of how we take the gifts of participant interviews or other information to a level that adds to existing knowledge. It is also how we understand our personal locations and how we are connected to our research. It's how we can make new meanings for some concepts that were interpreted by western researchers in disconnected ways. In other disciplines such as the broader social sciences, contributions to practice may differ; however, the meaning-making process remains as an integral part of Indigenous research methods. For example, in her article on early childhood development and Indigenous research, Michele Sam (2011) states the following:

> Within Indigenous societies, knowledges have traditionally been co-constructed according to local experiences, reflecting environmental, social, ethical, cultural, and relational characteristics. Accordingly, Indigenous knowledges have been validly interpreted and transformed into community action, if they built upon those local environmental, social, ethical, cultural, and relational considerations. In addition, Indigenous Peoples have processes that are rooted in a tradition of orality, and that function to support knowledge transformation. (Sam, 2011, p. 315)

Meaning making takes many forms, but there are several tools to assist in this unravelling of information, and in recent years Indigenous scholars have made contributions to how this occurs in a culturally meaningful way. As Potts and Brown (2015) remind us, however, "power lurks in all our reflections and decisions" (p. 30), and as researchers we "are often challenged with the underlying hierarchies inherent in our relationships" (p. 30). These are cautions that I often discuss with graduate students; relationships are essential to meaning making and foundational components to Indigenous research. As Penak (2018) states, stories "require a relationship with the audience, making the need for research to be engaging and accessible" (p. 268). This inspires how meaning making and relationship are two entities that are connected together. Lavallée (2009) describes this as "weaving points" in a collective story (p. 34). Weaving points and meaning making are how we build the connectedness of Indigenous research.

GENDER RELATIONS

In my years as a supervisor/mentor, one of my learnings has been the significance of gender and research conversations. I ask how a gendered analysis is used or missing in literature and how gendered roles and relationships influence their meaning making. I often clarify with students why they feel this aspect of research matters. We have thoughtful exchanges that highlight the importance of dismantling ongoing colonial discourses impacting gender inequity and violence. Sarah Hunt has been an inspirational Indigenous scholar for many Indigenous students who refer to her writing in their research. In her discussion of colonial violence, Hunt (2018) describes how "gender violence is central to our on-going dispossession" which has caused Hunt to examine their "understanding of the power dynamics of academia and processes of knowledge production" (p. 284). Hunt further describes the importance of understanding their "role as witness to colonial violence" (p. 284). As Indigenous researchers this statement should stop us in our tracks, and we should question our own witnessing or complicity in perpetuating violence. Hunt calls us to reduce or eliminate the harm caused to Indigenous people through academic research. As a thesis supervisor this call to action requires me to encourage Indigenous graduate students to consider their witnessing obligations such as consent and reciprocity. Through research we are given gifts of stories and information that can make a difference in future generations. This creates a place of honour and privilege for Indigenous researchers. In this book many Indigenous graduate students have examined issues of power, gender, and the colonial impacts on their families and communities. Their witnessing efforts contribute to our resistance as Indigenous researchers who continue to struggle in western academic institutions that have created and maintained false imagery and information about Canada's colonial history with Indigenous people. As graduate-level supervisors, we can use our engagement in solidarity with Indigenous students to reverse the impacts of a colonial history in Canada and in our post-secondary institutions. This is another pathway to healing for our communities.

CONCLUSION

In this chapter we discussed the importance of mentoring and supervision, which can be lifelines for Indigenous graduate students. It can be overwhelming for students to be a good relative within a research process. A supervisor can help a student tie their research shoelaces and help them back to facing the storm so to speak. While this is happening, their friends, families, and communities are also holding them up to accomplish a dream. This can be quite overwhelming, and that sense of accountability and responsibility can either inspire a student or immobilize them. In closing, what would we suggest as the recipe for meaningful Indigenous graduate student supervision? (And yes, we are back to the culinary references.)

For me (Jeannine) it has been in caring for students in a way that is meaningful to them. I want to hear from them at the onset of our relationship what feels helpful and what feels overbearing. How often do they need to hear from me? What are their dreams, and how can I help to achieve those? What resources would help as they try and complete their never-ending thesis writing? I am clear that there are times where I might come across as a pushy relative and then there are times where I might step back a bit.

Honesty and realism in this relationship is key, and so far I am pleased to report that Indigenous graduate students who have engaged with me as their supervisor have all completed. I can't be everything to a graduate student, but I can certainly aim to support them in accomplishing their dreams for a graduate education that is meaningful to them, their families, and their communities. To those Indigenous students entering graduate education, I advise you to remember your teachings in your academic pursuits and research. Choose your supervisor wisely, and welcome to the circle of Indigenous knowledge building and sharing. All my relations.

REFERENCES

Adams, H. (1995). *Prison of grass: Canada from a Native point of view* (Rev. ed.). Saskatoon: Fifth House Books.

Adams, H. (1997). *A tortured people: The politics of colonization*. Penticton, BC: Theytus Books.

Allen, S. (2020). What's the secret ingredient to great mentorship? KelloggInsight, Kellogg School of Management at Northwestern University. July 7, 2020. https://insight.kellogg.northwestern.edu/article/great-mentorship-research

Arnott, J. (1995). *Breasting the waves: On writing and healing*. Vancouver: Press Gang.

Barkwell, L. J., Dorion, L. M., & Hourie, A. (2006). *Métis legacy II: Michif culture, heritage and folkways*. Saskatoon: Gabriel Dumont Institute.

Canada, D. (2012). *The strength of the sash: The Métis people and the British Columbia child welfare system* [Doctoral dissertation, University of British Columbia]. cIRcle. UBC Library Open Collections. http://hdl.handle.net/2429/42150

Cajete, G. (2021). Native Americans and science: Enhancing participation of Native Americans in the science and technology workforce through culturally responsive science education. *Engaged Scholar Journal: Community-Engaged Research, Teaching and Learning, 7*(1), 122–139.

Cariou, W. (2002). *Lake of the prairies*. Toronto: Doubleday Canada.

Carrière, J. (2005). Connectedness and health for First Nation adoptees. *Paediatrics & Child Health, 10*(9), 545–548. https://doi.org/10.1093/pch/10.9.545

Carrière, J. (2007). Promising practice for maintaining identities in First Nation adoption. *First Peoples Child & Family Review, 3*(1), 46–64. https://doi.org/10.7202/1069526

Carrière, J., & Richardson, C. (2009). From longing to belonging: An Indigenous critique of applying attachment theory to work with Indigenous families. In

S. McKay, D. Fuchs, & I. Brown (Eds.), *Passion for action in child and family services* (pp. 49–67). Regina: Canadian Plains Research Centre Press.

Carrière, J., & Sinclair, R. (2009). Considerations for cultural planning in Aboriginal adoptions. In S. Strega & J. Carrière (Eds.), *Walking this path together: Anti-oppressive child welfare* (pp. 62–77). Winnipeg: Fernwood Publishing.

Evans, M., Andersen, C., Dietrich, D., Bourassa, C., Logan, T., Berg, L. D., & Devolder, E. (2012). Funding and ethics in Métis community based research: The complications of a contemporary context. *International Journal of Critical Indigenous Studies, 5*(1), 34–66.

Hart, M. (2009). For Indigenous people, by Indigenous people, with Indigenous people: Towards an Indigenist research paradigm. In R. Sinclair, M. A. Hart, & G. Bruyere (Eds.), *Wicihitowin: Aboriginal social work in Canada* (pp. 153–168). Winnipeg: Fernwood Publishing.

Hunt, S. (2018). Research within relations of violence: Witnessing as methodology. In D. McGregor, J. P. Restoule, & R. Johnston (Eds.), *Indigenous research: Theories, practices, and relationships* (pp. 289–295). Toronto: Canadian Scholars' Press.

Howe, K. R. (1998). The interpretive turn and the new debate in education. *Educational Researcher, 27*(8), 13–21.

Jennissen, T., & Lundy, C. (2006). Keeping sight of social justice: 80 years of building CASW. Canadian Association of Social Workers. https://www.casw-acts.ca/files/attachements/casw_history.pdf

Kimelman, E. C. (1985). *No quiet place: Final report of the review committee on Indian and Métis adoptions and placements.* Winnipeg: Manitoba Community Services.

Kumar, M. B., Wesche, S., & McGuire, C. (2012). Trends in Métis-related health research (1980–2009): Identification of research gaps. *Canadian Journal of Public Health, 103*(1), 23–28. https://www.jstor.org/stable/41995701

Lavallée, L. F. (2009). Practical application of an Indigenous research framework and two qualitative Indigenous research methods: Sharing circles and Anishinaabe symbol-based reflection. *International Journal for Qualitative Methodology, 8*(1), 21–40. https://doi.org/10.1177/160940690900800103

Logan, T. (2001). *The lost generations: The silent Métis of the residential school system.* Winnipeg: Southwest Region Manitoba Métis Federation.

McLaughlin, C. (2010). Mentoring: What is it? How do we do it and how do we get more of it? *Health Services Research, 45*(3), 871–884. https://doi.org/10.1111/j.1475-6773.2010.01090.x

Menard, A. (2002). The halfbreed blues [Song]. On *The velvet devil*. Velvet & Hawk Productions.

Métis Nation of Ontario. (n.d.) Frequently Asked Questions. https://www.metisnation.org/registry/citizenship/frequently-asked-questions/

Native American and Indigenous Scholars Collaborative. (n.d.) Native mentors and models. NAISC *Project Activities*, San Diego State University. https://education2.sdsu.edu/csp/research-projects/naisc/activities/mentors-models

Nelson, C. A., & Youngbull, N. R. (2015). Indigenous knowledge realized: Understanding the role of service learning at the intersection of being a mentor and a college-going American Indian. *In Education*, 21(2), 89–109. https://doi.org/10.37119/ojs2015.v21i2

Penak, N. (2018). A story pathway: Restoring wholeness in the research process. In D. McGregor, J. P. Restoule, & R. Johnston (Eds.), *Indigenous research: Theories, practices, and relationships* (pp. 256–270). Toronto: Canadian Scholars' Press.

Potts, K. L., & Brown, L. (2015). Becoming an anti-oppressive researcher. In S. Strega & L. Brown (Eds.), *Research as resistance: Revisiting critical, Indigenous, and anti-opressive approaches* (2nd ed., pp. 17–42). Toronto: Canadian Scholars' Press.

Reynolds, V. (2010a). *Doing justice as a path to sustainability in community work* [Doctoral dissertation, The Taos Institute]. https://www.taosinstitute.net/education/taos-phd-program/completed-dissertations/vikki-reynolds-dissertation

Reynolds, V. (2010b). Doing justice: A witnessing stance in therapeutic work alongside survivors of torture and political violence. In J. Raskin, S. Bridges, & R. Neimeyer (Eds.), *Studies in meaning 4: Constructivist perspectives on theory, practice and social justice* (pp. 157–184). New York: Pace University Press.

Reynolds, V. (2014). A solidarity approach: The rhizome & messy inquiry. In Simon, G., & Chard, A. (Eds.), *Systemic inquiry: Innovations in reflexive practice research* (pp. 127–154). London, UK: Everything Is Connected Books. Retrieved from https://vikkireynolds.ca/wp-content/uploads/2017/12/2014reynoldsasolidarityapproachtherhizomeandmessypracticeinsystemicinquirysimonandchardeds.pdf

Richardson, C. (2003). Stories that map the way home: A process of self creation. *Platforum: Journal of Graduate Students in Anthropology*, 5, Cultural Reflections,, 21–27.

Richardson, C. (2004). *Becoming Métis: The relationship between the sense of Métis self and cultural stories* [Doctoral dissertation, University of Victoria]. Dspace. https://dspace.library.uvic.ca/server/api/core/bitstreams/1942fd9f-47e4-4f27-9ccf-d598279f4208/content

Richardson, C. (2005). Cultural stories and the creation of the self. *Relational Child and Youth Care Practice*, 18(1), 55–63.

Richardson, C. (2008). A word is worth a thousand pictures: Working with Aboriginal women who have experienced violence. In L. R. Ross (Ed.), *Feminist counselling: Theories, issues and practice*. Toronto: Women's Press.

Richardson, C. (2009). Métis experiences of social work practice. In S. Strega & J. Carrière (Eds.), *Walking this path together: Anti-racist and anti-oppressive child welfare practice* (pp. 146–161). Winnipeg: Fernwood Publishing.

Richardson, C., & Carrière, J. (2017). Métis methodology: A possible map for ethical positioning and congruency in research. In J. Carrière & C. Richardson (Eds.), *Calling our families home: Métis peoples' experiences with child welfare*. Vernon: JCharlton Publishing.

Richardson, C., & Nelson, B. (2007). A change of residence: Government schools and foster homes as sites of forced Aboriginal assimilation – A paper designed to provoke thought and systemic change. *First Peoples Child & Family Review*, 3(2), 75–83. https://www.responsebasedpractice.com/wp-content/uploads/2020/04/A-Change-of-Residence.pdf

Richardson, C., & Seaborn, D. (2009). Beyond audacity to aplomb: Understanding the Métis. In R. Sinclair, M. A. Hart, & G. Bruyere (Eds.), *Wícihitowin: Aboriginal Social Work in Canada* (pp. 114–131). Winnipeg: Fernwood Publishing.

Sam, M. A. (Ktunaxa) (2011). An Indigenous knowledges perspective on valid meaning making: A commentary on research with the EDI and Aboriginal communities. *Social Indicators Research*, 103, 315–325.

Scofield, G. (1999). *Thunder through my veins: Memories of a Métis childhood*. Toronto: HarperFlamingo Canada.

Smith, L. T. (1999). *Decolonizing methodologies: Research and Indigenous peoples*. London: Zed Books.

Truth and Reconciliation Commission of Canada. (2015) *Truth and Reconciliation Commission of Canada: Interim report*. Winnipeg: Truth and Reconciliation Commission of Canada.

Young, T. K. (2003). Review of research on Aboriginal populations in Canada: Relevance to their health needs. *BMJ (Clinical research ed.)*, 327(7412), 419–422. https://doi.org/10.1136/bmj.327.7412.419

PART ONE

Embedding Child Welfare Research into Indigenous Methodologies

Researching Culturally Informed Approaches

Supporting Indigenous Youth Aging Out of Ministry Care

Robert Mahikwa

ABSTRACT

This chapter is a meta-narrative exploring how the incorporation of Indigenous oral traditions, storytelling practices, and the Medicine Wheel led to the emergence of an Indigenous research paradigm that was utilized to examine culturally informed approaches to supporting Indigenous youth aging out of the child welfare system in British Columbia. The author also discusses their own struggles and successes as an Indigenous-identifying graduate student trying to navigate a western academic context. In addition, words of encouragement and recommendations for present-day and future Indigenous-identifying graduate students are offered.

Keywords: *Indigenous identity, aging out, foster care, cultural disconnectedness, Indigenous research methodologies, Medicine Wheel, oral traditions, storytelling, thesis research*

INTRODUCTION

Aanii (Hello)! I would like to begin by acknowledging my sincere gratitude to the ləkʷəŋən, W̱SÁNEĆ, Songhees, and Esquimalt peoples on whose territories the University of Victoria has had the honour and privilege of being located, and wherein my thesis research had the opportunity to be conducted. In the spirit of reciprocity, I pray to Creator, the ancestors, and all our relations, that the following chapter will help contribute to the wholistic health and well-being of Indigenous-identifying children, youth, and families of these territories, as well as those for whom the following topics resonate.

SELF-LOCATING PROLOGUE

I self-locate as an Indigenous-identifying educator and researcher whose ancestral composition includes French-Canadian, American, Algonquin (Anishinaabe), Onondaga (Haudenosaunee), and Mi'kmaq peoples. I hold a Bachelor of Social Work and a Master of Indigenous Social Work from the University of Victoria. I have also taught sessionally in the School of Social Work at UVic, as well as Indigenous Studies in the Centre for Indigenous Education and Community Connections at Camosun College. I have been a humble visitor on the territories of Coast Salish, Nuu-chah-nulth, and Kwakwaka'wakw peoples since 2014, which is an gift for which I am forever grateful. Key areas of my scholarly work include Indigenous research methodologies, Indigenous social work, and Indigenous mentorship.

CONNECTION TO MY THESIS TOPIC

I have been mentored culturally by many Indigenous Elders and Indigenous scholars since the early 2000s. This mentorship has occurred on the land, in ceremony, in-person and via distance, in Indigenous/First Nation communities, within Indigenous organizations and centres, and at several post-secondary institutions.

Often, my mentors have reminded me that when it comes to "Indigenous identity" there is no single catch-all definition, nor a one-size-fits-all criteria. This is particularly accurate in Canada, whose colonial history and present-day relations with Indigenous populations remain disproportionately steeped in westernized thinking, assimilatory discourses, and intergenerational traumas. As such, like so many Indigenous-identifying graduate students, my cultural connections, cultural embodiment, and ancestry make for a complex relationship.

I was initially raised away from my cultural knowledges, traditions, and community. As such, I have since spent the majority of my life working towards a genuine re-connection with, and re-understanding of, my cultural knowledges, traditions, and ancestral peoples. It is a journey that I continue to traverse to this very day. The effects of colonization have put many obstacles along my path, but thanks to the cultural mentors in my life, I have come to know myself and connect with my Indigeneity more so than I ever thought possible. I could not and have not done this alone.

As will be soon evident in these pages, I feel most connected and aligned with Anishinaabe ways of knowing and being because these are the cultural knowledges and traditions within which I have been mentored. I know my Spirt name, and I was given a clanhood, and my ceremonial colours. All of the above continue to inform and guide essentially all aspects of my personal life, professional practice, community service, and scholarly work.

The focus of my thesis was about utilizing Indigenous research methodologies to explore culturally informed approaches to supporting Indigenous youth aging out of the child welfare system in British Columbia. Although I was not raised in the foster care system as a young person, I can relate to the effects of the cultural disconnectedness so prevalent among Indigenous-identifying youth who are, or who were, in the Canadian child welfare system. I also related with those who are seeking their own re-connection with their Indigeneity after having been culturally disconnected, for any number of possible reasons. In many ways, I think my story and my thesis topic are more linked than I had initially considered as a graduate student.

CULTURAL DISCONNECTEDNESS IN
CHILD WELFARE AND AGING OUT

It is widely acknowledged that there is an overrepresentation of Indigenous-identifying children and youth within the Canadian child welfare system (Blackstock, 2009; Fluke et al., 2010; Ministry of Children and Family Development [MCFD], 2018; Sinha & Kozlowski, 2013; Statistics Canada, 2013; Trocmé et al., 2004), many of whom age out of the system in their late teens or early twenties. As such, supporting Indigenous-identifying youth in culturally informed ways as they age out of the foster care system continues to be a rapidly emerging area of interest in the literature and in professional practice.

Here in Canada, and around the world, it is widely agreed that youth who age out of the child welfare system are at a significantly high risk of experiencing a lack of adequate housing; addiction(s); mental, emotional, and physical health concerns; limited employment options; incarceration; incomplete academics credentials; and marginalization, stigmatization, and an over-reliance on social services (Barker et al., 2014; Carrière, 2010; Cashmore & Paxman, 2006; Evans et al., 2017; Gomez et al., 2015; Jackson et al., 2011; MCFD, 2017; Mendes et al., 2013; Naccarato & DeLorenzo, 2008; Provincial Advocate for Children and Youth [PACY], 2012; Rutman et al., 2007; and Tweddle, 2007). Moreover, death by suicide or overdose is especially prevalent among this population (Adams, 2015; Culbert, 2017; Meissener, 2017; Rankin & Brend, 2016; Sherlock, 2016; and Stueck, 2017), and many of these youth do not live to see their twenty-first birthday. This is tragic, unacceptable, and arguably preventable.

The importance of nurturing, protecting, and maintaining the wholistic health and well-being of Indigenous-identifying children and youth whilst in the care of the child welfare system is paramount (Carrière & Richardson, 2013). Alienation and separation from one's cultural identity, community, and traditions are major contributing factors among Indigenous-identifying children and youth who are or were involved in the child welfare system (Blackstock, 2009; Blackstock et al., 2004; Carrière, 2010; Carrière & Richardson, 2013; Carrière & Strega, 2015; Cross & Simmons, 2000; Kirmayer et al., 2000; PACY, 2012; Richard, 2004; and Simard & Blight,

2011). This is of particular concern given that the legacy of the child welfare system in Canada stems from the Indian Residential School system, followed by the Sixties Scoop era. Prior to conducting my thesis research, I had initially underestimated the intergenerational impacts of these histories, issues, and barriers. But I soon came to the realization that knowing one's cultural identity and being able to embody this identity is essential to fostering this sense of wholistic health and well-being.

INSPIRATION FOR MY THESIS RESEARCH

While working at an Indigenous youth crisis and transitional housing centre, I met a Métis-identifying youth named "Charlie" who was aging out of the provincial foster care system.

I witnessed Charlie's attempts to access transitional support services for aging-out youth, albeit with little to no progression. Charlie was overcome with debilitating fear and distress about being forced to transition into adulthood and away from the services he had been relying on for so long during his formative years of life. Moreover, at that time, I noticed that these aging-out transitional services were not culturally specific.

My time with Charlie was brief; however, he had a lasting impact on me which continues to this day. In many ways, Charlie was the inspiration for my thesis research upon deciding to pursue graduate-level studies shortly thereafter. I do not know what happened to Charlie after he aged out, but I do hope and pray that he is doing well and is happy.

RESEARCH QUESTION AND SIGNIFICANCE

How can we support Indigenous youth who are aging out of foster care (or child welfare in general) and transitioning into adulthood, in more culturally informed ways?

The significance of my thesis is that it is solutions-focused, pragmatic, and intended to be highly transferable. It also emphasizes the voices of Indigenous-identifying adults who previously aged out of the foster care system in British Columbia, as well as the voices of community members, family members, and professionals who support aging-out/aged-out Indigenous-identifying youth and adults, either directly or indirectly. Too often these voices have been left out of the literature. However, my thesis is one of the few studies to make available the official transcripts, in full, and as approved by the Story-Sharers (research participants) themselves. They are the experts of their lives and lived experiences, and of their cultural journeys and identities; I am not. They have a right to be heard, and they hold the right to tell their Story in a manner that they deemed fit to tell. I invite you to read the thesis and the stories themselves in full; however, I provide a brief summary of this work below.

MY RESEARCH PARADIGM

A goal of my thesis research was to explore culturally informed ways to support Indigenous-identifying youth who are aging out, or have aged out, of the foster care system. As such, early on in my graduate studies, I decided that my research paradigm itself had to be culturally informed in order to produce culturally informed findings. But knowing a decolonial/decolonized path and following it can be easier said than done.

Typically, a "research paradigm" represents the lens through which research data is gathered, viewed, interpreted, understood, and re-presented. The same is true for Indigenous research paradigms and methodologies. However, a unique feature of Indigenous research paradigms and methodologies is that they are rooted in Indigenous theories that are based on Indigenous knowledges, traditions, values, principles, and protocols (Archibald, 2008; Hart, 2010; Kovach, 2021; Smith, 2021; Wilson, 2008). It is also often a misconception that Indigenous methodologies outright reject western approaches to research (Archibald et al., 2019); but this is not entirely true. Rather, Indigenous methodologies are simply approaches to research that are informed by, and/or centred within, Indigenous ways of thinking and doing.

The following image is a visual representation of the research paradigm I designed and constructed for my thesis research (extracted from Mahikwa

2018, p. 12), which is based on the cultural knowledges and iconography of an Anishinaabe Medicine Wheel, as was taught to me in community and by the Elders many years ago.

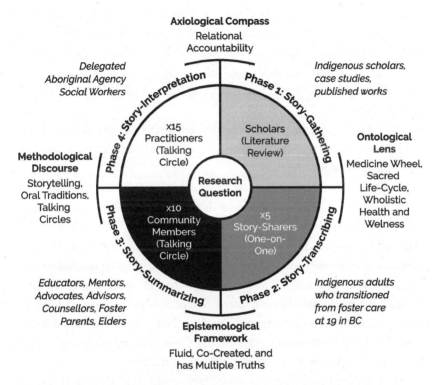

Medicine Wheel as a Research Paradigm: Interconnected, Interdependent, Interrelational, and Intergenerational. *Courtesy of the author.*

An Indigenous research paradigm is comprised of four key pillars: *ontology, epistemology, methods,* and *axiology* (Wilson, 2008), as is my thesis research paradigm, as follows.

At the core of my design is the *Medicine Wheel,* which is comprised of four equal quadrants. Not all Medicine Wheels are the same, but typically these quadrants represent the four aspects of *the self* (physical, emotional, mental, and spiritual), the four *sacred seasons* (spring, summer, fall, and winter), and the four *sacred directions* (east, south, west, and north) (Hill, 2021; Surprenant & Brady, 2021). These quadrants can also represent the four *sacred cycles of life* (birth, adolescence, adulthood/parenthood, and Eldership) (Anderson, 2011).

Thus, in my research paradigm, each quadrant represents the four phases of my research process (Story gathering, transcribing, summarizing, and interpretation), which are held together by the four research pillars (ontology, epistemology, methods, and axiology), and within each quadrant I identify the "communities" (samples) from whence the data (Stories) were gathered.

My research paradigm is also guided by what I call the four *Is* of the Medicine Wheel: *interconnectedness, interdependence, interrelationality,* and *intergenerationality.*

As the classic metaphor goes, when a pebble is dropped into a calm lake, a ripple effect emerges outward from the centre until the ripples meet the edge of the lake and then return back to the centre again. The pebble in my research paradigm is my research question from which each element of my research design emerges, and feeds back into the research question once again, thus representing the *interconnectedness* of my research paradigm.

With regards to representing *interdependence,* the idea here is that if you removed any aspects of the research design, the entire model would come apart. Each aspect plays an integral role. All roles are reliant on each other to ensure that the research design is present and active.

Each research participant (Story-Sharers and Circle Members) carries a commonality between them and around them, in that each person has a relationship with the child welfare system as someone who either received these supports and service, and/or as someone who delivered these supports and services. In some cases, research participants were both. It is for this reason that we see how *intergenerationality* is represented in the research design, given that some of the participants had, at the time, aged out recently, or aged out many decades prior, and of these individuals, some had gone on to work with aging-out/aged-out Indigenous-identifying youth.

STORYTELLING AND ORAL TRADITIONS AS METHODS

For many Indigenous cultural groups, oral traditions and storytelling practices have existed since time immemorial. This is how knowledges have been passed from one generation to another. The same is arguably true with all form of Indigenous and "non-Indigenous" research.

Oral traditions and storytelling practices can be effective and appropriate methods in Indigenous research methodology when it comes to gathering data (Stories), albeit not without its challenges. Namely, having to navigate oral traditions within a contemporary text-based format (Qwul'sih'yah'maht, 2015). Storywork as an Indigenous research methodology was famously coined by Stó:lō scholar Dr. Jo-ann Archibald (2008), which is an approach informed by seven cultural principles: *respect, responsibility, reverence, reciprocity, wholism, interrelatedness,* and *synergy*. Dr. Archibald's work has shaped countless Indigenous research projects and Indigenous-identifying students and scholars worldwide, myself included.

I incorporated Storywork as my methodology, and I incorporated oral traditions and storytelling practices as my methods. However, in order to achieve this within a text-based format, I decided that a number of *re-narrations* were needed. These were not simply "semantical revisions." Rather, these changes helped decolonize, Indigenize, and contextualize my Indigenous paradigmatic methodology and methods, as follows:

- **Knowledge(s)**: written with a capitalized *K* to represent knowledge(s) as a sacred lifeforce or entity because it is imbued with the spirit of each generation of those who (or what) carried it and share it.

- **Story**: referring to "data." It too is capitalized for the same reason as Knowledges above. It is spirit-imbued story, and thus is considered sacred and alive.

- **Story-Gatherer**: referring to "the researcher"; a sacred responsibility and thus capitalized.

- **Story-Gathering Process**: referring to the data-gathering process; also, a sacred process, like a ceremony.

- **Story-Sharer(s)**: referring to the "research participant(s)"; similar to how we might refer to an Elder as a Knowledge-Keeper, Knowledge-Carrier, or Knowledge-Sharer.

- **Story-Sharing Session(s)**: referring to what we might call "one-on-one interviews," albeit from within a cultural context and akin to what Kovach (2019) refers to as a "conversational method."

- **Talking Circle Session(s)**: referring to what we might call "group interviews," albeit from within a more culturally rooted context. Basically, these are Story-Sharing sessions but with more than one person being "interviewed."

- **Circle Member(s)**: referring to Story-Sharers who participated in at least one of two Talking Circles as part of Story-Gathering process for my thesis research.

Although these revisions may seem inconsequential at first glance, the implications of such changes were deeply profound and significant to ensuring that the thesis research and subsequent findings would also be culturally rooted.

On a personal note, my life changed forever when I realized I could adapt these commonly accepted western terms and concepts into more Indigenous culturally rooted ways of knowing and being that were congruent with the knowledges and traditions which I have been mentored in and have since carried.

But I could not have achieved this alone. These endeavours had to be, and were, heavily encouraged, mentored, and supported by my thesis supervisor, Sokhi Aski Esquao (Dr. Jeannine Carrière). My thesis proposal was also approved by the research ethics boards at the University of Victoria and the Ministry of Children and Family Development, with very few questions or revisions needed—for which I was grateful. This demonstrated to me that all parties involved in the thesis carried an authentic commitment to decolonizing and Indigenizing graduate level studies and research. I appreciate their trust, leadership, and allyship.

SUMMARY OF THESIS FINDINGS

Much like the *Medicine Bundles* carried by Indigenous Medicine People (Young et al., 2015), I grouped my findings into four distinct "Bundles" which build upon one another:

- **Bundle #1**: Goals and Outcomes (achievements for aging-out/aged-out Indigenous-identifying youth to pursue or achieve during and after their transition from child welfare to adulthood, and those which caregivers can help these youth pursue and achieve);

- **Bundle #2**: Supports and Services (those that are available, or need to be available, to help Indigenous-identifying youth/adults achieve the above Goals and Outcomes);

- **Bundle #3**: Values, Principles, and Philosophies (those which can, should, or must inform and guide the above Supports and Services); and

- **Bundle #4**: Essential Commitments (those which are needed to help build the necessary capacity for all of the above to be achieved).

The following table provides a brief description of findings for each of the above Bundles. For more in-depth descriptions of the following, please see Mahikwa, 2018 (pp. 75–81).

Bundle #1 Goals/Outcomes	Bundle #2 Supports/ Services	Bundle #3 Values/Principles/ Philosophies	Bundle #4 Essential Commitments
• Sense of Identity • Sense of Belonging • Sense of Esteem • Sense of Health/ Wellness • Sense of Competency • Sense of Agency • Sense of Direction	• Introduce Culture Early • Involve the Family • Create a Circle of Care • Positive Role Models • Social Outlets/ Activities • Cultural Mentorship • Life Skills Training • Contextualize History • Nurture Wholistic Healing • Celebrate Rites of Passage • Provide Essential Needs • Build a "Forever Home"	• Relationality • Trust • Be Humanizing • Authenticity • Presence • Unconditional Love • Honour Sacred Life Cycle • Wholism • Decolonization • Strengths-Centred • Advocacy-Oriented • Resourcefulness	• Specialized Training • Quality Helpers/ Workers • Indigenous-Led • Centre Youth Voices • Transparency • Accountability • Sustainable Funding • Affordability • Accessibility • Safe Cultural Spaces • Trauma-Informed • Organizational Wellness

ACKNOWLEDGEMENTS

I am, and will forever be, hugely grateful and appreciative to each Story-Sharer who gifted their voices, knowledges, insights, and recommendations to my thesis research. With these entrusted offerings I was able to weave together the above findings to help decolonize and Indigenize how we support the wholistic health and well-being of aging-out/aged-out Indigenous-identifying youth and adults, and their transition away from the child welfare system.

I also want to acknowledge my thesis supervisor, Sokhi Aski Esquao (Dr. Jeannine Carrière), for allowing me the opportunity to explore and discover myself as an Indigenous-identifying researcher by allowing me the safe space to explore and discover my interconnected relationships to, and with, my Indigenous research methodologies and paradigm.

In my mind, heart, and spirit, I believe this thesis "belongs" to everyone who contributed to its pages, and to everyone who can relate with its content, whether directly or indirectly.

LIFE SKILLS COACHING AND CULTURAL MENTORSHIP

One of the most prominent themes that stood out to me in my thesis findings was the frequent call for adequate *life skills coaching* and *cultural mentorship*, as a key way to support aging-out/aged-out Indigenous-identifying youth.

As it was articulated in the thesis, most Indigenous-identifying youth will need to know how to navigate and survive a *two-world adulthood*. One world represents their Indigenous identity (e.g., connecting with, and knowing, one's cultural knowledges, traditions, values, protocols, communities, and governance); and the other world represents their non-Indigenous identity (e.g., western ways of knowing and being within colonial-based systems and societies).

More specifically, the *life skills* coaching of these particular youth should focus on key, real-world topics such as budget management and opening/managing a bank account, verbal/non-verbal and written communication skills, study habits in school, skills on how to secure employment and housing, parenting skills, time management skills, learning how to drive a car, and learning how to shop effectively at grocery stores, to name a few; and their *cultural mentorship* would focus on helping them re-learn, re-connect, and re-embody their own cultural ways of knowing and being.

In many ways, and based on my own experiences in graduate studies, I see parallels between this area of research and how we can also support Indigenous-identifying graduate students. For instance, the "life skills coaching" would be equivalent to *learning how to conduct a literature review, constructing a research paradigm, writing a research proposal, undergoing an ethics review, recruiting research participants, conducting research methods, analysing data, engaging in an oral defense,* and *publishing,* to name a few. Whereas the "cultural mentorship" would focus on how to achieve all of the above whilst maintaining and interweaving one's own cultural knowledges, traditions, values, and principles within a westernized academic context.

In fact, I have seen such promise in these parallels that I have since decided to pursue Doctoral studies in Educational Studies, with a focus on exploring Indigenous (or Indigenized) approaches to supporting Indigenous-identifying graduate students in research-streamed programs in British Columbia, for my dissertation.

COMING TO KNOW MYSELF IN GRADUATE RESEARCH

This section is mostly intended for Indigenous-identifying graduate students who are, or who will, be pursuing Masters or Doctoral research-streamed studies, especially if they will be utilizing Indigenous research methodologies for the very first time.

For me, my thesis experience was incredibly informative and transformative. Of course I learned a lot about my thesis topic area, thesis structure, and the research process overall. But I also learned a lot about myself along the way because I utilized Indigenous methodologies for the first time ever. I hope the same will be true for you as well.

Specifically, while learning about Indigenous methodologies, I soon realized that my Indigenized research paradigm was essentially an extension of who I am as an Indigenous-identifying graduate student. This meant that exploring and discovering my research paradigm was simultaneously, and unexpectedly, a very deep inward journey of self-exploration and self-discovery. This was unlike anything I had ever anticipated. If you choose to follow a similar path, I pray that your journey will be much smoother and clearer than mine.

I say this because determining my research paradigm and design did not emerge overnight, nor did it emerge with any great ease. At times, the struggle was agonizing. I had to unlearn what I thought a research paradigm *had to look like* or *had to be* within an academic setting. I needed to be creative and tenacious about figuring out how to weave the cultural knowledges and traditions I carried together with the rigorous expectations of a graduate-level research program. As it turns out, the path towards decolonizing my research methodologies was also the path towards decolonizing myself as a researcher.

I experienced many trials, made many errors, and had many restarts along the way. It was like traversing a vast fog that stretched out all around me. I could see glimmers of distant lights, only to end in getting lost, confused, and turned around more often than not. My recommendation would be to have at least one person on your supervisory team who is familiar with Indigenous methodologies and can help guide you along your research journey.

But perhaps the most difficult aspect of this inward journey involved tapping into that inner part of me where self-doubt and questioning my sense of belonging and self-worth tends to reside. Asking myself, *What am I doing here in higher education? Am I "smart" enough to be here? Are my cultural knowledges safe here? Am I safe here? Am I "Indigenous-enough" to be utilizing Indigenous research methodologies? Am I incorporating, or appropriating? Am I being respectful? What if my research isn't "good enough" or for graduate-level research because it doesn't adhere to a western research paradigm and I will have to start all over again? What if the research ethics board won't understand my methodologies and will thus not approve my application? Maybe I should just stick to using a western research paradigm like everyone else? What makes "me" qualified to research this topic?* and the list goes on. I think most Indigenous-identifying graduate students will inevitably confront questions like these at various points during their graduate research journey. It might even be a necessary step along the way.

But if (or when) this is happening to you, I recommend leaning into these thoughts and discomforts. Maybe write them down in a journal and then find an Indigenous-identifying graduate student and/or faculty member with whom you can connect and discuss these worries and questions together. This could be someone in your program, at your institution, or at another institution. Find someone who can mentor and guide you through these thoughts and feelings.

In the end, the journey of coming to know myself through the process of pursuing and completing graduate-level thesis research was exciting, but also very difficult to endure. But looking back at it all now, I can say with confidence that it was completely worth it. I pray that the same will be true for you as well, and if I can be of assistance, please reach out.

YOU MATTER

As many Indigenous scholars have said to me, I now want to remind you: always remember *that you matter! No one has ever walked the same path in life as you have. Your experiences are unique. Your contributions to the literature and to your community are, and will be, special. You might be the person that you, or someone else, is waiting for and needing. You are among many Indigenous-identifying researchers and scholars who came before you so that you could walk this path today. Your ancestors and Creator brought you to this moment. You are here. We need you and we are happy you have arrived.*

Whether you are or were involved in the child welfare system, or whether you are or will be pursuing graduate thesis research work, I pray that you will trust the path and trust the process. You matter, you are sacred, and I hope that these pages are, or will be, helpful to you along your academic, professional, cultural, and/or life's journey.

Miigwetch. All my relations.

REFERENCES

Adams, C. (2015, October 21). Paige's story: In search of a name. *GlobalNews*. Retrieved from https://globalnews.ca/news/2290502/paiges-story-in-search-of-a-name/

Archibald, J. (2008). *Indigenous storywork: Educating the heart, mind, body, and spirit*. Vancouver: UBC Press.

Archibald, J., Lee-Morgan, J., & De Santolo, J. (2019). *Decolonizing research: Indigenous storywork as methodology*. London: Zed Books.

Anderson, K. (2011). *Life stages and Native women: Memories, teachings, and story medicine*. Winnipeg: University of Manitoba Press.

Barker, B., Kerr, T., Alfred, G. T., Fortin, M., Nguyen, P., Wood, E., & DeBeck, K. (2014). High prevalence of exposure to the child welfare system among street-involved youth in a Canadian setting: Implications for policy and practice. *Journal of Biomedical Central Public Health*, 14(197), 1–7. https://doi.org/10.1186/1471-2458-14-197

Blackstock, C. (2009). After the apology: Why are so many First Nations children still in foster care? *Children Australia*, 34(1), 22–29. https://doi.org/10.1017/S103507720000050X

Blackstock, C., Trocmé, N., & Bennett, M. (2004). Child maltreatment investigations among Aboriginal and non-Aboriginal families in Canada. *Violence Against Women*, 10(8), 901–916. https://doi.org/10.1177/1077801204266312

Cajete, G. (2000). Indigenous knowledge: The Pueblo metaphor of Indigenous education. In M. Battiste (Ed.), *Reclaiming Indigenous voice and vision* (pp. 181–191). Vancouver: UBC Press.

Carrière, J. (2010). *Aski awasis / Children of the earth: First peoples speaking on adoption*. Halifax: Fernwood Publishing.

Carrière, J., & Richardson, C. (2013). Relationship is everything: Holistic approaches to Aboriginal child and youth mental health. *First Peoples Child & Family Review*, 7(2), 8–26. https://doi.org/10.7202/1068837ar

Carrière, J., & Strega, S. (Eds.). (2015). *Walking this path together: Anti-racist, anti-oppressive child welfare practice* (2nd ed.). Halifax: Fernwood Publishing.

Cashmore, J., & Paxman, M. (2006). Predicting after-care outcomes: The importance of 'felt' security. *Child & Family Social Work*, 11(3), 232–241.

Cross, T., & Simmons, D. (2000). *Development and implementation of tribal foster care standards*. (J. Chase, Ed.). National Indian Child Welfare Association.

Culbert, L. (2017, July 7). She was known as the girl in the tent: Her family wants you to know the real Santanna. *Vancouver Sun*. Retrieved from https://vancouversun.com/news/local-news/she-was-known-only-as-the-girl-in-the-tent-but-her-family-wants-you-to-know-the-real-santanna

Evans, R., White, J., Turley, R., Slater, T., Morgan, H., Strange, H., & Scourfield, J. (2017). Comparison of suicidal ideation, suicide attempt and suicide in children and young people in care and non-care populations: Systematic review and meta-analysis of prevalence. *Children and Youth Services Review*, 82, 122–129. https://doi.org/10.1016/j.childyouth.2017.09.020

Fluke, J. D., Chabot, M., Fallon, B., MacLaurin, B., & Blackstock, C. (2010). Placement decisions and disparities among Aboriginal groups: An application of the decision making ecology through multi-level analysis. *Journal of Child Abuse and Neglect*, 34(1), 57–69.

Gomez, R. J., Ryan, T. N., Norton, C. L., Jones, C., & Galán-Cisneros, P. (2015). Perceptions of learned helplessness among emerging adults aging out of foster care. *Child and Adolescent Social Work Journal*, 32, 507–516. https://doi.org/10.1007/s10560-015-0389-1

Hart, M. A. (2010). Indigenous worldviews, knowledge, and research: The development of an Indigenous research paradigm. *Journal of Indigenous Voices in Social Work*, 1(1A), 1–16.

Hill, G. (2021). *Indigenous healing: Voices of Elders and healers.* Vernon: JCharlton Publishing.

Jackson, L. J., O'Brien, K., & Pecora, P. J. (2011). Posttraumatic stress disorder among foster care alumni: The role of race, gender, and foster care context. *Child Welfare*, 90(5), 71–93.

Kirmayer, L. J., Brass, G. M., & Tait, C. L. (2000). The mental health of Aboriginal peoples: Transformations of identity and community. *Canadian Journal of Psychiatry*, 45(7), 607–616. https://doi.org/10.1177/070674370004500702

Kovach, M. (2019). Conversational method in Indigenous research. *First Peoples Child and Family Review*, 14(1), 124–136.

Kovach, M. (2021). *Indigenous methodologies: Characteristics, conversations, and contexts* (2nd ed.). Toronto: University of Toronto Press.

Mahikwa, R. (2018). *The next chapter: A practical guide for individuals, families, communities, social workers, and organizations supporting Indigenous youth aging-out of care* [Master's thesis, University of Victoria]. Dspace. https://dspace.library.uvic.ca/server/api/core/bitstreams/a0783153-4916-498f-9bce-b1b96290caae/content

Meissener, D. (2017). Alex Gervais, Métis teen who took his own life, was "abandoned" by gov't: Report. *HuffPost.* Retrieved July 23, 2017, from http://www.huffingtonpost.ca/2017/02/06/alex-gervais-report_n_14633308.html

Mendes, P., Baidawi, S., & Snow, P. (2013). Young people transitioning from out-of-home care: A critical analysis of leaving care policy, legislation and housing support in the Australian state of Victoria. *Child Abuse Review*, 23(1), 402–414. https://doi.org/10.1002/car.2302

Ministry of Children and Family Development (British Columbia). (2017). *Ministry of Children and Family Development: Performance management report*, 9. https://www2.gov.bc.ca/assets/gov/family-and-social-supports/services-supports-for-parents-with-young-children/reporting-monitoring/00-public-ministry-reports/volume_9_mar_2017.pdf

Ministry of Children and Family Development (British Columbia). (2018). *Ministry of Children and Family Development: 2018/19–2020/21 service plan.* https://bcbudget.gov.bc.ca/2018/sp/pdf/ministry/cfd.pdf

Naccarato, T., & DeLorenzo, E. (2008). Transitional youth services: Practice implications from a systematic review. *Child and Adolescent Social Work Journal, 25,* 287–308.

Oliveria, K. (2019). Wisdom maps: Metaphors as maps. In H. Tomlins-Jahnke, S. Styres, S. Lilley, & D. Zinga (Eds.), *Indigenous education: New directions in theory and practice* (pp. 171–188). Edmonton: University of Alberta Press.

Provincial Advocate for Children and Youth (Ontario). (2012). *My real-life book: Report from the Youth Leaving Care Hearings.* http://cwrp.ca/sites/default/files/publications/en/YLC_REPORT_ENG.pdf

Qwul'sih'yah'maht (Thomas, R. A.). (2015). Honouring the oral traditions of the Ta't Mustimuxw (Ancestors) through storytelling. In S. Strega & L. Brown (Eds.), *Research as resistance: Revisiting critical, Indigenous, and anti-oppressive approaches* (2nd ed., pp. 177–198). Toronto: Canadian Scholars' Press.

Rankin, E., & Brend, Y. (2016, March 15). Dead teen Patricia Lee 'Indigo' Evoy lacked support, say friends. *CBC News.* Retrieved from https://www.cbc.ca/news/canada/british-columbia/patricia-lee-indigo-evoy-death-mcfd-youth-case-1.3491326

Richard, K. (2004). A commentary against Aboriginal to non-Aboriginal adoption. *First Peoples Child & Family Review, 1*(1), 101–109. https://doi.org/10.7202/1069588ar

Rutman, D., Hubberstey, C., Feduniw, A., & Brown, E. (2007). *When youth age out of care – Where to from there?: Final report based on a three-year longitudinal study.* Research Initiatives for Social Change unit, School of Social Work, University of Victoria. https://www.uvic.ca/hsd/socialwork/assets/docs/research/WhenYouthAge2007.pdf

Sherlock, T. (2016, March 15). BCTF calls for children's minister to resign after latest teen death. *Vancouver Sun.* Retrieved from https://vancouversun.com/news/metro/bctf-calls-for-childrens-minister-to-resign-after-latest-teen-death

Simard, E., & Blight, S. (2011). Developing a culturally restorative approach to aboriginal child and youth development: Transitions to adulthood. *First Peoples Child & Family Review, 6*(1), 28–55. https://fpcfr.com/index.php/FPCFR/article/view/104/168

Sinha, V., & Kozlowski, A. (2013). The structure of Aboriginal child welfare in Canada. *International Indigenous Policy Journal, 4*(2), 1–21. http://ir.lib.uwo.ca/iipj/vol4/iss2/2/

Smith, L. T. (2021). *Decolonizing methodologies: Research and Indigenous peoples* (3rd ed.). London: Zed Books.

Statistics Canada. (2011). *Aboriginal peoples in Canada: First Nations people, Métis and Inuit.* Retrieved May 2, 2024, from https://www12.statcan.gc.ca/nhs-enm/2011/as-sa/99-011-x/99-011-x2011001-eng.cfm.

Stueck, W. (2017, July 3). BC's coroner to review deaths of children who 'age out' of government care. *The Globe and Mail.* Retrieved from https://www.theglobeandmail.com/news/british-columbia/bcs-coroner-to-review-deaths-of-children-who-age-out-of-government-care/article35784188/

Surprenant, F. (Cree Elder), & Brady, A. (2021). *Medicine Wheel teachings.* Brantford: Indigenous Education Press.

Tachine, A. R. (2018). Story rug: Weaving stories into research. In R. Minthorn & H. J. Shotton (Eds.), *Reclaiming Indigenous research in higher education* (pp. 64–75). New Brunswick, NJ: Rutgers University Press.

Trocmé, N., Knoke, D., & Blackstock, C. (2004). Pathways to the overrepresentation of Aboriginal children in Canada's child welfare system. *Social Service Review, 78*(4), 577–600. https://doi.org/10.1086/424545

Tweddle, A. (2007). Youth leaving care: How do they fare? *New Directions for Youth Development, 2007*(113), 15–31. https://doi.org/10.1002/yd.199

Wilson, S. (2008). *Research is ceremony: Indigenous research methods.* Halifax: Fernwood Publishing.

Windchief, S. (2018). Stealing horses: Indigenous student metaphors for success in graduate education. In R. Minthorn & H. J. Shotton (Eds.), *Reclaiming Indigenous research in higher education* (pp. 76–87). New Brunswick, NJ: Rutgers University Press.

Young, D., Rogers, R., and Willier, R. (2015). *A Cree healer and his Medicine Bundle: Revelations of Indigenous wisdom—Healing plants, practices, and stories.* Berkeley: North Atlantic Books.

A Métis Grandmother's Knowledge

Stories of Grandmother Teachings and Métis Child Welfare in British Columbia

Shelley LaFrance

INTRODUCTION

Despite decades of evidence in Canada of injustices involving child welfare systems and outstanding recommendations, the overrepresentation of harm to Indigenous children, youth, and families remains (Blackstock, 2011, 2016). The Indigenous child welfare literature reveals a need to build on Métis-focused research related to child welfare systems that address noticeable gaps in the stories and knowledges of Métis grandmothers (Allan & Smylie, 2015; Campbell, 1973; Carrière & Richardson, 2017; Monchalin et al., 2019; Richardson, 2016). This chapter centres on a Métis grandmother's story and my own experiences as a Métis social worker in relation to child welfare experiences within the framework of Métis kinship care and mothering.

Through storytelling and autoethnography, I addressed the following research question: *How can the lived experiences and teachings of a Métis*

grandmother and Métis women enhance social work practices for social work-
ers and community members, as well as organizations and agencies that
serve Métis children and families? Significantly the findings of this study
centre ways that Métis grandmothers and mothers carry inherent knowledge about child, family, and community care; utilize resistance strategies
in their experiences with child welfare; and explore the social work implications that can disrupt colonial systems to inform agency and community responses.

In this chapter, I respectfully acknowledge I am an uninvited visitor and
settler on the ləkʷəŋən people's traditional territories of the Songhees and
Esquimalt First Nations in what is known as Victoria, British Columbia. I
am very grateful to the ləkʷəŋən people, to the Knowledge Keepers, caretakers of the lands and waterways, the ancestors, and all relations connected
to these beautiful territories. I also acknowledge that I have responsibilities
and ways of being and learning connected to my unearned privileges in
living on ləkʷəŋən territories.

This research was inspired by children, youth, families, and communities in my work and life, as well as Indigenous scholars and allies featured
in this research. Furthermore, I was influenced by the painful storytelling
of residential school survivors, as well as child and family experiences of
child welfare systems. In setting out on the journey of my thesis in 2019, I
reflected on the loss of and harm to loved ones whose experiences of colonization are related to historical and contemporary child welfare systems.

Despite many decades of research on colonial violence related to these
systems, colonial structures and approaches continue to influence these
unacceptable and heartbreaking losses and harms where the child welfare system is failing (Blackstock, 2004, 2011, 2016; Hart, 2009; Kline, 1993;
Maiter, 2015; National Inquiry into Missing and Murdered Indigenous
Women and Girls [NIMMIWG], 2019; Sinclair, 2016; Strega & Sohki Aski
Esquao [Carrière], 2015; Strega et al., 2013; Representative for Children and
Youth British Columbia [RCYBC], 2020). These failures in serving children
and families are often related to a lack of support or access to culturally
safe health care or services (Allan & Smylie, 2015; Monchalin et al., 2019).
Children should not lose their parents, nor parents lose children. These

sentiments are stated in the following RCYBC report (2020a): "Over a year has passed since the government released the National Inquiry's Final Report into Missing and Murdered Indigenous Women and Girls (NIM-MIWG) without substantive progress on addressing many of the recommendations relevant to child welfare" (p. 4). The concerns are related to issues involving social inequities, social control, racialization, and oppressive structures. Additionally, the report reveals ways that Métis grandmothers, women, and literature identify as helpful and essential that centre family and culturally centred knowledge of child and family caring systems.

With this research I wanted to influence social work practices, leadership, and community roles to strengthen and build upon the practices that dismantle oppressive systems and expose marginalized knowledges within child welfare. By contributing to Métis-focused research, the intention of this study was to influence further research to be done with women and families in roles caring for children. This research centres relationships and responsibilities that I carry as I stand alongside the grandmother who was centred as a participant with our mutual goals for justice and equity for Métis children now and for generations of Métis children to come. Additionally, this research may be relevant to First Nations and Inuit peoples as well as Black and other equity-seeking families who are also disproportionately represented in child welfare (Strega et al., 2013).

PERSONAL LOCATION

It is important for me to share who I am and where I come from since, as Shawn Wilson (2008) points out, the researcher's experiences and story cannot be separated from their own life in the research. While I was born on the Qayqayt First Nation's territories in New Westminster, British Columbia, I have lived on the ləkʷəŋən peoples' traditional territories most of my life, but also on the northern and mid-island territories on Vancouver Island, of the Kwakwaka'wakw and Nuu-chah-nulth First Nation peoples.

I am Métis on my father's side with Cree and French ancestry from St. Boniface of the Red River Métis. My Cree grandmothers came from Green Lake. My family names include LaFrance, Bruneau, and Landry. On my mother's side, I am from Ireland and of mixed European ancestry. My family names include Murphy and Hansen. My roles include being a mother, daughter, auntie, sister, niece, and cousin to many. My employment roles have been with urban Indigenous agencies for the past seven years, and I am a proud member of the Métis Nation and community.

LITERATURE REVIEW

This next section is a summary of the literature review and begins with understandings of the harms, deaths, and injustices of colonization dating back hundreds of years in the links to contemporary discrimination and harm related to child welfare (Blackstock, 2004, 2011, 2016; Kline, 1993; Maiter, 2015; NIMMIWG, 2019; RCYBC, 2020; Sinclair, 2016; Sinclair et al., 2009; Strega & Sohki Aski Esquao [Carrière], 2015; Strega et al., 2013). These systemic injustices are rooted in colonial structures such as the *Indian Act* and residential schools; however, these so-called schools are often compared to institutions and prisons where horrendous abuse, neglect, and crimes occur (RCYBC, 2020; Truth and Reconciliation Commission of Canada [TRC], 2015). Residential and day schools facilitated violence against Indigenous children and youth, including banning and punishment to children for speaking their language in these schools and forcibly removing children from their homes (RCYBC, 2020; TRC, 2015). An example of other residential school violence includes Blackstock's research, which cites a 1907 government report that confirmed 25 percent of children in residential schools needlessly died each year because of the government's refusal to provide children with tuberculosis treatment (Blackstock, 2016).

Research also illustrates compounding contemporary concerns involving the Canadian government in "the obstruction of Indigenous self-determination, failure to recognize treaty and land rights, and over-surveillance by criminal justice and child welfare systems" (Allan & Smylie, 2015, p. 5). Colonial violence and harm is evidenced by data, as revealed in Dr. Jeannine Carrière's research, which shows that "between 1971 and 1981, 70% to 80% of Manitoba's First Nations and Métis adoptions went to non-Native homes" (Sohki Aski Esquao [Carrière], 2017, p. 83). Gosek

(2017) points out that countless non-status and Métis Indigenous children were adopted out with estimates of close to 20,000 children being adopted, who were "often lost for decades or permanently displaced from their families and communities" (p. 32), which resulted in completely severing connections to family, community, and home territories. These forms of discrimination continued and shifted to contemporary child welfare systems. For example, census data from 2016 shows that "while nearly eight per cent of the child population in Canada is Indigenous (7.7 per cent), 52.2 per cent of children in foster care are Indigenous" (RCYBC, 2020a, p. 4). While concerns of overrepresentation are evident, issues connected to the misrepresentation of Métis children and youth render them invisible and underrepresented (Carrière & Richardson, 2017; Richardson, 2016). For example, reports in 2020 continue to demonstrate a lack of effort to identify Métis children and families, as well as an overall lack of awareness about Métis people (RCYBC, 2020b). Additionally, Carrière and Richardson point out that "until recently, both the federal and provincial governments have denied the existence of Métis rights" (2017, p. 105).

In May 2020, the RCYBC (2020b) reported that there were "764 children and youth in May 2020 and 844 children and youth in December 2017" connected to child welfare systems in British Columbia (p. 8). Child welfare systems continue to ignore both the inherent rights and well-being of Métis children, the ones that Carrière and Richardson refer to as "the hidden children of child welfare" (2017, p. 89). There also continues to be a lack of clarity in adoption policies alongside inadequate efforts to fund adoption programs and to engage in cultural planning for Métis children and families (p. 87). This lack of care and concern includes the lack of tracking of Métis caregivers by the Ministry of Child and Family Development (RCYBC, 2020b, p. 31). Furthermore, formal supports are needed in kinship care, including adjusting financial supports to prioritize kin and extended-family carers over non-Indigenous foster parents (Mann-Johnson, 2017, p. 224). Mann-Johnson also highlights how decisions around kinship care or any assessment of care for Indigenous children and youth are often made in isolation from Indigenous communities, which is a colonial practice (p. 229).

Other failings and structural inequalities also persist. For example, 60 percent of Indigenous families targeted by child welfare are living in poverty without adequate supports or access to culturally safe health care or services (Strega & Sohki Aski Esquao [Carrière], 2015). The program known as "Jordan's Principle" is a response to jurisdictional funding inequities and disputes that puts the child first and addresses payment issues later (Blackstock, 2016). Jordan's Principle is named after Jordan River Anderson, a Cree boy from Norway House Cree Nation, who spent over two years in a hospital unnecessarily and tragically died in the hospital at the age of five because the various government parties refused to pay for his care (2016). Furthermore, Jordan's tragic situation was not an isolated incident. Case studies found that hundreds of children had been denied or received delayed services available to other children (2016). Issues and concerns related to Jordan's Principle remain today with significant health disparities and failures for children and youth. Bureaucratic obstacles continue to exist for those applying for this funding today and, in most cases, applications must be submitted before the service is provided. Additionally, Jordan's Principle does not apply to Métis children unless they live on reserve, further alienating Métis families in the struggle for Indigenous rights. Reports in 2020 also describe how "federal funding models for Delegated Indigenous Agencies are flawed and discriminatory, leading to more children ending up in care" (RCYBC, 2017, p. 3). These concerns include leaving agencies short-staffed and unable to provide services, including culturally appropriate prevention services (2017).

Colonial structures and policies not only disempower land-based systems but centre intersecting sites of disadvantage and oppression for Métis women (Kline, 1993). In the absence of child-centred child welfare, children are removed from the home, often from mothers, rather than a professional ensuring they enact a collective, family-centred approach to addressing poverty, inequalities, and violence (Carrière & Richardson, 2017). These failures involve mother-blaming discourses that hold mothers responsible for male violence; social workers then make superficial judgments about her mental health, her ability to parent, even though the violence was not her fault. These types of child welfare inventions, which are all too common, include expectations about the abilities of mothers to predict risk, and react appropriately, as well as end violence enacted by men (Strega et al., 2013). As well, social workers tend to overlook the ways in which the mother had been trying to protect herself and the children all along, in favour of pathologizing discourses (Carrière & Richardson, 2017). Despite decades of "calling out" this sexist and ineffective practice, systems have made little to no change in this regard and Indigenous children continue to be removed, unnecessarily, from their mothers. This raises the question, who is responsible for keeping women safe in society from domestic, family, and systemic violence? Surely we cannot leave that up to individual women who may already be isolated and disconnected from family and community.

Métis author and lawyer Jean Teillet (2019) highlights that, in 2014, homicide, or rather "femicide," rates were six times higher for Indigenous women and girls than for non-Indigenous females. Furthermore, Teillet reveals that "no one has teased out the numbers of Métis women victims from these bundles of pan-Indigenous statistics" (p. 467). The 2019 NIMMIWG final report outlines imperative "Calls to Justice," which includes calls to social workers and those implicated in child welfare systems. Research reveals that substantive progress has yet to be made (NIMMIWG, 2019).

The literature has identified many concerns that inform this research. The failings of Métis rights, concerns connected to identity, as well as structural and colonial systems that continue to harm Métis mothers, children, families, and communities are the backdrop to this study. The literature also reveals a gap regarding Métis women's stories and knowledge that can strengthen understandings related to grandmother's teachings, motherhood, and child and family well-being in a child welfare context in British Columbia. Monchalin et al. (2019) point out that Métis women's knowledge is vital to the well-being and health of Métis communities, can address gaps in knowledge about socially and culturally safe services, and provide relevance in an urban context (p. 148). Elders often voice the importance of mothers in Métis culture, which include child welfare approaches to have a stronger focus on motherhood that supports mothering roles, identity, and healing processes (Carrière & Richardson, 2017, p. 108).

METHODOLOGY

The methodology of this research was guided by decolonizing theory that examines ways knowledge has been diminished through forced assimilations, modernization, and globalization (Battiste, 2011). Further decolonizing theory rejects colonial powers and works to restore local control of Indigenous knowledge, traditions, and values (Hart, 2009). Sinclair (2009) explains how a decolonizing context in social work works to address racism and injustices related to child welfare. While some scholars such as Sinclair support Indigenous adoption, they continue to critique the colonial and unjust adoption practices of the past. These injustices are manifested in colonial culture, social suppression, and intrusive and controlling legislation (Sinclair, 2009, p. 23). Furthermore, Hart (2009) states that

> colonialism continues to exist, occasionally transforming shape like the tricksters in our traditional stories. We need to continually reflect on our practice to see how it represents the characteristics and goals of Indigenism and anti-colonialism. (p. 41)

Understandings of shifting colonialism point to the rationale centred in this research question, given how examination of both a personal and systemic analysis is essential in social work practices. In some cases, Indigenous-run services may be the answer, particularly when communities may redesign services to align with their values and collective, cultural practices.

Anti-oppressive theory guides this research through an analysis of power, as well as examines how language, assumptions, and biases connect to our subjective experiences (Green & Thomas, 2007). Decolonizing practices and theory influence ways this research is framed through my understandings of historic and contemporary colonization and reflection on my own internalized colonial impacts. For example, decolonial practice includes my use of language and examining my perceptions, biases, and understandings of the world around me (2007, p. 91). These theories support the ways that knowledge is understood and gathered in this research, as well as connections in the meaning making of the analysis.

Although I remain in early learning, I was drawn to the Cree Medicine Wheel teachings to guide this research and my analysis in terms of such values as wholeness, balance, respect, and interrelationships (Hart, 2009). The importance and teachings of the Medicine Wheel include how Kundoqk (Green) and Qwul'sih'yah'maht (Thomas) (2015) describe the quadrants as relational between the past, present, and future which offer holistic ways to guide journeys and visions to address imbalances and ways to seek harmony with all our relations. The Cree Medicine Wheel provides an Indigenous framework that, as Hart (2009) shares, supports the helping of relationships, community and familial relationships, and commitments and views in relation to the natural world including ways this draws upon traditions to uphold the rights of Indigenous people.

Métis storytelling protocols guided my relationships and ethics, which included asking permission, visiting, gifting, and sharing food (Canada, 2017). Furthermore, Qwul'sih'yah'maht (Thomas, 2015) describes how an Indigenous storytelling methodology requires being inclusive of Indigenous voices and practices that are fluid, relational, and non-linear in the wisdom of the storyteller. The autoethnographic approach combines storytelling, experiences, and observations of my personal memories, as well as reflective and external information (Chang, 2016). The ethical principles that have guided this research also include the National Aboriginal Health Organization (NAHO) Métis Centre's "Principles of Ethical Métis Research." These principles were developed some time ago but remain culturally relevant to Métis research principles which include reciprocal relationships, respectful inclusion of ideas both individually and collectively, inclusive and safe environments, as well as a diversity of concepts and ways of knowing (NAHO, 2018). I was also guided by the First Nations Centre's principles of OCAP (Ownership, Control, Access, and Possession) in the governance of First Nations in the data, knowledge, control, and ownership of research (NAHO, 2007). The Canadian Institute of Health Research et al. (2010) Tri-Council policy statement, Ethical Conduct for Research Involving Humans, includes conduct centred in respectful relationships, collaboration, and respecting community customs.

My accountabilities included a thorough review and receipt of participant consent, including understandings of the possible risks and benefits of the research. Furthermore, we created a support plan together in the event of emotional distress that prioritizes the safety and care of participants. My ethics also sought to demonstrate reciprocity through gifting and centring relationships in my responsibilities. The process of seeking participants included connecting with an Elder, as well as community leaders and members, by listening to feedback and protocols. My intention is to demonstrate respect for and responsibility towards my community. In all these conversations, I received expressions of individual support and offers to share my research participant invitation poster with the community.

In the following section, I present a brief summary of how Métis grandmother Lynn's and other women's stories attest to the damage caused by child welfare. I will discuss the relationship between these stories and the concerns articulated in the child welfare literature. As well, the importance of storytelling will be discussed in the finding and analysis sections.

Lynn began by sharing her story about her family and the knowledge passed down to her by her grandmother. Lynn's experiences with child welfare took place from 2014 to 2018. Throughout her story, she described her experiences as upsetting and scary due to feelings of isolation and confusion. Her interaction with child protection workers began after her daughter experienced domestic violence. Child protection workers stated concerns for her daughter's well-being, which led to Lynn caring for and receiving legal custody of her grandson. Throughout this time, Lynn found the local Métis nation to be helpful through the services and programs offered.

Lynn described a time of difficulty when working with child protection workers. She was given safety plans with new and revised sets of instructions; she was not given important and relevant information that she needed to inform her care. There were frequent and ongoing worker changes, including a period where there was no worker at all. Calls she made to social workers were sometimes unanswered for weeks or longer. Lynn was promised daycare services that never materialized, forcing Lynn to leave her job twice in four years. On a number of occasions, social workers threatened to remove her grandson from her care. Lynn shared the following: "I will never forget that one social worker who always ended with, 'If you do not adhere to all that we have said...he will be removed...and placed with a foster family.'" Lynn shared that she would wake up worrying that social workers would come and take her grandson; it was debilitating. It should be noted that this form of practice flies in the face of the anti-oppressive practice taught in many social work programs. Threats and coercion have no place in the social work profession, and it was devastating to Lynn to have to experience this kind of treatment, as if she was an "enemy."

LYNN'S STORY

Lynn described that she received support from a family member, learned of complaints processes, and connected to a team leader. However, she said that both the complaints process and meeting with a team leader turned out to be unhelpful, caused further stress, and included racist responses. For example, she shared how she arranged with her lawyer to meet with a team leader, yet her lawyer was unable to attend because the team leader arrived so late. Lynn said when she met with the team leader, he was barefoot and had uncombed hair. After sharing her concerns with the team leader, Lynn said "his reply was the new computer system is slow and also, and I quote, us being Métis complicates things." She said that, despite his promise to follow up with her, she never heard from him again.

Lynn shared that her grandson was returned to his mom for a time. In a meeting, her daughter cried because this experience with child welfare was finally over, and then the social worker said, "I don't know why you are crying; it could have been worse." Lynn also described witnessing her daughter being treated roughly by a social worker when she cried when the worker took a sample of her hair, which left Lynn feeling very angry, Lynn expressed. "I said nothing...because they held all the cards; I felt if I voiced any concerns...I feared he would be taken from me." Lynn described her experiences with four different child welfare offices where she said staff at the last office helped to address child care and processes in legal next steps.

Ultimately, Lynn stated that she experienced a broken system. Social workers took her decision-making powers from her, as well as her dignity. She shared that they should have been working as a team instead of them treating her as an adversary. Lynn expressed that she felt like she was reliving the trauma of her ancestor's experiences of colonization. She said she still sometimes feels nervous that her grandson will be taken from her and believes this feeling is the result of this traumatizing experience. I acknowledge that Lynn shared some very personal, harmful, and tragic experiences when sharing her story. I am honoured to be a witness to her experience and do my best to receive and treat this story with respect and care. No family should be experiencing such disrespect and systemic violence, especially in a helping profession.

SHELLEY'S STORY

My autoethnography begins with reflections on my grandmother's teachings. These teachings have influenced me within my family, community, and work experiences. These reflections include teachings related to motherhood, belonging, and identity, as well as child nurturing and family care. Influential literature about grandmother teachings includes Métis author and grandmother Maria Campbell's novel *Halfbreed* (1973), which shares how her grandmother was foundational to her life by centring family, community care, and decision making, as well as teachings that disrupt colonial oppression surrounding identity. This novel was very powerful and impactful for me in gleaning a greater understanding of colonization, grandmothers, and identity.

My experiences in community and the knowledge of stories from Métis women and scholars have provided me with teachings centred in the values of respect, dignity, and belonging, including experiences in ceremonies and community ways of knowing. These teachings include Métis-informed approaches as described by Catherine Richardson (2016) which involve Métis perspectives on well-being, advocacy to address systemic barriers in systems, and concepts of human dignity in the foundations of social work. Richardson expresses that "helping Métis people find their way home should be the main task of social work" (p. 61). Furthermore, she adds that "this means helping families to find and reconnect with those taken and lost in foster care and adoption, and those lying in unmarked graves" (p. 161). Additionally, she emphasizes the higher likelihood for Métis women to become homeless, have their children removed into care, or even be killed after reporting violence (p. 175).

My work experiences include being a member of a committee that sought to address the Calls to Justice in the NIMMIWG final report (2019). While structural barriers persist, changes have been made and this work continues. While I am aware of expanding Indigenous services, there continue to be many challenges, barriers, gaps, and concerns for the safety of women and families. Richardson (2016) points out that these challenges include access for families to services in remote regions, lack of positive social responses, and connections to social class and race. These issues are centred in discrimination related to identity and safety for Métis women, given the increased likelihood to be blamed or stereotyped. Richardson also states that "Métis people are less likely to receive culturally appropriate services" (p. 175).

I have also witnessed the immense health needs of Indigenous children and youth in care, in which significant disparities in health can be related to barriers, inconsistencies, as well as discriminations associated with Jordan's Principle funding to support these services. Health disparities for Métis children and youth in care, as indicated in the McCreary Centre Society (2019) findings, are connected to disproportionate concerns of suicide, self-harm, sexual abuse, and mental health compared to non-Indigenous youth.

While I have shared significant knowledge and literature related to failures to Indigenous children and families in child welfare, I also want to acknowledge exceptions within Indigenous agencies in British Columbia that I have witnessed. This has included work that strives and fights against systemic barriers for equity in services for children and families. These barriers include increased needs in staffing, programs, health, and prevention services where community and culture are centred.

The analysis and findings are guided by the Cree Medicine Wheel, which is divided into four directions. Kundoqk (Green) and Qwul'sih'yah'maht (Thomas) (2015) share how the Medicine Wheel "is an ancient teaching tool. It has no beginning and no end and teaches us that all things are interrelated" (p. 27).

Nabigon and Mawhiney (2011) share how the north direction represents the symbols of winter, preservation, and caring. I have centred these symbols and values in relation to remembering and resistance. The theme of resistance in Lynn's story connects to her persistence in navigating systems despite the many indignities and humiliation. She continued to fight for services for her family and to do what was right, in the face of indifference, disrespect, and racism.

Lynn's story revealed the patterns of her resistance to experiences in these systems that promoted fear rather than demonstrating caring, respect, or dignity. These involved a lack of communication from workers and ignoring her decision-making abilities. For example, Lynn described receiving workers' safety plans that she was not involved in creating. They were decontextualized and did not seek "family knowledge" and Lynn's perspective. Lynn also described the ways that fear was present repeatedly, in the face of intimidation, threats, humiliation, and coercion. For example, she states, "There is no need to continually threaten removal; that just invokes fear in the recipient of that threat." Lynn also shared the unnecessary distress this has left her with: "I still sometimes feel nervous that he will be taken from me and I believe it is a trauma."

Lynn also exercised other strategies of resistance after being subjected to racist responses connected to her identity, which implied that, somehow, her identity was a problem that "complicated things." Furthermore, these child welfare responses lacked clarity and transparency, which served to impede the process of care. Lynn responded by asking for clarity, by wondering about what to do next, by trying to assess the best ways to get help for her family in navigating the system. In addition to the harm Lynn experienced, her story also centres her power, her responses, and her resistance. She never gave up and kept working with the state for the well-being of her grandchild. Through storytelling, Lynn exposed the truths of such harmful treatment, and she provides recommendations for helpful approaches to social work. For example, she shared:

> If only a phone call would have been returned, paperwork or court documents provided, then that would have allowed me to understand it all

better and why things were happening the way they were...And when you say a service will be provided, then follow through with what you are offering.

Here, she only demands what the system promises to provide. As civil servants, child protection workers have a duty of care and responsibility for administrative justice, returning calls in a timely manner and keeping families informed of decisions, resources, and necessary actions. Lynn's resistance to being dismissed and made invisible included ongoing attempts to connect with workers, taking issues up the hierarchy to team leaders, learning about her rights, and strategizing with family members about how to navigate the oppressive child welfare system. Even talking about it, refusing to remain silent, was an act of resistance for Lynn.

The findings of my research include remembering through stories both Lynn and I shared of grandmothers and family influences. Lynn shared, "My grandmother is Métis, her mother was Cree and her father French... my cousins and I are trying to bring what we lost back to our children and grandchildren." Through sharing family and cultural knowledge, she also demonstrates both remembering and resistance. Qwul'sih'yah'maht (Thomas, 2015) highlights how stories are reflections of teachings rooted in kinship responsibilities, such as ways these are passed from grandmothers to granddaughters centred in culture, identity, and belonging (p. 182). Stories that were shared by both Lynn and me included teachings passed down such as gardening, knitting, as well as relearning cultural knowledge and language that were lost through the generations.

Themes in these accounts related to issues such as lack of culturally relevant resources, preventative services, and discriminatory inequities related to funding for delegated Indigenous agencies. Lynn's social workers had a number of excuses for treating her and her family badly and one of those was race-based. Anti-Indigenous racism is a theme in the literature, which may account for the inadequate or inequitable funding compared to that received by non-Indigenous families and agencies (Allan & Smylie, 2015; Blackstock, 2016; Métis Nation British Columbia [MNBC], 2020; RCYBC 2017, 2020a; Richardson, 2016). These issues of inequities include a lack of health or preventative services are connected to harm of children and youth in care, as well as mothers and families (Graham & Davoren, 2015; Monchalin et al., 2019; NIMMIWG, 2019; Tait et al., 2013).

The themes connected to the north also include Métis-informed practices centring values of care, respect, and inter-relations that are connected to and represented in Cree language and the cultural concept *wahkootowin*, which Macdougall (2006) describes as follows:

> Wahkootowin is the Cree cultural concept that best represents how family, place, and economic realities were historically interconnected, the expression of a world view that laid out a system of social obligation and mutual responsibility between related individuals—between members of a family—as the foundational relationship within communities. (pp. 432–33)

The east direction represents spring, responsibilities, renewal, and identity. Meaning making centred in responsibility involves responses to mothers and families. For example, approaches in child welfare to address the need for culturally centred family care and health services. Responsibilities include the imperative Calls for Justice in the NIMMIWG related to social work and child welfare. In Lynn's story, she was concerned that her daughter might lose her housing, and support was needed for daycare in caring for her grandson. Lynn shared having to leave her job on two occasions due to lack of daycare for her grandson and stated that she did not receive any supports during those times that lasted many months. She described eventually receiving some helpful services such as a child care subsidy.

Responsibilities related to child welfare were also connected to themes of power linked to mothers' experiences in child welfare. For example, as Richardson (2016) points out, there are often unrealistic timelines for mothers to address child welfare concerns, especially in relation to experiences of domestic violence and health-related issues. She believes the system sets up mothers to fail with such short timelines in which to get one's life in order and recover from grief, loss, and family disruption.

Richardson also believes there are many creative solutions to family care and safety planning that do not involve decimating family structures at the request of a social worker. Lynn's story reveals her daughter's experiences of domestic violence in which child welfare responses were unhelpful. This experience is not unique. The literature also revealed concerns of mother's experiences of domestic violence that involve victim-blaming by child welfare workers, which includes lack of appropriate or effective responses in safety for mothers and children (Carrière & Richardson, 2017; Kline, 1993; NIMMIWG, 2019; Richardson & Wade, 2013; Strega et al., 2013; Teillet, 2019). Again, with enough support, creativity, and mother-centred practices, children don't need to be unnecessarily removed in certain situations where the mothering is being attacked or undermined. If that is the only alternative, then social workers should obviously work with families, in the spirit of "family group conferencing" style procedures to devise safety plans since families best know themselves and those who are the most appropriate caregivers in any given situation.

The justice system, along with the child welfare system and its responses, tend to fail women and their children. For example, findings throughout this research agreed that "the lack of prevention services meant that social workers had limited resources to stabilize family situations and prevent First Nations children from coming into child welfare care" (Blackstock, 2016, p. 292). As well, social workers may demand that a woman leave her violent partner without taking into account the reality that most women are murdered after they leave. Many women stay in the home as a way to monitor the violent behaviour and best ensure safety for the child. One aspect of Lynn's experience involved being given brochures for treatment centres. Lynn followed up with these resources only to be told there were lengthy waitlists. The family should not have to bear the brunt of such gaps in the system. In Lynn's story, the theme of her persistence in strategizing and navigating rules and systems with little support or information included responses that marginalized or ignored her knowledge and isolated her. She did what social workers asked her to do. When it didn't work, Lynn and her family were held responsible, and they continued to be punished by the social workers.

In relation to responsibilities, these represent collective responsibilities in the well-being and future of children and youth as identified by Métis Nation British Columbia (MNBC, 2024). This includes striving to "honour the traditional concept of Takaki Awasisiwin, which means a good childhood for the future of our people" (2024, para. 1). In reflecting on concepts of a good childhood, this includes our kinship networks and family, love, care, and nurturing children's talents and gifts.

The direction of the south relates to summer and relationships. These findings include how Métis people cannot be separated from the context of our relatives, identity, and caring systems. The themes of a lack of relational approaches, as witnessed in Lynn's experiences of trauma, speak to needs for a collective, family approach in all areas of child welfare.

Themes related to the concerns about identity included the underrepresentation and misrepresentation of Métis children and youth in child welfare. Exclusions of Métis identity were also related to NIMMIWG. Further revealed in the literature was how Métis experiences of residential and day school were overlooked until recently, as well as how this carried through in adoptions of children away from family and out of community. It was noted, as well, in the lack of tracking of Métis caregivers in these systems. These issues connected to identity perpetuate invisibility and discrimination in the ways Carrière and Richardson (2017) describe how Métis children's inherent rights and well-being continue to be ignored, so much so that these children are known as "the hidden children of child welfare" (p. 89). The Métis Commission also indicated that "there is an overall lack of awareness of who the Métis people are throughout the child welfare system" (RCYBC, 2020b, p. 30).

The literature also reveals how Métis state relationships relate to delegated service agencies in the discriminatory funding practices compared to non-Indigenous child welfare organizations. Themes of relationships in Lynn's story were of minimal positive interactions in her experiences with child welfare. Lynn shared that while nearing the end of her experiences, the staff at one of the offices was helpful, as was the worker for the home study. However, the overall theme with relationships in her experiences were very poor and connected to ways she expressed feelings of trauma related to child welfare responses. Lynn shared, "From my first encounter to that final court date, this was a very stressful and confusing time my common law and myself were put under." The literature also spoke of the need for Métis-informed approaches that centre collective, family-centred approaches. This involves decision-making abilities, respect, and approaches in a Métis context (Carrière & Richardson, 2017; Kinewesquao [Richardson], 2015; Richardson, 2016).

Relationship-centred knowledge is also described in the literature connected to kinship care; for example, how kinship care practices "respect the familial and communal networks of the Métis culture" centring mutual respect, support, and care (Mann-Johnson, 2017, p. 218). The care of children in kinship networks as described by Métis Nation British Columbia (2019) centres teachings and values of miyo-ohpikihawasowin:

> When we look out for one another, when we fellowship, spend time on the land, and live together with one another, we are "living well." When our children are connected to their community as family they are living well as Métis people. Our children are safe in our kinship networks. When we live these two values, we practice *miyo-ohpikihawasowin*, "good child-rearing." (p. 11)

The fall direction of the west relates to respect, dignity, and decision-making. Practices and values of respect and dignity include respect for oneself and others in balance, not mistreating any life, and the worth of all. Respect connected to identity includes both respecting self-identification but how language and responses related to identity must be respectful to uphold dignity. There was a theme of a lack of respect, as shared by Lynn, and the themes in the literature included a need for practice approaches that involve both individual and family decision-making abilities, improved communication and understandings, as well as not having experiences of isolation. For example, Lynn shared her experiences: "I was really confused and not one of my phone calls were returned."

In my autoethnography, respect was highlighted in family and community-centred approaches in family goals and advocacy around their identified needs. Respect is also centred in the Medicine Wheel relational worldview. This worldview demonstrates the many nurturing gifts, blessings, and opportunities from Creator and sacred relationships that centre "understandings of respectful individualism and communitism. The Wheel holds spirituality as its central pillar and has several key concepts: wholeness, balance, relationships, growth and healing Mino-pimatisiwin [the good-life]" (Hart, 2009, p. 35).

In this analysis and findings, Lynn's story revealed harsh treatment that attests to a "system" that needs to change. My experiences and observations confirm this reality as well. The literature and these stories demonstrate that services to Métis children and their families suffer from gaps that leave Métis women, such as Lynn, to navigate systems that induce fear and inequities in family and cultural supports, and that run counter to what a child caring system should maintain.

CONCLUSION

In seeking to answer the question of how the lived experiences and teachings of Métis grandmothers and women can enhance social work, this research revealed many implications. Implications for social work practice and approaches include the need to address the "Calls for Social Workers and Those Implicated in Child Welfare" as well as the "Métis Specific Calls to Justice" from the National Inquiry into Missing and Murdered Indigenous Women and Girls (NIMMIWG, 2019, pp. 197–99, 213–17). These objectives centre actions such as upholding Indigenous self-determination and improving support for families to keep children with their family homes, including family caregivers having equal supports. Further actions include providing culturally safe programs as well as relevant education for workers to name just a few of these calls to justice (NIMMIWG, 2019, p. 198).

Implications include addressing gaps in services related to funding and instabilities for Indigenous agencies. These service inequities and failures are connected to not only the needs for children and youth but also supports for mothers, women, and those affected by domestic violence, mental health, and substance use, as well as services for fathers and family care.

Furthermore, themes included how gaps in services involve ignoring or marginalizing cultural knowledge that produce cultural safety concerns and, therefore, the need for education in child welfare.

Further implications are related to practice approaches of respect, upholding dignity as well as Métis-informed practice and aspirations. This implication includes respect to self-identification and identity given the exclusions of Métis identity historically and currently in many areas of child welfare. The final implication as captured throughout the literature and stories is the need for increased awareness of Métis people, histories, and traditional knowledges with well-being in Métis family and community collective contexts. This awareness and understanding include the centring and respect of grandmothers' teachings, motherhood, and community knowing and being in child and family caring systems. This importance of grandmothers' knowledge centres the resistance by grandmothers historically and with the present, collective community resistance to colonial systems in child welfare.

My hope for future research is alongside Métis grandmothers and mothers in their knowledge and experiences related to child welfare. My goal for this research in storytelling and autoethnography is to share testimony of Métis grandmother's teachings and women's knowledges and related literature. The objectives include ways that challenge and disrupt colonial systems through meaning making related to social work implications that influence self-determination, equity, and justice. In this research, I demonstrated how we remain on a journey to accomplish these in the field of child and family services.

In Lynn's hopes in sharing her story in this research, she expressed: "My hope is my story can be one of the many ripples needed to be a voice for our children who end up in the system." The spiritual teachings of the Cree Medicine Wheel bring balance and wholeness that guides approaches and values related to the self, self in relation, and in the connections to resistance, remembering, relationships, responsibilities, and respect.

In closing, with honour to the late Métis child welfare advocate and scholar Deborah Canada, whose legacy work aimed to enhance social work practices:

Culturally safe practices, and beyond that, any culturally appropriate service delivery framework for the Métis people in British Columbia must respect the voices of the people. Additionally, it needs to be understood that Métis people are the experts in the care and custody of their children. (Canada, 2017, p. 242)

I believe Métis grandmother's teachings and Métis-informed approaches centring equity and justice in child and family services will continue to be realized through the momentum of collective engagement including building on Métis-focused research. All my relations!

REFERENCES

Allan, B., & Smylie, J. (2015). *First peoples, second class treatment: The role of racism in the health and well-being of Indigenous peoples in Canada.* Toronto: Wellesley Institute. https://www.wellesleyinstitute.com/wp-content/uploads/2015/02/Summary-First-Peoples-Second-Class-Treatment-Final.pdf

Battiste, M. (2011). *Marie Battiste: Knowledge as a key site for decolonization* [Video file]. YouTube. https://www.youtube.com/watch?gl=US&v=Evxptou4tOU

Blackstock, C. (2011). Wanted: Moral courage in Canadian child welfare. *First Peoples Child & Family Review*, 6(2), 35–46. https://fpcfr.com/index.php/FPCFR/article/view/114

Blackstock, C. (2016). The complainant: The Canadian human rights case on First Nations child welfare. *McGill Law Journal*, 62(2), 285–328. https://lawjournal.mcgill.ca/article/the-complainant-the-canadian-human-rights-case-on-first-nations-child-welfare/

Campbell, M. (1973). *Halfbreed.* McClelland & Stewart.

Canada, D. (2017). The strength of the sash. In J. Carrière & C. Richardson (Eds.), *Calling our families home: Métis peoples' experiences with child welfare* (pp. 9–30). JCharlton Publishing.

Carrière, J. (2007). Promising practice for maintaining identities in First Nation adoption. *First Peoples Child & Family Review*, 3(1), 46–64. https://doi.org/10.7202/1069526ar

Carrière, J., & Richardson, C. (2013). Relationship is everything: Holistic approaches to Aboriginal child and youth mental health. First Peoples Child & Family Review, 7(2), 8–26. https://doi.org/10.7202/1068837ar

Carrière, J., & Richardson, C. (2017). *Calling our families home: Métis peoples' experiences with child welfare*. Vernon: JCharlton Publishing.

Chang, H. (2016). *Autoethnography as method*. London: Routledge. https://doi.org/10.4324/9781315433370

Canadian Institutes of Health Research, Natural Sciences and Engineering Research Council of Canada, and Social Sciences and Humanities Research Council of Canada. (2010). *Tri-council policy statement: Ethical conduct for research involving humans*. http://publications.gc.ca/collections/collection_2011/ger-pre/MR21-18-2010-eng.pdf

Gosek, G. M. (2017). *The Aboriginal Justice Inquiry-Child Welfare Initiative in Manitoba: A study of the process and outcomes for Indigenous families and communities from a front-line perspective* [Doctoral dissertation, University of Victoria]. Dspace. https://dspace.library.uvic.ca/server/api/core/bitstreams/e7c1ed98-7749-406e-bc5f-64329b59c999/content

Graham, C., & Davoren, T. (2015). *Sharing their stories: Narratives of young Métis parents and Elders about parenting*. National Collaborating Centre for Aboriginal Health.

Green, J., & Thomas, R. (2007). Learning through our children, healing for our children: Best practice in First Nations communities." In L. Dominelli (Ed.), *Revitalizing communities in a globalising world*. London: Routledge.

Hart, M. A. (Kaskitémahikan). (2009). Anti-colonial Indigenous social work: Reflections on an Aboriginal approach. In R. Sinclair, M. A. Hart, & G. Bruyere (Eds.), *Wícihitowin: Aboriginal social work in Canada* (pp. 25–41). Winnipeg: Fernwood Publishing.

Kinewesquao [Cathy Richardson]. (2015). Preparing social workers to support Métis families. In Sohki Aski Esquao [J. Carrière] & S. Strega (Eds.), *Walking this path together: Anti-racist and anti-oppressive child welfare practice* (2nd ed.). Winnipeg: Fernwood Publishing.

Kline, M. (1993). Complicating the ideology of motherhood: Child welfare law and First Nation women. *Queen's Law Journal*, 18(2), 306–342.

Kovach, M. (2015). Emerging from the margins: Indigenous methodologies. In S. Strega & L. Brown (Eds.), *Research as resistance: Revisiting critical, Indigenous, and anti-opressive approaches* (2nd ed., pp. 119–152). Toronto: Canadian Scholars' Press.

Kundoqk (Green, J.) & Qwul'sih'yah'maht (Thomas, R.). (2015). Indigenous children in the centre: Indigenous perspectives on anti-oppressive child welfare practice. In Sohki Aski Esquao [J. Carrière] & S. Strega (Eds.), *Walking this path together: Anti-racist and anti-oppressive child welfare practice* (2nd ed.). Winnipeg: Fernwood Publishing.

Macdougall, B. (2006). Wahkootowin: Family and cultural identity in northwestern Saskatchewan Métis communities. *Canadian Historical Review*, 87(3), 431–462. http://dx.doi.org/10.1353/can.2006.0082

Maiter, S., (2015). Race matters: Social justice, not assimilation or cultural competence. In Sohki Aski Esquao [J. Carrière] & S. Strega (Eds.), *Walking this path together: Anti-racist and anti-oppressive child welfare practice* (2nd ed., pp. 87–104). Winnipeg: Fernwood Publishing.

Mann-Johnson, J. (2017). Kiikwookew kwizin and kinship care: Attending to the hearts of Métis children. In J. Carrière & C. Richardson (Eds.), *Calling our families home: Métis peoples' experiences with child welfare*. JCharlton Publishing.

McCreary Centre Society (2019), *Ta Saantii Deu/Neso: A profile of Métis youth health in BC*. https://www.mcs.bc.ca/pdf/ta_saantii_deu_neso.pdf

Métis Nation British Columbia. (2019) *Understanding the Métis in British Columbia: A guide for social workers, legislators, and policy makers*. Surrey, BC: Métis Nation British Columbia. https://documentcloud. adobe.com/link/track?uri=urn%3Aaaid%3Ascds%3AUS%3A9e95 3aa4-27b4-40e5-899d-14a178d650b7#pageNum=1

Métis Nation British Columbia. (2024). Children and Families. *MNBC Work & Programs*. Retrieved May 3, 2024, from https://www.mnbc.ca/ work-programs/ ministries/children-and-families

Monchalin, R., Smylie, J., Bourgeois, C., & Firestone, M. (2019). "I would prefer to have my health care provided over a cup of tea any day": Recommendations by urban Métis women to improve access to health and social services in Toronto for the Métis community. *AlterNative: An International Journal of Indigenous Peoples*, 15(3), 217–225. https://doi.org/10.1177/1177180119866515

Nabigon, H., & Mawhiney, A. M. (2011) Aboriginal theory: A Cree Medicine Wheel guide for healing First Nations. In F. J. Turner (Ed.), *Social Work Treatment* (5th ed., pp. 15–29). New York: Oxford University Press.

National Aboriginal Health Organization. (2007). *OCAP: Ownership, control, access and possession*. Ottawa: National Aboriginal Health Organization. https:// icwrn.uvic.ca/wp-content/uploads/2013/08/FNC-OCAP.pdf

National Aboriginal Health Organization. (2018). *Principles of ethical Métis research*. Métis Centre. https://achh.ca/wp-content/uploads/2018/07/Guide_Ethics_ NAHOMetisCentre.pdf

National Inquiry into Missing and Murdered Indigenous Women and Girls (Canada). (2019). *Reclaiming power and place: The final report of the National Inquiry into Missing and Murdered Indigenous Women and Girls*. Vol. 1b. https://www.mmiwg-ffada.ca/final-report/

Qwul'sih'yah'maht (Thomas, R. A.) (2015). Honouring the oral traditions of the Ta't Mustimuxw (Ancestors) through storytelling. In S. Strega & L. Brown (Eds.), *Research as resistance: Revisiting critical, Indigenous, and anti-oppressive approaches* (2nd ed., pp. 177–198). Toronto: Canadian Scholars' Press.

Representative for Children and Youth British Columbia. (2017). *Delegated Aboriginal agencies: How resourcing affects service delivery.* https://rcybc.ca/sites/default/files/documents/pdf/reports_publications/rcy-daa-2017.pdf

Representative for Children and Youth British Columbia. (2020a). *Illuminating service experience: A descriptive analysis of injury and death reports for First Nations children and youth in BC, 2015–2017.* https://rcybc.ca/wp-content/uploads/2020/12/IlluminatingServiceExperience.pdf

Representative for Children and Youth British Columbia. (2020b). *Invisible children: A descriptive analysis of injury and death reports for Métis children and youth in British Columbia, 2015 to 2017.* Victoria: Representative for Children and Youth. https://rcybc.ca/wp-content/uploads/2020/07/RCY_Me%CC%81tis-InvisibleChildren_July2020_FINAL.pdf

Richardson, C. L. (2016). *Belonging Métis.* Vernon: JCharlton Publishing.

Richardson, C., & Carrière, J. (2017). Métis methodology: A possible map for ethical positioning and congruency in research. In J. Carrière & C. Richardson (Eds.), *Calling our families home: Métis peoples' experiences with child welfare.* Vernon: JCharlton Publishing.

Richardson, C., & Wade, A. (2013). Creating islands of safety: Contesting failure to protect and mother-blaming in child protection cases of paternal violence against children and mothers. In S. Strega, J. Krane, S. LaPierre, C. Richardson, & Carlton R. (Eds.), *Failure to protect: Moving beyond gendered responses to violence.* Winnipeg: Fernwood Publishing.

Sinclair, R. (2009). Bridging the past and the future: An introduction to Indigenous social work issues. In R. Sinclair, M. A. Hart, & G. Bruyere (Eds.), *Wícihitowin: Aboriginal social work in Canada* (pp. 19–24). Winnipeg: Fernwood Publishing.

Sinclair, R. (2016). The Indigenous child removal system in Canada: An examination of legal decision-making and racial bias. *First Peoples Child & Family Review, 11*(2), 8–18. https://doi.org/10.7202/1082333ar

Sinclair, R., Hart, M. A., & Bruyere, G. (Eds.). (2009). *Wícihitowin: Aboriginal Social Work in Canada.* Winnipeg: Fernwood Publishing.

Sohki Aski Esquao [Carrière, J.]. (2017).

Strega, S., & Sohki Aski Esquao [Carrière, J.]. (2015). Introduction: Anti-racist and anti-oppressive child welfare. In Sohki Aski Esquao [J. Carrière] & S. Strega (Eds.), *Walking this path together: Anti-racist and anti-oppressive child welfare practice* (2nd ed.). Winnipeg: Fernwood Publishing.

Strega, S., Krane, J., Lapierre, S., Richardson, C., & Carlton, R. (2013). *Failure to protect: Moving beyond gendered responses.* Winnipeg: Fernwood Publishing.

Tait, C. L., Henry, R., & Walker, R. L. (2013). Child welfare: A social determinant of health for Canadian First Nations and Métis children. *Pimatisiwin: A Journal for Aboriginal and Indigenous Community Health,* 11(1), 39–53. https://gladue.usask.ca/sites/gladue1.usask.ca/files/gladue//resource461-2de50430.pdf

Teillet, J. (2019). *The north-west is our mother: The story of Louis Riel's people, the Métis Nation.* Patrick Crean Editions/Harper Collins.

Thomas, R., & Green, J. (2019) A way of life: Indigenous perspectives on anti-oppressive living. *First Peoples Child & Family Review,* 14(1), 81–93. https://doi.org/10.7202/1071288ar

Truth and Reconciliation Commission of Canada. (2015). *Canada's residential schools: The Métis experience: The final report of the Truth and Reconciliation Commission of Canada: Vol. 3.* Retrieved from https://nctr.ca/records/reports/#trc-reports

Wilson, S. (2008). *Research is ceremony: Indigenous research methods.* Halifax: Fernwood Publishing.

4

An Inquiry into the Stories of Indigenous Fathers and Their Paths into Fatherhood

A Narrative Analysis Conducted with Kwakwaka'wakw Fathers

Tanille Johnston

ABSTRACT

This chapter focuses on key elements offered by my Indigenous Master of Social Work thesis, which was motivated by a promise to a late friend and colleague that I would actively acknowledge and do something about the gap of services and supports for our Indigenous male counterparts. Embarking on this journey also brought forward the lack of other literary works that focus on the area of Kwakwaka'wakw Fatherhood. My primary goal was to contribute to a shift in child welfare practice, away from mother-centrism and towards equitable parental involvement through creating an opportunity for understanding Kwakwaka'wakw Fatherhood (Ball, 2009; Strega et al., 2008). It is my hope that this piece encourages social workers to strive for Father inclusion in their daily practice and to hold themselves to a high level of accountability regarding the British Columbia Ministry of Children and Family Development's (MCFD) goal of supporting all children and youth in British Columbia to live in safe, healthy, and nurturing families (MCFD, 2018).

Historically Indigenous men have been a focus in anthropological works; however, it's only been the last fifteen to twenty years that they have been asked about their roles in child raising. It's an honour to have created and supported an opportunity to listen to our Kwakwaka'wakw Fathers speak about themselves as parents (Dominelli et al., 2011; Strega et al., 2008). Through a thematic analysis and a storytelling methodology, this thesis began to answer the following question: *What reflections do Kwakwaka'wakw Fathers have when asked about their journey of coming into Fatherhood?* Kwakwaka'wakw Fathers were asked to share their stories of their experiences along their paths of Fatherhood. The analysis of their stories and a thorough literature review brought forward themes of Grandparents' Roles, Men in Culture, and Fishing. These themes were used to look at the various challenges that Kwakwaka'wakw Fathers face living in a colonized world and to create recommendations for social workers with files involving Kwakwaka'wakw Fathers. In conclusion, defining characteristics of a Father role in a Kwakwaka'wakw community are offered, as well as a call for a change not only in practice, but in policy, and in hearts for the future work between front-line social workers at MCFD and our Kwakwaka'wakw Fathers. **Keywords:** *Kwakwaka'wakw, Fatherhood, First Nation, protective factors, child welfare*

DEDICATION

A friend and colleague, Mark, challenged me in a conversation about services and supports to seek out each of those opportunities for males and to acknowledge that although patriarchal society favours my male counterparts, this is not the case in many of our First Nation communities. Our men are trying to thrive without many of the supports and programs that are available to our sisters, mothers, daughters, and aunties. Approaching this discrepancy needs to be inclusive of the fact that our women are also underserved by what is currently available in the ways of services and supports for families involved with the child welfare system. In the challenging conversation with my friend and colleague, I told him I would bring attention to that discrepancy, and this is my step to doing so. Rest peacefully, Mark. I'll try to make waves.

DEFINITION OF TERMS

First Nation(s): First Nation does not have a legal definition. In this work, First Nation is used to describe an individual person that self-identifies as being First Nation and/or belonging to a First Nation; First Nation can often refer to a band, reserve-based community, or a larger nation. Many First Nations are status Indians under the *Indian Act*, but many are not, and in this work the term First Nation applies to both; on and off reserve, status and non-status (Indigenous Foundations, 2009).

Father: This word is purposefully capitalized. We capitalized persons, places and/or things, and these Fathers are people and this work is aimed to uphold them in every way possible, even when it comes to their representation in the English language. Father, for the purpose of this work, is defined as a Kwakwaka'wakw individual that carries or acts as a parental figure to a child and/or youth of their own biologically or of another.

Our: As a First Nations woman belonging to a sister nation of the Kwakwaka'wakw, the Ligwilda'xw, when I use the word "our" I'm speaking to this relationship and belonging to families that are interconnected between these two language and family groups.

ABOUT THE AUTHOR

My name is Laqwalaogwa, and I'm from the Ligwilda'xw people of the We Wai Kai Nation. I lived and learned on the lands of the Coast Salish and Strait Salish people for over ten years until my move in 2016, back to my traditional territory where I was born and raised. Although there is no grounding like being home, I am very grateful for the opportunities that the South Island gifted me. I have practiced social work in the areas of Guardianship, Resources, Child Protection, and Health. I have been a practicing social worker for more than ten years and continue to find great meaning in this work.

✺✺✺✺✺✺✺✺✺ ✺✺✺✺✺✺✺

THE PROTECTIVE POTENTIAL OF FATHERHOOD

My current literary work is focused on defining what Fatherhood means in Kwakwaka'wakw communities in order to help front-line workers understand more about First Nation Fathers. My goal is that doing so will support social service workers to find new meaning, reach out in different ways, and view our Fathers as potentially protective rather than harmful factors (Ball, 2009; Ball & Daly, 2012; Ball et al., 2013; Strega et al., 2008, 2009). This is to honour those Fathers who are ready and striving to be meaningful role models in their children's lives, and to also acknowledge that accountability for children should be placed on both parents equitably and not solely weighted on our Mothers.

> Fathers may well be the greatest untapped resource in the lives of Aboriginal children today. If we could understand and support them to get involved and stay connected with their children, that would be a big protective factor for these youngsters as they grow up. (John, 2004)

Although focused on implications for influence within the social work world, the results of my research highlight the huge impact that a loss of fishing rights, loss of accessibility of the fishing industry, and the loss of the fish themselves has had on traditional methods of fathering for First Nations fathers. The Department of Fisheries and Oceans has played a pivotal role in dismantling opportunities for fathering and generativity of knowledge. In this chapter I will further outline why I chose Fatherhood, the methodology I applied, the three key concepts that came forward through my research, as well as my thoughts on findings and words for future Indigenous graduate researchers.

WHY KWAKWAKA'WAKW FATHERHOOD?

When asking my social work colleagues if they've ever received training on how to work with and engage with Fathers that have perhaps never been consulted about their children's open files, the answer is often "no" or "well, we've received like domestic-violence training and like how to reintegrate a sex offender training" (anonymous, personal communication, February 21, 2020).

I don't want to dismiss the alarming statistical information about the frequency of male-bodied persons perpetrating multiple forms of abuse against women. But there is a lot to say that isn't said about the men who don't fit in this stereotype. I want North America to take a break from only conceiving of Fathers as absent or abusive and explore the idea of Fathers as a potential protective element in their families and communities (Strega et al., 2008). Let's harness that potential and provide accessible and supportive opportunities for Fathers to learn, grow, and demonstrate their strengths. The following will outline how I, as an Indigenous researcher, engaged with the question *What reflections do Kwakwaka'wakw Fathers have when asked about their journey of coming into Fatherhood?* and the key concepts that emerged from sitting in story with Kwakwaka'wakw Fathers.

SELF AND METHODOLOGY

Indigenous people are at a stage where they want
research and research design to contribute to their
self-determination and liberation. (Rigney, 1997, p.3)

Our people have been inappropriately researched and misrepresented for centuries. My dedication to completing research in a good way comes from a place of wanting to contribute to the pool of other First Nation writers that are pushing for our stories to be recognized as legitimate forms of knowledge.

I hold my role as a First Nation researcher with purpose. I believe it is my utmost responsibility to ensure that the way I work does not replicate an invasive and destructive history. I believe that to complete research in a good way I need to look to our traditional governance structures to guide me. One of my cultural advisors throughout this process, Alex Nelson, taught me that everything we do in life should align with the teachings of the Gukzi (Big House). Each of the four posts in the Gukzi represent a value: 1) Respect, 2) Integrity, 3) Honesty, and 4) Trust (RIHT). I took these values and applied them to my work as the RIHT methodology. Trust is a virtue that I hold very dear to my heart. I believe that trust is the ultimate connection you can have with a person. It requires vulnerability, dedication, and transparency. It requires the presence of the other three virtues in the Gukzi: Honesty, Respect, and Integrity. These four corners of the Big House have been with me throughout this work and have been reflected upon with each phase of research.

In addition to looking at research through Kwakwaka'wakw protocol, I also had a small group of Kwakwaka'wakw Advisors that were in place to support me. They were utilized to vet the language I used to seek research partners (Fathers) as well as to review the questions I was going to be asking. I confided in them to debrief with, to ask questions of curiosity to in a safe space, and to remind me that this is hard work and needed work. This group was important to ensure that my colonized brain would not take over and produce western research. They were also fundamental in supporting my own personal journey of decolonization within myself.

> There was once, for all of us, a fire in the night... To talk, to tell our stories, to teach each other, is as necessary to our growth as water. We're all storytellers. We always were. But most of us have forgotten that... (Schorcht, 2008)

Applying a storytelling approach to this research was a glaringly obvious path. It is a commonly known and well-recorded fact that First Nations cultures are oral (Cajete, 1999). And that the history of our people lives within that oral history, which is represented through stories. Further to this, "through the retelling of stories, First Nations represent their identities and societies" (Fraser, 2004, p. 180), making this approach all that more appropriate to begin to define and identify what it means to be a Kwakwaka'wakw Father (Isaac, 2010; Schorcht, 2008).

A storytelling methodology creates space to honour the traditional way of knowledge sharing in First Nation communities (Kovach, 2009; Qwul'sih'yah'maht [Thomas], 2015). A conversational method of research is a relatively new way of researching and aligns with an Indigenous paradigm that is arguably less invasive than other methods of research (Kovach, 2009; Qwul'sih'yah'maht [Thomas], 2015; Wilson, 2008).

My use of a storytelling approach is also passively influenced by other methodologies committed to social justice and decolonizing. Active decolonization and an equity approach to social justice have been an ingrained part of my social work practice. I am dedicated to practising in a way that enforces equity and equality for all First Nation, Métis, and Inuit (Baskin, 2011; Brown & Strega, 2015; Ladson-Billings, 1998; Smith, 1999; Wilson, 2008).

Through the process of hosting conversations with Kwakwaka'wakw Fathers, I learned that the barriers they face are bigger than simply "stepping up to the plate." As I spoke with these fathers, three recurring themes emerged that helped to frame the challenges they face when it comes to being involved and connected with their children. I believe understanding these three themes can help social service workers better understand and support the fathers they work with in their communities. Before exploring the three key concepts from my research, I want to acknowledge that although these findings may project knowledge that reflects the thoughts and feelings of other Indigenous and non-Indigenous Fathers, my research has been done specifically with Kwakwaka'wakw Fathers as I am a family member of this community and this relationship has allowed me to conduct research in a safer space, amongst family (Wilson, 2008).

FATHERS AND FISHING

Historically, "men [would] define fishing—especially salmon fishing—as their most important economic activity" and while "many men could earn a great deal more money through logging…they [choose] not to" (Rohner & Rohner, 1970, p. 30). However, the Department of Fisheries and Oceans (DFO) has, over time, made fishing inaccessible as a trade and thus removed a vital part of what has been considered Fathering from the lives of our men.

In the past, the boats were where our men were actively learning how to parent. It's where they learned how to be responsible, where they listened to their Elders' stories, where they began to step into their parents' and grandparents' boots. A place where they brought up the next generation, and it has been taken away. The loss of access to fishing removes food security for many First Nations as well as the financial stability required by the western world. Perhaps worse, it also removes our culture and severs the intergenerational knowledge transfer necessary to our survival as First Nations people.

It's on those boats that our Fathers learn about problem-solving and sacrifice, hard work, creativity, failure, and perseverance. Fishing has served as a vehicle to ground us in our culture and has always been a part of our identity. But since the establishment of the DFO, we have been losing all these things. If residential, boarding, and day schools wiped out the opportunity for generations of children to learn from healthy parental role models, the DFO is doing a really good job of removing any remaining opportunity for our Fathers to do so.

A prime example of this is the price tags put on the licenses required to fish commercially. These licenses were created and then bought up by colonizers and now cost so much that only the upper class can afford to own one; there is only a very small number of owner-operators. The hot hands that hold these licenses now lease them out at exorbitant rates that make it extremely difficult to make a living after paying for the lease, the crew, the gas, the equipment, and food.

This forces First Nations with boats to work harder for less, often taking out smaller crews to handle the massive job of bringing in enough fish both to sell and to feed their Elders and community members. The pressure to bring in a big-enough catch doesn't allow for the younger generations to be present on the boats in the way they have in the past. The high-pressure environment is not conducive to teaching and the stakes are too high to have extras on board to feed and care for.

This loss of inter-generational knowledge does more than just put First Nations food security at risk. Since the knowledge of how to harvest fish is primarily attained through commercial means, remote First Nations communities are also losing access to the social and ceremonial aspects of fish and fishing. This is resulting in the destruction of culture, belonging, and self for many First Nations Fathers.

FATHERS AS GRANDPARENTS

Grandparents were, and continue to be, a vital source of learning and parenting. Each of the Fathers that I spoke with commented numerous times on the roles their Grandparents played in their upbringing. Grandparents were referenced over sixty times between the three conversations. It was very common for children's parents to leave the village to work for months at a time. Men would primarily head out fishing for months at a time, and the women often worked in the canneries. Children were left in the villages to be raised by their Grandparents and other community members. This was never viewed as neglect or as shirking responsibility but was simply the way of life.

In the book *Assu of Cape Mudge: Recollections of a Coastal Indian Chief*, Harry Assu reflects, "When I was a young boy, I spent a lot of time with my Grandfather. He told me stories of his life time on these waters. I learned many things from him" (Assu, 1989, p. 25). In Irene Isaac's work, Elder Vera Newman "had just about every night with my grandparents" and said "Grandfather sometimes told us legends" and "sometimes he danced for us" and was "always teaching us" (Isaac, 2010). Ray, one of the Fathers involved in this work, named one of his Grandfathers as a mentor, "one of my Grandfathers, my dad's Father, I grew up with him on the fishing boat as well. So learned some things from him, my mom's Father not so much, he died at a very young age, so I didn't really know him" (Wilson, 2018). Western style of child-rearing sees the responsibility primarily held by the biological parents. However, in First Nations this responsibility is held by the community with an emphasis on the Grandparents. When parents are accessing their parents, their sisters, their brothers, and their partners, relatives for support and responsibility of their children, this is not neglect or the ditching of responsibility but a cultural norm of parenting. It is an important part of child-rearing in First Nation communities; establishing a child's village. It's with exposure to the village that a child learns to accept help and the support of a variety of persons, where they learn about their family tree, delegation, social skills, and the ability to be empathic (Rohner & Rohner, 1970).

Today families struggle with the western world's imposition of children being the sole responsibility of the parents—especially when child welfare becomes involved. Child welfare assessments demand the primary parenting responsibility be defined and placed on one or two persons. This is a very limiting factor and is culturally inappropriate. In many First Nation communities there is no easily identifiable primary parent, and the responsibility of ensuring a child's safety is the responsibility of the community just as much as the parents'.

FATHERS IN CULTURE

Our men hold the responsibility of carrying and passing of names, passing of dances, carrying and sharing of secrets. They're the owners of the honour of hamatsa, they are our composers, our singers, the hosts of our potlaches, our fishermen, and they are our Chiefs (Boas, 1897, 1920, 1921, 1925). First-born sons in our families are taught early on about the importance of upholding their family's name since they are in line to inherit their family's Chieftainship (Spradley, 1967, p. 9; Walkus, 2018). The eldest sons of our families also commonly carry the responsibility of all the younger siblings. They are given parenting roles very early and help to ensure their siblings' safety and health.

Over and above the responsibilities given to them by their community, they also hold all the responsibilities that western society has placed on Fathers. They must be "all-star" dads and be present and available and have meaningful time with their children. They must also be breadwinners and be able to fully provide for the children and their partners. They must be the do-it-all and know how to accomplish the various tasks associated with masculinity—fixing the sink, putting broken toys back together, building a

shed, etc. The cultural expectations and demands of Fathers are also extensive, such as their ceremonial community obligations.

Many of our Fathers have not been able to take the time to step back
and look at all the weight that society has put on them or the extreme
expectations they face. Instead of thinking and planning how they want to
carry themselves in community, they are stuck trying to constantly live up
to or prove wrong the labels and personas placed on them by the western
world. I believe that we need to talk more openly about how many roles
our Fathers are trying to fill, the places and activities where learning has
historically come from, and the changes that have happened to spaces and
practices. We need to create space for Fathers to take a breath, regroup, and
regain their place in the community and their power.

RETHINKING FATHERHOOD

Jessica Ball (2009) states that Indigenous Fathers are "arguably the most
socially excluded" persons and that the intergenerational disruptions, residential schools, incarceration, and racism are all key influences on their
ability to successfully parent (p. 29, 30). I would add to this list the DFO's
role in removing the intergenerational knowledge transfer and mentorship (which is so vital in First Nations communities) by making fishing
inaccessible. So, what do we do?

A recent study by Caroline Mniszak, *Exploring the Information Contexts of
Young Fathers in Two British Columbian Cities*, looked at the lack of appropriate resources for young Fathers (Mniszak, 2018). According to her work, very
little research has been done in the area of young Fatherhood and there are
extremely "disproportionate amounts of services and information resources
available for young mothers versus young Fathers" (2018).[1] Her work echoes
that of Ball, Strega, and Brown which also calls for appropriate programs
and services designed specifically for Fathers (Ball, 2010; Ball & Daly, 2012;
Ball et al., 2013; Brown & Strega, 2015; Mniszak, 2018; Strega, 2007).

---

1   Mniszak defined young as fourteen to twenty-four years of age for the purposes of
    her research.

In order to see our Fathers differently—as protective factors that contribute to children's well-being—there must be a number of changes: policy reform, patience, positive media representation, new programs, and paternity testing (Ball & Daly, 2012). There also needs to be a mentality shift among front-line workers where greater involvement of fathers is sought out and supported rather than labelled as "absent" when the system doesn't create space for them.

There would be value for front-line workers to learn more about the traditional and potential roles of First Nation Fathers and how they can better and more creatively support and engage all Fathers. Working to increase the involvement and engagement of Fathers will not only increase the health and well-being of their children but of the Fathers as well. And this, in turn, will serve to create "safe, healthy, and nurturing families [that are] strongly connected to their communities and culture" (MCFD, 2018).

My research is dedicated to creating change in our systems of care—change that recognizes the value and supports the involvement of Fathers, Sons, Brothers, and Uncles within our communities and within the systems that we encounter. Although western, patriarchal society favours my male counterparts, this is not the case in many First Nation communities. Our men are attempting to thrive without many of the supports and programs that are available to our Sisters, Mothers, Daughters, and Aunties, and we all need to work to look at opportunities to raise up our men. It's also important that this work must not discount the fact that although there are programs and services available to Mothers, they are not nearly sufficient enough to support them. Collectively more needs to be done.

AN OFFERING

This connectivity that is embodied in storytelling is a
continuation of Indigenous existence. (Sium & Ritskes, 2013)

It's important to remind ourselves that conducting traditional research is more than simply identifying as an Indigenous, Aboriginal, Métis, Inuit, or First Nations person and then following the path of western colonial

researchers before us and accomplishing research through undesired solic-
itation without reciprocity. Carrying respect, integrity, honesty, and trust
with you as a researcher and actively answering the questions that the
Gukzi or your own cultural protocols requires of you will create a deeper
connection between you and your work, and will ensure that you're stepping lightly, taking the time that's needed, and dedicating your work for
the purposes of benefiting participants and Indigenous communities, not
solely an institution.

I hold my hands up to the Fathers that have been with me through this
process and thank them for all they have offered me and hope that this
work has offered them a sense of value and ownership over its influence.
It's been an honour to represent their stories in these findings and to continue to speak to this work when space is provided. My motivation for this
research came from a place of wanting to make ripples in the child welfare
system of British Columbia that will ultimately result in Fathers far and
wide being brought into their children's lives, and has grown to look at
the impacts of the Department of Fisheries and Oceans in dismantling a
vital platform for Fatherhood generativity. The impact of colonialism is
undoubtedly riddled through our Fathers and is consistently imposed on
them. It hurt my heart to see our Fathers trying to do it all, reignite our culture and traditional ways while working full-time, often more than one job,
in an attempt to single-handedly provide for their families in this expense-
driven world, and also be a primary parent. I see colonialism eroding our
Fathers through the historical establishment of elected systems of government in communities and through the loss of fishing sovereignty.

The stories that these Fathers shared offered insight into the reality of
the impositions placed on Fathers today, not only through the western
world's definition and expectations of a Father, but their commitment to
their role to community and to their children. They spoke to the importance of culture generativity, and their lack of personal opportunity for this
in the past due to choices that had to be made in life to pursue education
and careers and being removed from their traditional territories to do so.
The societal pressure to perform, earn, purchase, and live independently in
your single-family home has encouraged an "all-American" ideal of moral

deliverance that has naturally separated parents, Fathers, from their families, and from vital opportunities for generativity. It felt as though these Fathers had never really had an opportunity to sit down and talk about their parenting role and what this means to them. This may not be factual, but it was definitely an honour to be able to have an opportunity to praise the role that they live in our communities. It is my hope that they're proud of the movement that this research will contribute to the importance of raising up our Fathers.

Having read these research findings and being in a position to create space for Fathers, I ask you to reflect on your social work practice and how you might be able to practise differently to support men in Fathering roles. Are you able to create more male-parent inspiring imagery in your waiting area? Are you in a position to create a program that supports Men that are parenting? Can you make it a priority to include a Father-figure in a file? Or make that extra call to reach out to the Dad? Together, let's support Fathers and recognize the untapped resource of their contributions to our communities.

OUR FUTURE RESEARCHERS

For many Indigenous persons such as our Elders, the written word has never been our way as it was a colonial way of sharing. Don't let that deter you from embracing it as an opportunity for a journey with yourself, with the future of Our people, as a mechanism for sustainability of Our stories, Our protocols, Our history. This is a tool to hold Ourselves up, to have a voice, to inspire, and to provide a path for those of us that feel lost, or don't know where to start with finding Our roots. Being able to pick up a book about your people when you feel as though you were abandoned or forgotten for decades is an extremely empowering moment. Being a part of bringing people home through providing a platform for learning right where some of our work can be found in a library, on Google, in the bookstore is a privilege. Write to provide a path home that's reachable from all over the world.

REFERENCES

Assu, H., & Inglis, J. (1989). *Assu of Cape Mudge: Recollections of a Coastal Indian Chief*. Vancouver: UBC Press.

Ball, J. (2009). Fathering in the shadows: Indigenous fathers and Canada's colonial legacies. *Annals of the American Academy of Political and Social Science*, 624(1), 29–48. https://doi.org/10.1177/0002716209334181

Ball, J. (2010). Indigenous fathers' involvement in reconstituting "circles of care." *American Journal of Community Psychology*, 45(1–2), 124–138. https://doi.org/10.1007/s10464-009-9293-1

Ball, J., & Daly, K. (Eds.). (2012). *Father involvement in Canada: Diversity, renewal, and transformation*. Vancouver: UBC Press.

Ball, J., Moselle, K., & Moselle, S. (2013). *Contributions of culture and language in Aboriginal Head Start in Urban and Northern Communities to children's health outcomes: A review of theory and research*. Public Health Agency of Canada. http://cahr. uvic. ca/nearbc/media/docs/cahr51foade9a51cf-phac-ashunc-languageand-culture-report.pdf.

Baskin, C. (2011). *Strong helpers' teachings: The value of Indigenous knowledges in the helping professions*. Toronto: Canadian Scholars' Press.

Boas, F. (1897). *The social organization and the secret societies of the Kwakiutl Indians*. Washington: US Government Printing Office.

Boas, F. (1920). The social organization of the Kwakiutl. *American Anthropologist*, 22(2), 111–126. https://www.jstor.org/stable/659966

Boas, F. (1921). *Ethnology of the Kwakiutl*. In *Thirty-fifth annual report of the Bureau of American Ethnology, 1913–1914* (pp. 43–794). Bureau of American Ethnology. Washington: US Government Printing Office.

Boas, F. (1925). *Contributions to the ethnology of the Kwakiutl*. (Vol. 3). New York: Columbia University Press.

Brown, L., & Strega, S. (2015). *Research as resistance: Revisiting critical, Indigenous, and anti-oppressive approaches* (2nd ed.). Toronto: Canadian Scholars' Press.

Cajete, G. A. (1999). *Igniting the sparkle: An Indigenous science education model*. Skyland, NC: Kivaki Press.

Dominelli, L., Strega, S., Walmsley, C., Callahan, M., & Brown, L. (2011). "Here's my story": Fathers of "looked after" children recount their experiences in the Canadian child welfare system. *British Journal of Social Work*, 41(2), 351–367. https://doi.org/10.1093/bjsw/bcq099

Fraser, H. (2004). Doing narrative research: Analysing personal stories line by line. *Qualitative Social Work*, 3(2), 179–201. https://doi.org/10.1177/1473325004043383

Indigenous Foundations. (2009). *Terminology*. Retrieved March 13, 2019, from https://indigenousfoundations.arts.ubc.ca/terminology/#firstnations

Isaac, I. (2010). *Understanding traditional ecological knowledge through Kwakwaka'wakw story* [Doctoral dissertation, University of Victoria]. Dspace. https://dspace.library.uvic.ca/server/api/core/bitstreams/fc72e4db-69d1-48e5-bbba-4eab028b828b/content

John, E. (Grand Chief) (2004, April 27–28). Closing Remarks, *British Columbia First Nations Summit*. Aboriginal Leadership Forum on Early Childhood Development, North Vancouver.

Kovach, M. (2009). *Indigenous methodologies: Characteristics, conversations and contexts*. Toronto: University of Toronto Press.

Ladson-Billings, G. (1998). Just what is critical race theory and what's it doing in a nice field like education? *International Journal of Qualitative Studies in Education*, 11(1), 7–24. http://dx.doi.org/10.1080/095183998236863

Ministry of Children and Family Development. (2018, April 24). Province proposes changes to improve Indigenous child welfare. *BC Gov News*. Retrieved July 2, 2019, from https://news.gov.bc.ca/releases/2018CFD0015-000722

Mniszak, C. (2018). *Exploring the information contexts of young fathers in two British Columbian cities* [Doctoral dissertation, University of British Columbia]. Open Collections. https://doi.org/10.14288/1.0365778

Qwul'sih'yah'maht (Thomas, R. A.) (2015). Honouring the oral traditions of the Ta't Mustimuxw (Ancestors) through storytelling. In S. Strega & L. Brown (Eds.), *Research as resistance: Revisiting critical, Indigenous, and anti-opressive approaches* (2nd ed., pp. 177–198). Toronto: Canadian Scholars' Press.

Rohner, R. P., & Rohner, E. C. (1970). *The Kwakiutl: Indians of British Columbia*. New York: Holt, Rinehart and Winston.

Schorcht, B. (2008). Story words: An interview with Richard Wagamese. *Studies in American Indian Literatures*, 20(3), 74–91. https://www.jstor.org/stable/20737425

Sium, A., & Ritskes, E. (2013). Speaking truth to power: Indigenous storytelling as an act of living resistance. *Decolonization: Indigeneity, Education & Society*, 2(1), i–x.

Smith, L. T. (1999). *Decolonizing methodologies: Research and Indigenous peoples*. London: Zed Books.

Spradley, J. P. (1967). *The Kwakiutl guardian spirit quest: An historical, functional, and comparative analysis* [Master's thesis, University of Washington].

Strega, S. (2007). Anti-oppressive practice in child welfare. In D. Baines (Ed.), *Doing anti-oppressive practice: Social justice social work* (2nd ed., pp. 67–82). Winnipeg: Fernwood Publishing.

Strega, S., Brown, L., Callahan, M., Dominelli, L., & Walmsley, C. (2009). Working with me, working at me: Fathers' narratives of child welfare. *Journal of Progressive Human Services*, 20(1), 72–91.

Strega, S., Fleet, C., Brown, L., Dominelli, L., Callahan, M., & Walmsley, C. (2008). Connecting father absence and mother blame in child welfare policies and practice. *Children and Youth Services Review*, 30(7), 705–716. https://doi.org/10.1016/j.childyouth.2007.11.012

Wilson, S. (2008). *Research is ceremony: Indigenous research methods*. Halifax: Fernwood Publishing.

PART TWO

Arts-Based Knowledges and Practices

5

centring stories by urban indigiqueers/trans/two-spirit people and indigenous women

on practices of decolonization, collective care, and self-care

mel lefebvre

ABSTRACT

centring the voices of indigiqueers, trans, two-spirit (2S) people, and indigenous women shines light where we find radical thought, grassroots action and rebellious forms of care. this revolutionary practice ultimately disturbs the systems of colonialism and heteronormativity that work to oppress qtbipoc (queer, trans, black, indigenous, people of colour) communities. the gendered processes of colonialism in so-called north america have disrupted the balance of gender roles and leadership responsibilities/ capacities traditionally held by non-binary, gender fluid, and trans folks in our communities. government legislation and policy such as the *indian act*, the reserve system, and residential schools have led to social and economic disparity for indigenous peoples and forced diaspora to urban centres, where indigenous community is now comprised of a variety of nations coming together in solidarity to share and support one another. edited into nine podcast episodes titled *kiyanâw maskihkîwakan: our medicines*, this research-creation project centres storytelling by urban indigiqueers, trans, two-spirit people, and indigenous women on their life journeys and decolonization, collective care, and self-care. storytellers touch on experiences related to identity and belonging, (re)connection, trauma, cultural teachings, creativity, gender and sexuality, body sovereignty, role in community, and notions of and relationships with land. they reveal how we kindle and keep alight kinship relations with each other and ourselves on the land—whether urban, rural, or cyber scapes—as we navigate these settled spaces towards possible indigenous futures. **keywords**: *indigenous, collective care, self-care, story, storytelling, storywork, indigiqueer, trans, two-spirit, 2S, queer, non-binary, gender fluid, gender, sexuality, women, bipoc, qtbipoc, sovereignty, colonialism, community, podcast, research creation, indigenous method, indigenous methodology*

TRIGGER & CONTENT WARNING

some content in this thesis may refer directly or indirectly to:

- colonization
- trauma/intergenerational trauma
- death and dying
- after-death care and funeral services
- child welfare system, the sixties scoop, residential schools
- physical/sexual violence
- child abuse
- emotional abuse
- slurs, stereotypes, racism
- addictions, including drug or alcohol abuse
- suicide and self-harm

LOWER CASE

this text is written deliberately in lower case. my traditional languages of michif and nêhiyawêwin using roman orthography have no capital letters, and syllabics as shapes are not about capitalizations—which brings about ideas of hierarchy—but are spirit markers illustrating timeless experience in this universe.

settler colonialism in canada attempted to wipe out indigenous languages and replace them with english and french, denying our right to exist as we are. i try to reframe that when i am able, through thought, writing, protest, and refusal. this is a small way of many to push back against the colonizer language, a defiance from within these constructs of academia, capitalism, patriarchy, and settler society, and instead a celebration of indigenous independence, choice, human rights, and freedom.

SELF LOCATION & THANKS

tansi nitotemtik. nitisikason mel. niya oma testawayak iyinew. niya oma apihtakosisan otipemsew ekwa nêhiyaw ekwa mooniyaw. niya oma asâsowêw. niya oma kakua okwimisa.

hello friends. my name is mel. i am a two-spirit (2S) red river métis/nêhiyaw/french/irish traditional tattoo practitioner. i am porcupine's helper.

i am a mother, community worker, artist, and phd student at concordia university in montreal.

my great grandparents were farmers in fisher branch (formerly wasoo), manitoba—the interlake region—where my great grandmother was born. before that, the family had lived in lac la ronge, saskatchewan, where some of my great aunts and uncles were born. family names include desjardins, st-laurent, delorme, guiboche, roque. in the early 1900s, they moved their six children to quebec where there was work for my grandfather at the textile factory. my grandmother was the seventh and last child to be born; she was the only one of the seven to be born in quebec. my grandmother was three when her mother died and the passing down of cultural knowledge was frayed…but not broken. my great aunts and uncles and their mother identified as cree. this is why i learn and am guided by nêhiyawêwin and michif as they are interconnected.

i work diligently and with care to restore these frayed threads, for my father, sister, and myself. my mother is our heart.

i want to acknowledge my elders: dr. mary wilson, blu waters, sedalia kawennotas fazio, vicky boldo, and joseph naytowhow.

a *huge* kinanâskomitin to the storytellers who made this possible and were so generous and open in sharing their stories.

a special loving kinanâskomitin to my supervisor and dear friend, liz fast, who is simply this: ◉ a pathway for us all to follow, that she's cleared with her diligence and care. like the golden mean, reminiscent of the spiral, used as a mode of creating symmetry, proportion, and harmony, she carefully crafts beauty and truth in our community. her guidance is so special, so needed. she channels an ancient wisdom that opens the way towards our true selves.

to moe clark, nîtisân, who makes me laugh, holds and shares so much knowledge, creativity, poetry, inspiration and commitment, you are the spiciest.

thank you to the social sciences and human resources council, concordia university's indigenous directions leadership group, and the school of graduate studies that made it possible to fund the research that informed this chapter.

〰〰〰〰〰〰〰〰

INTRODUCTION

centring stories by urban indigiqueers/trans/two-spirit and indigenous women on practices of decolonization, collective care and self-care

Settler colonialism in so-called north america is a gendered process that has forced and reproduced heteropatriarchal socio-economic systems on/in indigenous communities, and has disrupted the balance of gender roles and leadership responsibilities/capacities traditionally held by indigiqueers,[2] trans, two-spirit[3] people, and indigenous women (jacobs, 2017; national inquiry into missing and murdered indigenous women and girls [nimmiwg], 2019). government legislation and policy such as the *indian act* (1867–) and the reserve system have led to social and economic disparity for indigenous peoples, as well as the disruption of indigenous families and communities (canadian feminist alliance et al., 2019; jacobs, 2017).

forced diaspora and lack of services on reserves have led many of us to live in urban centres where indigenous community is comprised of a variety of nations coming together in solidarity to share and support one another. the final report of the national inquiry into missing and murdered indigenous women and girls (nimmiwg) supports the necessity to practice collective and self-care as it finds that the violence against indigenous women, girls, and gender-diverse people are a direct result of colonial policy and actions like the indian act, the sixties scoop, residential schools and breaches of human and indigenous rights (nimmiwg, 2019, p. 50)—the practices of collective and self-care counter that violence by creating community that fosters well-being, resilience, and pride in being and knowing who we are as indigenous people.

edited into nine podcast episodes titled *kiyanâw maskihkîwakan: our medicines*, this research-creation project centres storytelling by urban indigiqueers, trans, two-spirit folks, and indigenous women on their life journeys and asks us to speak specifically to decolonization, collective care, and self-care. storytellers were asked to speak on a variety of topics depending on their life journey and practices with common themes touching on growing up, professions and practices, kinship relations kindled and kept alight in city spaces, caring for ourselves and one another, and healing as we move through these settled spaces towards possible futures while in the context of our indigenous traditions.

---

2   the term indigiqueer was created by thirza jean cuthand in 2004 as "indigequeer" for vancouver queer film festival's indigenous/two-spirit program.
3   two-spirit/2S—created by cree teacher myra laramee who shared it with a gathering of indigenous lgbtqi people from throughout north america, held in southern manitoba in 1990 (wilson, 2015).

in the research that informs this chapter i have sought to hold space for us to speak freely about our lives, offer insight into challenges regarding colonialism, build on the indigenous knowledge base that informs about our roles and needs as indigenous 2Slgbtq+ and women, present practices of how we are claiming our identities and wellness, and tell our stories through an accessible oral medium. indigenous people are still here despite the structures in place that work to harm us. we are governing our own bodies and minds in this effort to decolonize, survive, and thrive (hill, 2013; vizenor, 2008), and create stronger kinship systems or *constellations of care* (danger, 2019).

the methodologies and methods to be discussed and used to ground this work and engage with participants include the nêhiyawêwin principles of wâhkôhtowin (nêhiyaw kinship ethics), miyo-wîchêtowin (care for others/collective care) and miyo-pimatisiwin (living a good life/self-care) (cardinal & hildebrandt, 2000; naytowhow & wilson, 2019); research creation (chapman and sawchuk, 2012); anti-colonialism and decolonization theory (fanon, 2004; smith, 2012); queer theory and queer indigenous ethics (danger, 2019; driskill, 2010; hunt & holmes, 2015; simpson, 2017; tuck & recollet, 2016; wilbur & keene, 2019; wilson, 2015); storywork (archibald, 1997, 2012); research as ceremony (wilson, 2008); circle method (chilisa, 2012); the conversation method (kovach, 2010); and podcasting to share indigenous ways of being and learning through a contemporary medium that is perhaps more attractive and accessible to the urban community—particularly for those who may not be interested or able to engage with academic text—as well as various learners and learning styles (day, 2017; mitchell, 2017).

LITERATURE & COMMUNITY KNOWLEDGE REVIEW

literature & community knowledge

the rigour through which academic literature goes is deeply appreciated, with many knowledgeable, dedicated, and thoughtful creators ensuring robust research, analysis, critique, reflection, and proper citation in caring for these wells of knowledge. within an indigenous framework, citing only literature that is deemed acceptable by the western academy is limiting: the experiences and knowledge that exist within our communities—urban, rural, and on reserve—are as valuable and have faced a fire comparable to any academic peer review. much of this knowledge is transferred through conversations, speeches, and sharing at gatherings—not necessarily as a written text with edits, but as stories that are told and retold, recorded in our minds and bodies. as such, some of these moments have been included in this review as vital sources of knowledge on this research topic.

this literature and knowledge review covers nêhiyawak (plains cree) kinship ethics as grounding this work; anti-colonial/decolonization theory and practice as it pertains to indigenous ways of overcoming colonial policy through personal and collective process; indigenous research paradigm/research as ceremony as ways in which indigenous peoples build on the indigenous knowledge base; indigenous queer theory and practice as modes of returning to ourselves and being in relation; collective care and self-care as acts situated in direct opposition to state-sanctioned heteronormativity; survivance and thrivance as continuation of our stories and flourishing into the future; notions of resurgence and sovereignty as potentially inaccessible to diverse genders; and social media and digital media as unprecedented access to thought dissemination and collective action. not included in this research is storywork with/by indigenous children. a bonus episode is included in the podcast of my daughter who is learning cree teachings from me and community; however, this research does not look in-depth at other young voices, as that is not the focus.

beyond settler colonialism, indigenous ways of knowing and being have existed and nurtured us since time immemorial. nêhiyaw (plains cree) kinship relations and care—relational ethics—holds that everything that comes from the land is related and as such, requires reciprocal accountability through relationship: wâhkôhtowin. in his book *research is ceremony*, plains cree scholar shawn wilson points to our ways of knowing ourselves in connection to the rest of the universe and that these systems of belief directly inform and guide "the tools we as researchers use in finding out more about the cosmos" (wilson, 2008, p. 13). as leaders, philosophers, educators, and caregivers in this dominant settler society, indigenous peoples have developed ways to decolonize and co-exist with the institutions that have sought to assimilate or disappear us. in the academy, where historically research has been done *on*, *to* and *about* indigenous peoples (smith, 2012, p. 1), our ways of being and knowing can shift *research* into *relationship*, to form an indigenous research paradigm based on our cultural ways of being in relation: in reciprocity and accountability (wilson, 2008).

we can look to african oral traditions where some of the first stories around decolonization were recorded, where cultures fought for self-determination and reclamation of land and knowledges (lunga, 2014). as a concept in the social sciences, french west indian psychiatrist, philosopher, and writer frantz fanon speaks about decolonization as "the basic claims of the colonized," the last becoming the first, a changing of the "social fabric" from within, and the colonizer as one who "fabricated and continues to fabricate the colonized subject" (fanon, 2004, p. 2).

as linda tuhiwai smith presents in *decolonizing methodologies: research and indigenous peoples* (2012), decolonization is concerned with research context: in this case, indigenous peoples and their communities and the western institutions and researchers throughout history that have implicated themselves in our communities to support the power and reach of imperialism that has sought or seeks to investigate, annihilate, and appropriate our knowledges and lifeways (smith, 2012). one can look to the ubiquity of christianity, heteronormativity, capitalism, and state violence within and surrounding our communities as structures of white supremacy that require dismantling to save the lives of black, indigenous, and people of colour (bipoc).

in this effort to decolonize and dismantle, michi saagiig nishnaabeg scholar, writer, and artist leanne betasamosake simpson suggests in her book *as we have always done* (2017) that decolonization is a personal and collective process of "returning to ourselves, a reengagement with the things we have left behind, a re-emergence, an unfolding from the inside out" (simpson, 2017, pp. 17–18). simpson brings us to the self as a driving force for collective change where we reach back to our ancestors, remember how we lived and thrived, and bring that knowledge and action into today.

an integral aspect of this remembrance and contemporary practice that simpson offers, cherokee two-spirit queer writer, activist, and performer qwo-li driskill sees the twenty-first century swelling with indigiqueer 2Slgbtq+ folks embracing our traditional gender identities and roles as a method of critiquing and struggling against colonialism, and as a result, has bolstered our perspectives and allowed us to foster more robust, creative actions of decolonization as we position ourselves as often central to decolonial agendas (driskill, 2010). in embracing our roles in community, indigiqueers and trans folks, indigenous women and girls are centred during gatherings and protests, drumming and singing to call in our ancestors and enact our sovereignty in direct opposition to heteronormative settler government, state violence, land theft, and resource extraction.

This acceptance of our varied, non-binary gender identities that have always existed is coined by two-spirit cree scholar alex wilson as "coming in [which does not] centre on the declaration of independence that characterizes 'coming out' in mainstream depictions of the lives of lgbtqi people. Rather, coming in is an act of returning, fully present in our selves, to resume our place as a valued part of our families, cultures, communities, and lands, in connection with all our relations" (wilson, 2015). (re)claiming our identities and continuing to practice our traditions and strengthen our communities, reconnect ourselves as members of a forced diaspora, care for each other *as we have always done* (simpson, 2017), we are not only in direct opposition to colonization, but dismantling it brick by brick and generating something new.

indigenous kinship relations have undergone profound mutations under the weight of settler colonialism, genocide, and environmental crises, that attempts to assimilate indigenous peoples to uphold the heteropatriarchal capitalist socio-economic structure we know today (vowel, 2014). in conversation on the podcast *all my relations*, dakota scholar kim tallbear provides a critical perspective on decolonizing relationships as well as heteronormativity and "compulsory monogamy" as oppressive and as an upholding the hierarchical settler structure which seeks to individualize us, disrupting our community relationships, and keeping us dependent on the state instead of each other for support (wilbur &keene, 2019). indigenous epistemologies regarding how we care for one another, such as wâhkôhtowin, help us to understand being in many loving relationships—polyamory—and practising "good relations" based on respect and reciprocity instead of ownership.

to challenge individualized heteronormative ways of being, tallbear suggests the need for knowledge sharing between indigenous and queer scholarship. indigenous queer scholar sarah hunt and queer scholar cindy holmes discuss how *queer* is not merely a term referring to gender and sexuality but extends beyond to *action* where we challenge ways of knowing and being entrenched into society by the settler state; the praxis of decolonization and queering are "active, interconnected, critical, and everyday practices that take place within and across diverse spaces and times" (hunt & holmes, 2015). what do these everyday practices look like in terms of decolonization and care?

in their keynote at concordia university's symposium *communities of care* in february of 2019, métis-saulteaux-polish 2S artist and community worker dayna danger pointed to the multitude of ways in which we build kin and hold space for each other. danger presents her art work and practice as opportunities for consent within appropriate time frames and indigenous protocol as it relates to respect, responsibility, and reciprocity; to challenge the assumption of ownership as the human subject the art portrays is more an owner than the artist themselves; to invite their muses to panels and participate in dialogue, challenging ideas of individualism; to explore and nurture romantic friendships as transformative kinship and constellations of care; to create sober spaces and respect boundaries; to cook in community and eat to nourish *before* dialogue; and to invite curators to be caregivers to artists and their work (danger, 2019). danger actively involves those she works with throughout the artistic process and holds collaborating institutions accountable to the same relational ethics they themselves practice.

actions of self and collective care have been and continue to be discussed as essentials of decolonization, resiliency, and *survivance*. anishinaabe writer and scholar gerald vizenor refers to survivance as an "active presence," a "practice," and the "continuation of stories" in our contemporary context that can be, as he references anthropologist dorothy d. lee's observations of dakota culture, a practice of relational responsibility wherein the dakota are responsible for and in relationship with "all things," creating a communal sense of survivance (vizenor, 2008).

beyond survivance as our continuation, kanyen'kehaka artist and curator greg hill posits in his story *afterword: looking back to sakahàn* (2013) set in the year 2038 that indigeneity springs from vizenor's foundational survivance to "thrivance" (hill, 2013). in comparing the first *sakahàn: international indigenous art* (2013) exhibition with one in a fictional future present, hill describes thrivance: a status-quo where indigenous peoples' art flourishes, recognized by the artworld, where "indigenous artists have asserted their aesthetic sovereignty and developed new forms of expression that maintain links to concepts and values of their heritage while also looking ahead" and together with curators, have created "a self-sustaining blaze" (hill, 2013, p. 14). while hill frames this as a fiction, he describes what is happening in indigenous art and community today and relates it directly to the new generation who "are adept at navigating the irony, incongruity, complexity and fertility contained in the concept of indigeneity. they give it form. they embody it. thrivance" (p. 17).

in the article *what do we mean by queer indigenous ethics?* featured in *canadian art* magazine, cree-métis-saulteaux curator and writer lindsay nixon speaks to cree poet, scholar, and author billy-ray belcourt about decolonization and queer indigenous ethics, pointing to indigenous decolonization over the last fifty years as having a clear thrust of resurgence philosophy which "often argues that indigenous peoples must rise above colonialism by asserting flattened conceptions of sovereignty and nationhood, thereby erasing women and two-spirit folks by centring solely activism that mirrors colonial-capitalist warring and legal scholarship" (nixon & belcourt, 2018, para. 8). *rising above* implies that all indigenous peoples have the means and space to do so, excluding many indigenous trans, queer, 2S, and women who often exist in precarious situations where the day-to-day is focused on surviving rather than planning potential futures within concepts of resurgence and sovereignty. centring and holding space for indigiqueers, trans, 2S, and women values their stories of daily care, disturbs heteronormativity, and shines light where we find radical thought and grassroots action related to intimately caring for one another.

these radical thoughts are being disseminated more broadly now than at any other time in history with indigenous people having access to and control over dissemination through social media and broadcasting tools like podcasts that have contributed to decolonizing cyberspace and the airwaves, empowering qtbipoc to connect globally, share ideas, rally together, create events, initiate change, practise solidarity, disseminate each other's work, support one another emotionally and financially, and shift the harmful narratives prevalent in mainstream media.

for chapman and sawchuk of concordia university who co-wrote *research-creation: intervention, analysis and "family resemblances,"* these types of research creation—and specifically creation-as-research—"involves the elaboration of projects where creation is required in order for research to emerge" and is the investigative process of "bringing together technology, gathering and revealing through creation" (chapman & sawchuk, 2012, p. 19). in line with indigenous ways of sharing knowledge through creation, this method has allowed for collaborative meaning making, intimacy, and reflection as well as deep analysis and critique, which serves efforts to decolonize by centring the experiences of these storytellers, some of whom have been pushed to and exist in the margins of society. this decolonization is caring for one another through transformative actions to create extensive kinship relations within which, as erica violet lee describes, "we find the knowledge to recreate all that our worlds *would've been* if not for the interruption of colonization" (lee, 2016, para. 7, emphasis in original).

gaps

there are numerous indigenous folks creating and disseminating relevant and crucial work, and i say kinanâskomitinaw to them for their generosity and commitment as i reference some of them here and have read and listened to many more. amongst all the fabulous works, i have yet to discover a podcast devoted strictly to indigiqueers/trans, 2S, and indigenous women's thoughts and practices of collective and self-care. if this does exist, i apologize for not mentioning it here.

in this light, i feel that together with participants we are shining a vibrant light on stories that often go unheard and providing a resource on how we as indigenous 2Slgbtq+ folks and indigenous women care for one another and ourselves, not only in desperate times but as daily practice. our community care is so necessary, especially when considering the heightened violence we experience (*see* mmiwg2S), especially those who are more racialized and/or more visibly existing outside the gender binary.

this research creation also demonstrates how any one of us can take control of media and use it to strengthen our communities and make meaning by centring our knowledge and perspectives. we do not have to wait for approval or permission from western institutions: we can get a recording device, have conversations, and post them online. that is not to say it will always be an easy process, but it is within our reach and it is happening.

grounding framework

grounding this research creation is the nêhiyaw teachings of kinship relational ethics: respect, reciprocity, responsibility, and accountability to our human and more-than-human kin—past, present, and future (wilson, 2008). nêhiyaw (plains cree) worldview and relational ethics requires this reciprocal accountability through relationship: wâhkôhtowin. as shared with me by elders mary wilson and joseph naytowhow, nêhiyaw epistemology, cosmology, and kinship systems are reflected in the medicine wheel, a representation of the life journey and the values that nêhiyawak live by in relation to all things: we honour and learn about the reciprocal relationships we have to the four directions, the seasons, the land, and our more-than-human kin (naytowhow & wilson, 2019). the stories told by elders and knowledge holders include the land and what it has to teach in order to live in mino-pimâtisiwin—a "conscious connection" with our human and more-than-human kin, including the land, to perpetuate balance (wilson, 2015). moving through the world in this good way is an act of decolonization.

METHODOLOGIES & METHODS

as research creation, this podcast is focused on co-created indigenous knowledge through the experiences of indigenous 2Slgbtq+ and women outside of western academic modes of storytelling and dissemination. as urban indigenous folks, we mobilize, engage with and (re)connect with our communities in creative ways to support each other in a commitment to justice and equity.

the discourse around and actions of producing knowledge by western institutions often excludes indigenous ways of being and knowing. settler intellectuals have studied us, put our belongings and bones behind museum glass, and deemed our epistemologies and how we embody those as primitive, lacking in scientific fact, while profiting from their inherent value. that knowledge-power dynamic is deeply rooted in imperialism that sought or seeks to extract our resources and control our minds and bodies (simpson, 2007).

"indigenous peoples have struggled for the legitimacy of indigenous knowledge and are wary, sceptical even, of academic attempts to over-determine [indigenous knowledge]…to ensure that it 'fits' existing academic regimes of control" (smith et al., 2016, p. 132). transmitted orally and through experience, indigenous knowledges are passed down through generations, determined by our land and language and reflecting our bodies, minds, and souls (native women's association of canada [nwac], 2015). i see research creation as a flexible path through which we can tell our stories and keep our relationships—past and present, with the animate and inanimate—intact.

podcast as research creation allows our beautiful and radical thoughts to be disseminated as storytelling more broadly than at any other time in history. we have access to and control over dissemination through these social media and broadcasting tools that have contributed to decolonizing cyberspace and the airwaves, empowering qtbipoc to connect globally, share ideas, rally together, create events, initiate change, practice solidarity, disseminate each other's work, support one another emotionally and financially, and shift the harmful narratives prevalent in mainstream media.

māori scholar linda tuhiwai smith says that indigenous methodology and methods (i.e., process) includes respect and potential transformation in the form of education and healing and that our indigenous epistemologies and ontologies should be "built in to research explicitly, to be thought about reflexively, to be declared openly as part of the research design, to be discussed as part of final results of a study and to be disseminated back to people in culturally appropriate ways and in a language that can be understood" (smith, 2012).

for each of the eight interviews (the ninth is my seven-year-old daughter who gets an allowance regularly!), participants were approached with respect and offered an honorarium of $200, gifted tobacco and handmade jewelry, and offered the convenience of meeting in their homes (including my willingness to travel to toronto and virginia at my own expense to interview participants, although both trips were cancelled due to the covid-19 virus). participants also read and edited interview questions prior to meeting and were provided draft episodes to provide feedback on and request changes to at their discretion before dissemination.

within this creation process, i have listened to and reflected on the stories of indigiqueers, trans, 2S, and indigenous women to do what stó:lō scholar jo-ann archibald has coined "storywork," the combination of these two words signalling the significance of this research and meaning making through oral tradition and lived experience (archibald, 2008). archibald suggests an open-ended approach to storywork and has said that indigenous stories invite us to listen, take time to reflect, and understand what they teach and what sort of action we can take: the story becomes a guide with the seven principles of respect, responsibility, reverence, reciprocity, holism, interrelatedness, and synergy (archibald, 1997, 2012). using storywork as methodology and method has provided guidance to stay connected to and present with participants during the interview process, remain grounded in the importance of storywork as it pertains to nêhiyaw teachings, and be flexible and patient with time and circumstances, especially during the pandemic.

as a member of the 2S queer indigenous community, i chose to be interviewed for this research before the other participants so that i could experience the process, ensure a level of safety, be more empathetic to those i interviewed, and be vulnerable in sharing my own stories. i wanted to show my solidarity with those who told their stories, as so often research is done *on* or *to* indigenous people instead of *with* or *by*. i also interviewed my daughter for this research, who i often invite to share in and collaborate with on my many projects. although only seven years old, she was able to share her perspective on decolonization and caring, subjects we have spoken together about and created around before. in nêhiyaw worldviews and practice, children have knowledge to teach us if we are open to listening. being in community, developing lasting relationships, and giving back through service has created a web of kinship that provides support such as those coming forward to offer their stories in an effort to build our indigenous wells of knowledge. in return, this kinship—wâhkôhtowin—requires me to do this research in a good way, with respect and humility, and ensuring the integrity of these stories moving forward.

many of our stories have been erased or gone unwritten as heteropatriarchy ensures men are in positions of power, defining gender norms of "male" and "female," suppressing gender diversity and womanhood (tuck & recollet, 2016). scholars eve tuck and karyn recollet remind us that indigenous women, queer, trans, and 2S people have been critical about colonialism since first contact and have identified the ways settler colonialism and heteropatriarchy are part of the same system of oppression that work to control us. we have had to reluctantly work within these systems to support ourselves and communities, essentially upholding them to survive, even in the face of the violence it perpetrates (tuck & recollet, 2016).

during a fish scale art and beading workshop at native montreal in december 2018 hosted by nêhiyaw/michif artist and educator jaime morse, participants were told the story of beadwork as métis mapping technology. morse had attended a talk by métis lawyer kathy hodgson-smith where she described research with saskatchewan métis elders for a land use and mapping study, and how métis women gave testimony about traditionally beading maps onto the clothing of men before they embarked on months-long seasonal trade journeys. according to morse, coats beaded with maps indicating various cache sites and reminders of particular duties could be taken off and consulted by those travelling long distances (native montreal, personal communication, december 2018). i was told personally by prominent métis cis-male historians that they had not heard these stories of traditional métis mapping and that they were, therefore, false. to date, i have yet to find this history recorded on paper or online, evidence of the unfortunate reality of the erasure of indigenous women and gender-diverse voices, stories, and experiences.

inviting indigiqueers/trans, 2S, and indigenous women to share their stories is a practice of centring and valuing their knowledge as experts highlighting their experience and responsibility to their communities and recognizing that parts or all of these perspectives are inherently existing outside of the colonial construct. leanne betasamosake simpson writes about *kwe as resurgent method* where kwe cannot be understood through colonial thought; kwe is "different than the word *woman* because it recognizes a spectrum of gender expressions and it exists embedded in grounded normativity" that is nishnaabeg, which "comes from the spiritual world and flows to humans through intimate relationships with human and nonhuman entities" (simpson, 2017, p. 28). *kwe as resurgent method* demonstrates that no matter the history of settler colonialism, we embody our traditions, our ancestors know us, and we can access this truth at any time. as a person who identifies as indigiqueer, this method was appropriate to explore and be mindful of: the variety of genders and sexualities that exist within our communities and the range and potential of intimacies outside of the heteropatriarchy allow for transformative thought and openness in welcoming and approaching participants.

FINDINGS

in-depth interviews are the primary source of data for this research, which allowed for nuanced exploration with a small group of indigenous people—eight indigiqueers/trans, 2S folks, and indigenous women, and one indigenous child—on a particular topic. face-to-face conversation—in person or over zoom—(re)kindled our relationships, enabled a more sensitive and frank discussion, and provided robust, detailed information.

a range of topics were presented depending on the individual's personal journey and practices. conversation prompts were:

- what is your name, nation and where are you from?
- can you tell me about your work/practice?

- what are your views on decolonization?
- what is self-care for you/how do you perform self-care?
- what are you working on now and/or what are your plans for the future?

common themes

while i did offer discussion prompts, conversations developed organically and were not prescriptive, with emerging threads of commonality, which follow here. rather than paraphrasing podcast participants, i have chosen to give space to the storytellers to express themselves fully, through extended quotes.

belonging/identity

participants expressed struggle with and search for their identity yet at some point in their lives turned a corner with their uncertainty through varying degrees of self-acceptance in order to embrace who they are and "come to terms." when speaking about exploring identity and searching for belonging, there was a running thread that vibrates with feelings of curiosity and fear, as storytellers grasped at different parts of a whole still unfound. and in parallel with their own self-doubt, some were perceived and labelled by society as other, as racialized, as indian or black or mixed, and yet, they themselves could not confirm this identity. others grew up knowing their identity clearly, living in community and belonging, only to be turned upside down by the outside world for their otherness. in some cases, other indigenous people accused storytellers of being too white, too mixed, attacking with colonized ideas of blood quantum. and still for some, violence brought with it the cold reality of how indians are perceived and treated in this colonized world. overall, there was a definite sense of grounding when storytellers spoke about their cultures and how they have come to navigate, embrace, and continue to cultivate that grounding. for those whose identity is a story of reconnection, there were echoes of relief at finding their kin, being welcomed by community and held in all their imperfections.

all participants discussed identity and belonging in some form or another, directly or indirectly. it seems to me that navigating these topics and sorting through all the noise that broader society pushes forward through mainstream media and colonial institutions is almost impossible to escape: the othering of our bodies and ways of knowing is a constant mind fuck that plays on our self-worth, our capacity to meaningfully connect and engage, and ultimately pass on what we have learned to others within our families and communities. there is also the lateral violence coming from within our own communities that upholds colonized notions of gender and blood quantum, creating more obstacles to reconnection for those who are dispossessed of their communities and lands. those storytellers who seemed more grounded in their identity with a more robust confidence are those who grew up in their communities or surrounded by their family, are able to clearly identify their lineage, and who have had access to their cultural teachings.

(re)connection

the act of finding a sense of belonging and identity, piece by piece, and nurturing this is a (re)connection to culture and community. navigating this (re)connection, participants tell stories about imposter syndrome, lacking the confidence to be who we are in community and in our own families, (re)claiming, discovery and acceptance, of ourselves. this act of reclamation has given storytellers a chance to share with family and friends, creating a wider web of knowledge and resistance to the colonial paradigm, while at the same time, they shared the discomfort and fear expressed by immediate family members as the storytellers learn more, create deeper relations within the indigenous community, speak more openly with knew knowledge, and become more of who they are. the reverberations of this deeper identity have meaning and consequences for family and friends too, as storytellers hold up the mirror that reflects love, lineage, responsibility, genocide, diaspora, resistance, reclamation, and allyship. the ways in which we connect and reconnect to our cultures as indigenous people are so rich and varied, from researching on the internet to service in the community, to performance and prayer. some storytellers found biological family members, others began to learn from community elders, and still others relearn the songs and language of their cultures to build bridges to the past and future.

colonization/trauma

storytellers concretely identify some of the ways colonization has manifested in society including capitalism, patriarchy, and racism that work to erase qtbipoc and break our ways of building relations with each other. we have been brainwashed to suspect each other and ourselves and simply accept the violence that our bodies and the land continue to experience. and yet, storytellers express their feelings and actions of recognizing that they have endured and how that endurance and resistance has strengthened them, bolstered their will to survive, work for their communities, demand change, have families, and pass on what they have learned. others are more matter of fact about the circumstance of colonization and, although they push back against it in various ways, express a kind of soberness mixed with a sarcasm that seemingly acts as a salve. many contemplate how we exist outside of colonization in the present, our lives beyond this imposed nation-state and the promises of the future.

traditional teachings[4]

many of the storytellers expressed some degree of disconnection from their cultural teachings, even some who grew up in their communities or with their indigenous relations. there was a variety of connection points which led to the topic of teachings such as death, gender and belonging, creativity, disconnection, reclamation, and sharing on social media. one participant went into great detail, describing actual teachings received from an elder, how they share through music and performance, and how, as a reconnecting indigenous person, this knowledge is a bridge for us to return to ourselves and our communities. another storyteller spoke about teachings as the search for self and ancestors and that, although there is much gratitude at being offered teachings from various nations, there is a certain quest to be fulfilled: to find one's own medicine. of incredible significance is that storytellers have such dynamic, contemporary, brilliant, full lives, spanning so many interests and directions, imagining and building futures, that

---

4 it should be noted that teachings are intimate points of connection to one's culture and some are never shared outside of community and/or ceremony.

stereotypes of who indigenous people are and what broader settler society tells us we should be doing simply fell away, interview after interview, like a decaying shed skin.

creativity

creativity in all its forms has long been a practice within indigenous cultures. artmaking often tells the stories of our epistemologies, survival, reclamation, and identity as we carve out new spaces and places of connection, kinship and medicine. post contact, this creativity also became part of our subsistence economies, providing us with modes of trade in an ever-changing world where some of our traditional methods of survivance dwindled or were eradicated altogether. essentially, the connections we experience between land, culture, and community have shaped our art-making processes and aesthetics.

some storytellers speak about music—voice and instruments—as transformative, a bridge between present worlds and to other dimensions and ancestors, as alleviating anxiety, as welcoming within self-exploration and into community, as legacy and mode of transferring stories/knowledge, as medicine, prayer, and ceremony. other forms of creation the storytellers work with include mixed media, digital and computation arts, and traditional tattooing as reclamation of self, community, and territory, as exploring new worlds of possibility, as points of connection and intimacy with and medicine for self and others.

gender/sexuality

storytellers discuss how colonization has impacted indigenous bodies, gender, and sexual identities, brought doubt into our indigenous ways of being, how we are navigating these often challenging topics and our own identities as well as finding new ways of coming together intergeneration-ally and finding common ground. one participant spoke extensively about their work in sex worker advocacy, laws and legislation that impact body sovereignty, and how to make room for conversations around sex work and the well-being of practitioners. capitalism and patriarchy influence the ways in which we see ourselves, producing gender stereotypes, which we push back against through this advocacy as well as creativity and kinship.

navigating, discovering, and perpetuating healthy sexualities can be found in indigenous language, within which binaries often disappear. one storyteller speaks on discovering a new word in their language that reframes two-spiritedness as existing between the binary and explores ways of seeing this new word/concept as between worlds/dimensions, which ultimately feels freer and more filled with possibility. traditional and contemporary ways of existing outside of the male/female binary, even to refuse to label ourselves, allows us to be potential bridges of knowledge and understanding between elders and youth, to create safe(r) spaces, and connect with the land as our true selves.

challenges related to practice

all challenges related to practice stem from oppression due to colonization. there are many moments we find ourselves restricted and unable to speak out due to repercussions: one participant edited out conversation about their work for fear of reprisals even though the discussion revolved around the necessity for change, accountability of the employer, racism, and discrimination. as we navigate these colonial spaces, we are mindful of what is appropriate to share with the settler community, and as some storytellers are reconnecting natives, what is appropriate for us to explore, speak about and embody. one storyteller shared the challenges of low-income families and the homeless—those in our communities hardest hit by capitalism—as unable to afford even the act of dying. for others, the challenge is at the intersection of harm reduction and how to be well while being mindful of the necessity to stay connected to our lands, basic needs, addiction, hiv, and mmiwg2S. stereotypes, tokenization, and representation came through in all the stories as obstacles to overcome—none of the participants addressed, referred to, or seemed to feel these were insurmountable.

land/urban spaces/territory

storytellers shared ideas of and connections to land as home and how that takes many shapes based on forced diaspora, ancestral lands, reserve land as well as land without borders, to live wherever we as indigenous people desire, despite colonial impositions such as capitalism and property of territory and body. colonization has forced us to understand and practice connection to land in new ways, to bring possibilities of reclamation forward for youth. it is a challenge for urban indigenous communities to find what we traditionally deem to be "land" as in "the bush" and connect with the soil, trees, waters. we are creating these opportunities for ourselves and youth so that we can create and renew systems of care. we are also speaking about recognizing city as land: underneath these seas of concrete lies earth that is still sacred. and many of us are comfortable here, our practical knowledge of surviving and thriving on the land lies dormant inside us. whether we awaken those aspects of ourselves is often dependent on accessibility and when so much of our land—the bush—is taken up by cottage country and owned by government, this can prove difficult. so how do we create access to safe, land-based experience especially for those who are most vulnerable? what does the future of territory/land look like? one participant considers and works extensively in/with cyberspace as territory, modelling lands with the intent of claiming and making space. can virtual land offer indigenous people respite from colonialism?

collective care & self-care

mental health was a major theme running through many of the stories. storytellers expressed how they navigate not only varying degrees of trauma directly associated with colonization, especially for those who are visibly qtbipoc, but those more subtle veins of pain, imbalance, and confusion. the disruption that capitalism has created within our bodies is evident and storytellers all work, in one capacity or another, to heal themselves and the broader community. what became very clear is the care, acceptance, and ingenuity with which participants approach their own health and that of the community. ranging from accepting to take medication and publicly validating that decision in support of others, to netflix, hugging, tattooing, gardening, and bringing harm reduction workshops into prisons, the pain storytellers have experienced has led them to more empathic modes of connecting and healing.

DISCUSSION
process & methods/methodologies

the findings of this research process proved robust and nuanced regarding the experiences of and issues surrounding the lives of indigiqueers, trans, 2S folks, and indigenous women. participants were eager and open, sharing information far beyond the expected outcome. as conversations touched on issues such as identity, colonization, diaspora, trauma, embodiment, body sovereignty, creativity, healing, community, leadership, and the future, it was evident through all the stories that there was an appreciation of being heard and included in this process.

it is interesting and relevant to reflect on the fact that my thesis is a research creation project. during the podcast and in my first draft of this document, i made no mention of research creation per se; however, as an indigenous person who exists, works, creates, and serves through an indigenous lens, research creation is simply the inherent nature of indigenous ways of being and knowing. we work *with* community, merging creative and academic practices like knowledge sharing, music, song, and art to experience and experiment, innovate, and support each other, finding new ways to tell old and contemporary stories. research creation is embodied and unspoken.

the methodologies and methods chosen to frame this research grounded the work and aided in guiding each stage from conception to protocol and preparation, to meeting storytellers in conversation and reflection. certainly nêhiyaw kinship relational ethics required this research be grounded in respect and responsibility: wâhkôhtowin prepared me to approach this process with care, understanding that our lives as indigenous peoples are complex in terms of our histories, and how we move through, navigate, and push back against this colonized world. although we had many concerns and experiences in common, each of our individual lives is so layered and dynamic, and each of our practices so different, it was necessary to sit in each storyteller's space, empathize deeply with their words and experience to truly hear their words and present them with dignity, during the process and after in dissemination. as māori scholar linda tuhiwai smith says, indigenous research methods and methodologies have inherent transformative properties and the potential for education and healing (smith, 2012), and together with participants we delved and explored themes with care. through and within this collective care our voices sounded, and the textures and nuances of our lives were touched as we unearthed new perspectives regarding our existence in and impact on urban indigenous spaces/places. in the light of what stó:lō scholar jo-ann archibald calls *storywork* (archibald, 2008), our conversations were open-ended without time limits, allowing for intimate deliberation and contemplation. participants were able to share what they felt was relevant and veer into a variety of tangential spaces, maintaining the spirit of storywork, which is to make meaning through traditional or lived experience (2008).

this work has shown indigiqueers, trans, 2S, and indigenous women to be powerful and caring, making meaning in our lives, finding our own individual voices and then implicating ourselves in and supporting community by sharing our practices, experiences, and values as medicine for ourselves and others. we have shown ourselves to be reflective and analytical about colonization and how we have survived this despite its efforts to erase us. although we have been forced to adopt some of these systems in order to survive and endure the violence that comes with that (tuck & recollet, 2016), these conversations have demonstrated a kind of transcendence that is reminiscent of leanne betasamosake simpson's *kwe as resurgent method*, discussed earlier, where kwe—different from the english *woman*—cannot be understood through a colonial lens as it reflects a "spectrum of gender expressions" and transforms how we understand ourselves and the relationships we have with humans, more-than-humans, and the creator (simpson, 2017). through these transformative relationships with ourselves and community, we overcome, create, explore, take risks, fail, succeed, educate, learn our cultures and languages, find ourselves and our relations, heal, and inspire.

the care we take and the values we live by within these urban indigenous spaces are similarly represented in the similar methodologies of botswanan scholar bagele chilisa and cree scholar margaret kovach are active in this research—respect, celebration, play, uninterrupted speaking/

sharing, conversation, the passing on of knowledge and memories (chilisa, 2012; kovach, 2010). less active was their practical method of forming circles to share experience, especially in relation to the interviews done over zoom due to the covid virus. this was an incredibly stressful time and maintaining the schedule for this research while balancing all the optics of covid was intense. although digital interventions proved useful during this pandemic period, they hindered somewhat the building of intimacy with participants during conversations, and by extension, it is possible that the comfort felt by participants during this process may have been affected.

conversation as method proved very useful in gathering stories about indigiqueer, trans, 2S, and indigenous women's experience with decolonization, collective care, and self-care. sensitive topics were explored in-depth through conversation with an indigenous listener who is part of the same community, and this helped participants move through and reflect on challenging experiences. these voices would not have been listened to or heard in the same way through an impersonal survey or less intimate focus group.

described as a "colonial hangover" by tasha beeds, professor at the university of sudbury's department of indigenous studies, communities that are oppressed sometimes turn on themselves using the same colonial tools and tactics as their oppressor (infocus, 2020). research points to residential schools as the impetus for behaviours within indigenous communities such as shaming, blaming, and bullying, also known as lateral violence— we turn on each other out of anger and frustration (bombay et al., 2014).

conversations around belonging and identity directly correlated with colonization in north america and the resulting trauma/suffering. as urban indigenous folks, all the participants are diasporic albeit with varied stories on where they now live and how they came to be there. the struggle to find identity as an urban indigenous person is a common story in the urban indigenous community and one that is often rife with feelings of shame, guilt, loneliness, and anger. creating programming and spaces where urban indigenous people can connect and reconnect with their indigenous culture is paramount in finding self-acceptance and self-worth, which in turn creates a stronger community. the benefits of land-based learning, for example, range from centring indigeneity and various gender identities, to regenerating intergenerational teachings and increasing the spiritual and cultural well-being (meyer, 2008; radu et al., 2014).

we would do well to open up and accept various ideas around and practices of engaging with land. participants spoke of urban land, being landless, searching for land, trying to understand our relationship to land, engaging with land creatively, looking to our ancestors to invoke land... urban land is land (tuck et al., 2014) as are our spiritual, emotional, and intellectual dimensions (styres et al., 2013; tuck et al., 2014). by bringing traditional and contemporary ideas together, we may be able to create more inclusive spaces that view all forms and experiences of indigeneity as valuable.

it is evident that learning our languages and cultures gives us a more grounded sense of place and self as evidenced by participants who did possess traditional teachings and integrate them in to their traditional and contemporary practices—community work, music/song, and death/dying services—whereas those who had less access to and knowledge of cultural teachings expressed a certain loss, self doubt, disconnection, and perpetual search for meaning. certainly within our creative practices and communities we have found solace and healing as well as in our individual expressions and reclamations of our genders/sexualities.

undoubtedly more work needs to be done in this area in terms of inclusiveness of indigenous gender-fluid voices and experiences. the knowledge base on indigenous non-binary experiences in pre-contact communities is limited; we can propose that we instead look at the present and future as how we teach ourselves about indigiqueer 2Slgbtqia+ experience, needs and care.

> i am interested less and less in uncovering a genre of experience from the graveyard of indigenous history that we might call *queer*. this means that i am most curious now about what queer indigeneity *does*: the sort of possibilities, affective spheres, intimacies, modes of ethical life, paradoxes, and temporal and atmospheric disturbances it elicits. (billy-ray belcourt, quoted in nixon & belcourt, 2018, para. 2)

as we move forward, podcasting as a method for indigenous peoples has proven to be flexible, viable, and accessible, for creators and as audience, to transfer our knowledges within urban centres and beyond. as my kin and i work within community with vulnerable populations existing on the streets, in shelters, in prisons, in low or no-income situations, podcasting is an easy way for us to get our stories out there for people to reflect on and empathize with, building a broader and stronger community that includes both indigenous people and non-indigenous accomplices. as more of us speak out on our lives, the harms we have lived and that were passed on to us, and to share our joys and possibilities, we can hope that our voices will travel further and become more relevant to broader society, informing and transforming the daily conversations and disseminations of life as indigenous queers, trans, two-spirit folks, and women.

REFERENCES

archibald, j. (1997). *coyote learns to make a storybasket: the place of first nations stories in education* [doctoral dissertation, simon fraser university]. summit research repository. https://summit.sfu.ca/_flysystem/fedora/sfu_migrate/7275/b18592806.pdf

archibald, j. (2008). *indigenous storywork: educating the heart, mind, body, and spirit.* vancouver: ubc press.

archibald, j. (2012, august 5). dr. jo-ann archibald—on indigenous stories and their framework [video]. vimeo. https://vimeo.com/46993624

bombay, a., matheson, k., & anisman, h. (2014). *origins of lateral violence in aboriginal communities: a preliminary study of student-to-student abuse in residential schools.* ottawa: aboriginal healing foundation.

canadian feminist alliance for international action, palmater, p., & canada without poverty. (2019). *a national action plan to end violence against indigenous women and girls: the time is now.* https://pampalmater.com/wp-content/uploads/2019/02/MMIW-Inquiry-Report.pdf

cardinal, h., & hildebrandt, w. (2000). *treaty elders of saskatchewan: our dream is that our peoples will one day be clearly recognized as nations.* calgary: university of calgary press.

chapman, o., & sawchuk, k. (2012). research-creation: intervention, analysis and "family resemblances." *canadian journal of communication, 37*(1), 5–26.

chilisa, b. (2012). *indigenous research methodologies.* thousand oaks, ca: sage publications.

danger, d. (2019, february 1–2). *keynote* [speech]. communities of care [graduate
 student symposium]. diversity in the arts at concordia, concordia university,
 montreal.

day, l. (2017). *reconciling how we live with water: the development and use of
 a collaborative podcasting methodology to explore and share diverse first
 nations, inuit, and métis perspectives* [master's thesis, university of guelph].
 atrium. https://atrium.lib.uoguelph.ca/server/api/core/bitstreams/
 abccoec3-7a07-4db5-8c88-f04af793affc/content

driskill, q.-l. (2010). doubleweaving two-spirit critiques: building alliances between
 native and queer studies. *journal of lesbian and gay studies*, 16(1–2), 69–92.
 https://doi.org/10.1215/10642684-2009-013

fanon, f. (2004). *the wretched of the earth* (r. philcox, trans.). new york: grove press.

hill, g. (2013). afterword: looking back to sakahàn. *art monthly australia*, 262, pp.
 13–17.

hunt, s., & holmes, c. (2015). everyday decolonization: living a decolonizing queer
 politics. *journal of lesbian studies*, 19(2), 154–172. https://doi.org/10.1080/10894
 160.2015.970975

infocus. (2020, january 9). lateral violence a "colonial hangover" we need to heal:
 prof [podcast]. *aptn national news*. retrieved from https://www.aptnnews.ca/
 infocus/lateral-violence-a-colonial-hangover-we-need-to-heal-prof/

jacobs, b. (2017). decolonizing the violence against indigenous women. in
 p. mcfarlane & n. schabus (eds.), *whose land is it anyway? a manual for
 decolonization* (pp. 47–51). vancouver: federation of post-secondary educators
 of bc.

kovach, m. (2010). conversational method in indigenous research. *first peoples child
 & family review*, 5(1), 40–48. https://doi.org/10.7202/1069060ar

lee, e. v. (2016, march 1). reconciling in the apocalypse. *the monitor*, canadian
 centre for policy alternatives. https://policyalternatives.ca/publications/
 monitor/reconciling-apocalypse

lunga, v. (2014). re: what is the origin of decolonization theories? [comment].
 retrieved from https://www.researchgate.net/post/What-is-the-origin-of-
 decolonization-theories/5a1e67d0f7b67e0eeeobf1fa/citation/download

meyer, m. a. (2008). indigenous and authentic: hawaiian epistemology and the
 triangulation of meaning. in n. k. denzin, y. s. lincoln, & l. t. smith (eds.),
 handbook of critical and indigenous methodologies (pp. 217–232). thousand
 oaks, ca: sage publishing.

mitchell, t. (2017). indigenous podcasting: resisting the colonial paradigm. *the
 grassroots journal*. retrieved july 16, 2020, from https://www.thegrassrootsjournal
 .org/post/2017/11/06/indigenous-podcasting-resisting-the-colonial-paradigm

national inquiry into missing and murdered indigenous women and girls (canada). (2019). *reclaiming power and place: the final report of the national inquiry into missing and murdered indigenous women and girls.* vol. 1a. https://www. mmiwg-ffada.ca/final-report/

native women's association of canada. (2015). *aboriginal women and aboriginal traditional knowledge (atk): input and insight on aboriginal traditional knowledge.* i-portal, university of saskatchewan. http://www.nwac.ca/ wp-content/uploads/2015/05/2014-NWAC-Aborignal-Women-and-Aborignal-Traditional-Knowledge-Report1.pdf

naytowhow, j., & wilson, m. (2019, may 15). pipe ceremony [ceremony], *congress of qualitative inquiry* [symposium], indigenous inquiries circle, university of illinois. https://icqi.org/wp-content/uploads/2019/08/QI2019-Final-Program.pdf

nixon, l., & belcourt, b.-r. (2018, may 23). what do we mean by queer indigenous ethics? *canadian art.* https://canadianart.ca/features/ what-do-we-mean-by-queerindigenousethics/

radu, i., house, l. m., & pashagumskum, e. (2014). land, life, and knowledge in chisasibi: intergenerational healing in the bush. *decolonization: indigeneity, education & society, 3*(3), 86–105.

simpson, a. (2007). on ethnographic refusal: indigeneity, 'voice' and colonial citizenship. *junctures,* (9). https://junctures.org/index.php/junctures/article/ view/66/60

simpson, l. b. (2017). *as we have always done: indigenous freedom through radical resistance.* minneapolis: university of minnesota press.

smith, l. t. (2012). *decolonizing methodologies: research and indigenous peoples* (2nd ed.). london: zed books.

smith, l. t., maxwell, t. k., puke, h., & temara, p. (2016). indigenous knowledge, methodology and mayhem: what is the role of methodology in producing indigenous insights? a discussion from mātauranga māori. *knowledge cultures, 4*(3), 131–156. https://researchcommons.waikato.ac.nz/server/api/core/ bitstreams/57927e69-83d1-43ea-b58a-e7e00cb4dcf5/content

styres, s., haig-brown, c., & blimkie, m. (2013). toward a pedagogy of land: the urban context. *canadian journal of education/revue canadienne de l'éducation, 36*(2), 34–67. https://journals.sfu.ca/cje/index.php/cje-rce/article/view/1293

tuck, e., mckenzie, m., & mccoy, k. (2014). land education: indigenous, post-colonial, and decolonizing perspectives on place and environmental education research. *environmental education research, 20*(1), 1–23. https://doi. org/10.1080/13504622.2013.877708

tuck, e., & recollet, k. (2016). introduction to native feminist texts. *english journal, 106*(1), 16–22. https://www.jstor.org/stable/26359311

vizenor, g. (ed.). (2008). *survivance: narratives of native presence*. lincoln: university of nebraska press.

vowel, c. (2014, april 21). indigenous women and two-spirited people: our work is decolonization! guts. https://gutsmagazine.ca/indigenous-women-two-spirited-people-work-decolonization/

wilbur, m., & keene, a. (hosts). (2019, march 19). decolonizing sex (no. 5) [audio podcast episode]. in *all my relations podcast*. https://www.allmyrelationspodcast.com/podcast/episode/468a0a6b/ep-5-decolonizing-sex

wilson, a. (2015). our coming in stories: cree identity, body sovereignty and gender self-determination. *journal of global indigeneity*, 1(1), 1–5. https://www.jstor.org/stable/48717629

wilson, s. (2008). *research is ceremony: indigenous research methods*. halifax: fernwood publishing.

6

Stitching Ourselves Back Together

Urban Indigenous Women's Experience of Reconnecting with Identity through Beadwork

Shawna Bowler

ABSTRACT

This chapter explores how urban Indigenous women experience reconnections to cultural identity when they take up the practice of traditional
beadwork. A beading methodology was used to explore the experiences
of five urban Indigenous women in Winnipeg. Within this methodology,
stories and conversations about beadwork are used to gather and share
knowledge in research. Participants were asked to share their experience of identity reconnections through beadwork stories. The major
elements of this beading methodology and its underlying theoretical,
epistemological, and ontological roots are told through the story of the
beaded medicine bags. These medicine bags were created for and gifted
to each participant for the knowledge they contributed to this research.

The author's own beaded medicine bag is also used as a framework for a thematic analysis and discussion of the research findings. The themes identified through this analysis suggest beading as a multi-faceted and action-oriented approach that facilitates processes of journeying, remembering, relationships, asserting the self, and healing. This chapter concludes by highlighting some of the important implications of beading as an Indigenous way of knowing, being, and doing in social work practice and research. Beading has potential to promote decolonization, resiliency, wellness, and healing in our work with Indigenous communities. **Keywords**: *Beadwork stories, decolonization, healing, identity, beading methodology, Indigenous women*

INTRODUCTION

This research features beading as a way to tell a story and convey knowledge of our embodied, wholistic, and deeply personal experience of healing and identity. Previous scholarship has noted, to varying degrees, the identity connections and healing experienced by Indigenous women when they engage with the practice of beadwork (Belcourt, 2010; Bourgeois, 2018; Gray, 2017; Hanson & Griffith, 2016; Ray, 2016). Within this research project, a beading methodology is utilized to develop a deeper understanding of urban Indigenous women's experience of reconnecting with identity through beadwork. Beadwork stories are significant to this methodology, which will be detailed in a later section of this paper. Five Indigenous women from Winnipeg participated in this research by sharing their personal experience through stories and conversations about beadwork and beading practices. Each of the participants shared a common experience of disconnection from culture and identity. Their stories reflect how beadwork became integrated into each woman's process of making meaning of her Indigenous identity. Five themes were identified as central to this process: journeying, remembering, relationships, asserting ourselves, and healing.

This research has also contributed to my own process of decolonization and healing. Much like the participants, I am also an urban Indigenous woman who did not grow up immersed in Indigenous culture or connected to my ancestral community. Having lived in Winnipeg all my life and not having a relationship with a significant portion of my family, I was further removed from the influence that land, culture, or community might have had on the formation of my identity. For me, taking up the practice of beadwork helped me begin to develop a deeper understanding of my Indigenous identity. Through my beadwork journey, I began to engage with my own traditional and ancestral Indigenous knowledges. I was eventually able to return to my ancestral community and was able to form a deeper relationship with my paternal grandmother, my Kookum. My ancestors are descended from the Red River Métis and the Dakota-Sioux people from Tatanka Najin (Standing Buffalo Dakota Nation) in southern Saskatchewan. Prior to beginning this research, I had never been to this community. I was inspired to return there by the beadwork stories the Indigenous women shared in this research. I am a self-taught beadworker. I am also a social worker. My practice in both of these areas has been guided by a desire to be involved in social justice for Indigenous communities in ways that uphold culture and tradition and contribute towards decolonization and resurgence. My beading and social work journey not only led me to the questions in this research, but also contribute to my understanding of the potential and power of beading as a way of knowing, being, and doing in research and social work.

UNRAVELLING THE STITCHES: THE CONTEXT OF BEADWORK

The practice of beading existed prior to European contact, where hair, quills, bone, stone, hoof, seeds, shells, and other things found within nature and on the land were used to adorn personal or ceremonial items (Belcourt, 2010; Gray, 2017; Hill, 2003). Some of these items are still used in traditional beadwork today. Beadwork was not only for embellishment. The styles, motifs, and materials often reflected social, spiritual, political, ceremonial, or personal relevance (Belcourt, 2010; Gray, 2017). European beads were introduced by trade to an already existing tradition of beading. Indigenous women held an important role in the process of incorporating and Indigenizing European trade goods into Indigenous life. Sherry Farrell Racette (2008), a Métis art historian, noted:

> The work of integrating new goods into everyday life was largely the cultural work of women... Language, symbolism, and continuity of practice "grandmothered" ancient meanings on to new forms; rather than marking a decline in material culture, they illustrate the important work of women in the creation and synthesis of knowledge systems. (p. 77)

Through the process of Indigenization, trade good such as beads have become incorporated to the point where they are now considered a part of traditional Indigenous art and culture. They reflect the important cultural work of our grandmothers, who were tasked with incorporating knowledges from these two worlds into the cultural and artistic forms we recognize today (Farrell Racette, 2008). With the onset of colonization, beaded objects gained material value as crafts, souvenirs, or art that were coveted by collectors and art connoisseurs among European settlers (Farrell Racette, 2008; Gray, 2017). This devalued and marginalized beading as a knowledge system. Beading became marginalized further when the Canadian government, recognizing beadwork as a symbol of Indigenous cultures and identity, banned the wearing and use of beaded items and, thus, the practice of beading itself, through the *Indian Act* until 1951 (Farrell Racette, 2017). The banning of these items not only disrupted the identities of Indigenous people, but also the intergenerational transmission of knowledge and culture, the important work of our grandmothers that Farrell Racette (2008) highlights. As a result, Indigenous women became disconnected from this way of knowing, being, and doing and were unable to pass this knowledge to subsequent generations.

The visual and aesthetic properties of traditional beadwork have led to a common association of this practice within the realm of art, where the aesthetics of Indigenous beadwork are considered a symbolic and creative expression of the cultural knowledge, experience, and identity of the artist (Belcourt, 2010; Farrell Racette, 2008, 2017; Robertson, 2017). When Indigenous artists reclaim these traditional forms of art that were once historically prohibited, this speaks to resiliency and resurgence within their work. There has been a movement by some contemporary Indigenous artists to reclaim and use beadwork to express the past and present impacts of colonization on Indigenous communities (Anderson, 2016; Farrell Racette, 2017; Robertson, 2017). In doing so, Indigenous artists are able to use their own traditional ways of doing and making art to reflect their own reality in a way that is decolonizing and healing.

The practice of artmaking also shares a close relationship with healing. The healing benefits that are inherent within creative and artistic activities are noted by Archibald and Dewar (2010), who propose that when these activities include aspects of traditional art and culture, there are additional benefits to Indigenous people, particularly if they have experienced loss in relation to culture. Artistic and creative processes were seen as enhancing or deepening the healing process by allowing artists to access inner and cultural knowledge, develop personal insights, and gain a greater understanding of the self (Archibald & Dewar, 2010). Identity is often an important and significant aspect of Indigenous healing. The ability of creative arts to foster healing with Indigenous identity is noted by Coholic, Cote-Meek, and Recollet (2012), who state that art-based processes can support Indigenous women to strengthen identity by contributing to the development of greater self-esteem, self-awareness, and confidence, which in turn, fosters resilience in the face of a shared experience of colonial oppression.

The conceptualization of beading as art does not originate within Indigenous communities. Hanson and Griffith (2016) note, "The distinctive valuation of handcrafted arts and crafts originates as a European concept, primarily defined in ways that have historically served the interests of male artists" (p. 226). There has been recent Indigenous scholarship that has critiqued the colonial construction of beading as "art." Beading is not merely art, it is an Indigenous way of knowing, being, and doing that has existed for generations among Indigenous women and communities. As such, beading as knowledge has important implications in how research might be conceptualized and approached within Indigenous contexts. Beading has been used as a method of inquiry positioned alongside Indigenous storytelling in research specific to Indigenous women that places emphasis on the contextualized knowledges embedded within the practices and stories of beadwork (Bourgeois, 2018; Hanson & Griffith, 2016; Ray, 2016). Beading as a method of inquiry also relates to how we think about knowledge in beadwork and what we believe can be known through this practice. Bourgeois (2018) suggests beading as "a valid and rigorous epistemology that is intimately connected to each practitioner's sense of identity and understanding of reality" (p. 43). Beadwork also conveys meaning. Symbols, patterns, and design reveal knowledge that can be cultural, personal, or political. Gray (2017) prompts us to consider the beaded wampum belts which transmit the history, values, and political and social standing of the Iroquois people as one example of how beadwork has been used as a visual language in communicating specific knowledges.

Beading knowledges are extended into the realm of academic research by Ray (2016) who proposes that by asserting these knowledges within research, beading provides "an outlet to collect, understand, and convey knowledges in a way that is meaningful and relevant within an Anishinaabe worldview and aligned with concepts of sovereignty and community wellness" (p. 376). Through a resurgence in the inclusion of such knowledges, not only within our personal lives but also within the way we go about doing research with Indigenous women, Ray (2016) asserts that values, identity, cultural ways of knowing, and relationships disrupted by the generational impacts of colonization may be healed and restored. This contributes to demarginalizing and decolonizing beading as a way of knowing and researching. Bourgeois (2018) and Ray (2016) have both drawn attention to the epistemological nature inherent within the practice of beading, emphasizing an understanding of beading practices as a distinct, Indigenous women's knowledge system and method of inquiry within academic research. This has created space for the inclusion of beading as an Indigenous way of knowing, being, and pursuing research with Indigenous women.

BEADING METHODOLOGY

The story of the beading methodology used in this research is connected to the beaded medicine bags I created and gifted to each of the Indigenous women who participated (Figure 1).

FIGURE 1. Beaded medicine bags. Winnipeg, Manitoba, December 8, 2018. Courtesy of the author.

The beaded medicine bags were created to illustrate my understanding of beading as methodology and its underlying epistemological and ontological roots. They were also created as part of relational accountability. They are meant to express my intention to go about doing research in a good way, to be a respectful and humble storyteller, and to share and give back beadwork and story in exchange for the same. Tobacco and sage were bundled in yellow cloth and tied with sinew, and the medicines were placed inside the bags. The inclusion of traditional medicine and choice of creating a beaded medicine bag was meant to acknowledge beading as medicine to heal.

The beaded flowers on the medicine bags convey the beliefs about knowledge that I approached this research with. Although each medicine bag is beaded with a four-petaled flower, each flower is unique. Each flower is beaded with different combinations of colours and no combination is the same. The uniqueness of the flowers demonstrates that there are potentially many knowledges to be uncovered through beadwork and stories, that none are invalid. The choice of a four-petaled flower was deliberate as it acknowledges the wholistic and relational nature of beading knowledge. Each petal is interconnected with the centre circle that signifies the self. The four petals are influenced by the four directions of the Medicine Wheel. They represent the heart, mind, body, and spirit as well as my belief that when we do beadwork, we engage with knowledge from all these parts of ourselves. Within one petal of each flower, a spirit bead has been stitched deliberately out of place. A spirit bead is an intentional flaw created within an otherwise perfect piece of beadwork to demonstrate humbleness before the Creator, and to show that nothing on Earth given to us by the Creator is perfect, including ourselves (Scofield & Briley, 2011). The inclusion of spirit beads is meant to demonstrate that spiritual knowledges are part of the beauty of Indigenous knowledges, subtly woven through them, not unlike the spirit beads in my medicine bags. Spirit beads invite the diversity of spiritual knowledge and experience into the research process. Spirit beads uphold spiritual knowledges as a valid part of the whole of what we can know through beading as a method of inquiry in research.

The beaded medicine bags were also created to become part of the research methods. Their inclusion prompted the reciprocal and communal process of story sharing and exchanging knowledge. Although I created a medicine bag for each participant, I also made one for myself. Within my medicine bag, I carried tobacco, sage, and a necklace beaded by my late Kookum. This beaded necklace is significant to my own journey of reconnecting with identity through beadwork. I began my interview with each Indigenous woman by sharing my beaded medicine bag and Kookum's beaded necklace within it, while also sharing some of my own story of reconnection and healing through beadwork. Participants were then gifted with the medicine bag I had created for them, thereby prompting them to share their own beadwork stories and creating a supportive space to receive these knowledges from them. The beadwork stories the women shared were not only about beadwork. At the core of these stories were the lives of the Indigenous women themselves and the stories of their ancestors. Their beadwork is an embodiment of their lived experience of healing and identity.

MEDICINE BAG FRAMEWORK

My own beaded medicine bag containing my Kookum's beaded necklace was used as a framework to organize and explain the research findings. Its inclusion is meant to honour researcher reflexivity in my thematic analysis of the patterns within the beadwork stories shared by the participants. Altogether, there were five distinct themes identified that speak to how beading facilitates connections to identity for urban Indigenous women. These themes are represented through the beaded flower on my medicine bag (Figure 2).

The four petals correspond with knowledge that participants shared from the heart, mind, body, and spirit. They represent four identified themes of beading journeys, remembering, relationships and asserting ourselves. Healing, the fifth theme, lies at the centre because it was found to be interwoven among all the other themes. The four petals emphasize the interconnectedness of the themes to one another and to the core underlying experience of personal healing that each woman described throughout her beading story. The themes suggest beading as a multifaceted, action-oriented and wholistic practice that becomes incorporated into urban Indigenous women's ways of making sense of themselves and their place within the world.

The first theme, **beading journeys**, is informed by knowledge from the spirit. Beading brought clarity to the Indigenous women's ongoing journeys of self-discovery. Through this practice, the participants were able to rely on their own ways of conducting self-research. Beading helped them to find guidance and direction on their journey. Each beading story is shared within the context of each Indigenous woman's ongoing journey

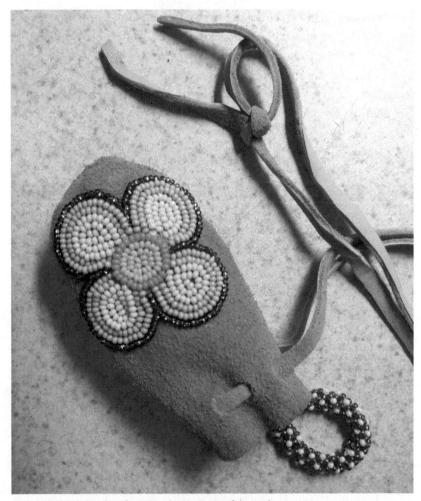

FIGURE 2. Medicine bag framework. Courtesy of the author.

of searching for traditional or cultural knowledge, ancestral connections, personal healing or belonging, and validation, which are all integrally connected to the recovery of an Indigenous sense of self. Their journeys are examples of how beading is a decolonized way of doing self-research. Roberta described beading as an outlet to start learning about herself and the ancestors and culture she had been disconnected from throughout most of her life:

I felt like I was constantly searching for something. I know nothing about my culture. I know nothing about who I am, who my ancestors are. I know my immediate family and that's it. I have memories of my grandmother. I have memories of my grandfather on my mom's side. That's all. I don't know my family. I don't know where I come from. I don't even know what my bloodline is. I had to go find these things out and I'm still looking. I still feel kind of lost but at least I feel like I'm not treading water anymore. I feel like I'm getting somewhere. And I have something to contribute instead of just being somebody that's asking questions and wants to know.

The journey through beading and self-researching also involved many of the women seeking out guidance through teachers, mentors, or in relying on spiritual guides and ways of knowing to support their journey. Through this guidance, some of the women asserted that they had not actively sought out a connection to beadwork but had been guided towards it in ways that are unseen but deeply meaningful and specific to them.

The theme of **remembering** is informed by beading knowledge from the mind or memory. Beading triggered a process of remembering that involved the recovery of blood memories, honouring grandmothers, and recognizing inherited gifts and their place and purpose within culture. Through remembering, the women described a greater sense of knowing who they are and how to be within the world. Several of the Indigenous women described beading as being part of their blood memories. They shared how they began to recognize beading knowledge and skill as already existing within their DNA and saw it as an inherent gift passed down through the bloodline of their ancestors. Most of the women who saw beading as a gift said they believed this gift came specifically from their grandmothers. This was true for Tamara, whose beaded medallions, the Kookum Collection, are part of her process of honouring and remembering her grandmother. She says:

I prayed every time I beaded and took every bead as a prayer. I spent a lot of time with myself. I started thinking about my Kookum a lot. I started wishing that I had a Kookum. I grew up in ceremony, going to sweat lodge, and I remember a lot of those teachings. I could never really connect them to real-life situations. They were just memories, stories. I guess when you get older, go through your life's journey, and you're learning about your identity and yourself, then you start to reflect on things like that. I'm starting to reflect on how my life would have been with my Kookum, if I'd had that interaction with her. I started to remember what I would want from my Kookum, and then the flowers started to really come. That's how I started the Kookum collection…these are the things I wish I had because I never had the opportunity to know my Kookum.

All the beadwork stories also touched upon how doing beadwork helped the women realize they have a place and purpose within culture and community. Remembering place and purpose involved a recognition among the women that they are meant to participate in culture and make their contribution to it through their specific role as a beadworker.

The theme of **relationships** is informed by knowledge from the heart. Relationships important to the participant's sense of self were strengthened and established through beadwork. This was inclusive of relationships held with family, land, community, culture, and traditions. Nurturing relationships through beading created a greater sense of belonging and connectivity. Violet shared how her involvement with a local beading group instilled a sense belonging within community and culture:

> I'm just more connected. You see more people. You feel like you're in there with them…I was so excited. I think, just to be able to create some of the cultural identities of the Métis and being in there with a lot of the other ladies. You get to see the people there and who has been beading for awhile and you listen to people talk…there's so much shared there, more than just a pattern for this or a pattern for that.

Through gifting family with beadwork, sharing beading knowledge with them, inviting them into their beading circles, and creating beadwork to honour family members, the women were able to strengthen and establish greater kinship bonds. Strengthening family connections helped the participants better understand themselves and their generational place. Each of the women also experienced a greater feeling of closeness to culture. This was especially important for those participants who felt they had no relationship to culture. Roberta had been estranged from culture throughout most of her life and shared how beading gave her greater confidence to begin to explore it:

> I think a lot of the time I was scared. I'm finding I don't feel so much of a stranger when I go ask people about culture because I feel like I'm doing something to contribute towards it. Beading just makes me feel connected when I'm with it. It feels amazing to be included and to learn about the things you want to know, especially when it comes to who you are. It led me to meet so many really awesome people who knew things I wanted to know about. I think if I carry this on, those people I'm going to meet are the people I want in my life. It's also helping my family talk about things. They see me going out to learn these cultural things and when I tell them about what I've learned, they're so amazed. It kind of motivates them to want to learn about it too. It feels good when we talk about it, there's just good energy, and I really want more of that in my life.

By providing a foundation through which to explore, understand, and be within it, creating beadwork helped the Indigenous women strengthen their relationships to culture.

Asserting ourselves is a theme concerned with the physical realm and with knowledge that is embodied. The women identified how they used beadwork to assert and express their identity and their own Indigenous ways of knowing, being, and doing. This was regarded by the participants as important to the continued existence and survival of Indigenous people and culture across space and time. Within the beading stories, there was also discussion around the physical *practice* of beading as a way of asserting the self that is rooted within decolonization and resistance. Crystal shared how beading her treaty card was intended to assert resistance towards oppressive definitions of Indigenous identity imposed through colonization:

I personally have a big problem with treaty cards. Why do I need to show you a card to prove that I've been colonized? It's a bone of contention with me. I took my treaty card, blew it up a little bit bigger and I'm going to bead it with my image on it. That's an act of resistance and an act of decolonizing. I didn't want to make it the size that fits in a wallet because it's hidden away like they've been trying to do to Indigenous people for so long—hide us.... If I can represent in some really visual, in-your-face, beautiful way, then let's do that. I think beadwork can do that.

She also shared that she does beadwork everywhere she goes and said this is part of her own practice of Indigenizing space:

I don't wear a lot of my own beadwork, but I represent by beading every-where I can—which is something I wasn't able to do before because I didn't have a lot of pride in that. I tried to work really hard to make sure I was safe from things like racism, but now I'm just like, no. I'm going to do it. Racism be damned, and if people are uncomfortable, well guess what? I'm going to claim this space.

The Indigenous women expressed a desire for continuity which speaks to the assertion of beading knowledges across generations. Beadwork knowl-edge transcends space and time and connects the women with future and past generations. The knowledge, memories, and stories the women put into their beadwork will continue to exist within their beadwork long after they are gone. Beadwork allows for the knowledge and stories of their ancestors to be kept alive. Embedded within the beadwork stories shared by each woman were also stories of her ancestors and their experiences of colonization and resilience.

Healing lies at the centre of my framework because it was a found to be linked within each of the previous four themes as the processes of journeying, remembering, connecting, and asserting the self through beading were essentially healing ones. Beading is a decolonized and Indigenous way of healing that instills both personal and cultural well-ness. Through this practice, the Indigenous women were able to remain grounded, process personal traumas, become more aware of what they sense and feel internally, and realize transformative personal change. The women's stories demonstrate beading as an Indigenous way of healing that bridges the mind-body connection and instills not only personal wellness, but cultural wellness. The act of beading helped the participants look towards their own ways of working through trauma and created the possibility for culture and tradition to become a part of how they heal. For Amy, doing beadwork helped her stay grounded and begin to process traumatic experiences:

> Part of beading and healing is having the opportunity to focus on something that your hands are doing while your brain is putting things back together. I'm pretty sure I have ADHD but have never been medicated or diagnosed. I'm not good at sitting still. My brain will start to race and do crazy things if I'm not busy. Beading has helped me to process a lot of the traumas in my life and has helped me to literally stitch myself back together. I was traumatized when my daughter fell out the window. Sundancing, prayers, beading her mukluks, and doing beading as the giveaways was part of me being able to process that trauma. The act of making and giving things has made a huge impact on my ability to process those traumas and the damage that it did to me. I feel like it gave me a way to control it. When my life felt incredibly out of control, it was very orderly. It's very much like pulling things together. It gave me a sense of order in my life.

The nature of healing was described by the Indigenous women in a wholistic way. Beading gifted them with the capacity to be more consciously engaged and aware of what they feel and sense within their hearts, minds, bodies, and spirits when they did beadwork. In terms of healing, this supports the potential for beading to help participants identify what parts of themselves they needed to nurture and attend to.

Finally, all the participants spoke about change and coming into new ways of being through beadwork. Through mindfulness and wholistic engagement, beading created the context for insight, contemplation, and self-reflection to occur. Amy shared how beading became a transformative process for her that prompted personal change and stimulated her creativity. She likened beading to "giving birth" where the ideas, visions, and knowledge are gestating inside of her. When she is ready, she brings this vision outside of herself and transfers it into finished beadwork. She herself is also transformed through this reflective process. She becomes the embodiment of the strength, healing, and beauty held within her beadwork. The women's stories demonstrate that beadwork is a catalyst that promotes personal change within their lives. By taking up a traditional and cultural practice and implementing the knowledge and skills they have learned through it into their lives, they are able to live a fuller, richer life and begin to restore their Indigenous ways of being within the world.

STITCHING BEADS INTO THE FABRIC OF SOCIAL WORK

The Indigenous women's beading stories and the experience of utilizing a beading methodology have also provided helpful insights around how the practice of beading holds important implications for social work. As social workers, it is important to acknowledge that our practices and the systems we work within have also served to divide and isolate Indigenous people from their culture and identity. It is therefore imperative for social workers to identify how to support Indigenous clients in reclaiming and healing cultural identity in ways that counter the settler-colonial social work practices and philosophies that have contributed to cultural and identity disconnections. This involves looking towards traditional and Indigenous approaches to helping and healing and centring decolonization and self-determination in our practices. This research sheds light on the significance of beading in this endeavour. Beading offers a way to reclaim and sustain cultural identity, and to maintain Indigenous ways of knowing, being, and doing in response to the colonial oppressions Indigenous people have faced, and continue to live, feel, and experience within contemporary society.

Beading is a resiliency-based practice that can foster strength in Indigenous culture and identity. Centring strengths and celebrating resiliency is foundational within social work practice. When we reclaim this traditional practice that was once suppressed, beadworking is an act of resiliency (Prete, 2019). As demonstrated within the Indigenous women's beading stories, it is a practice that prompts remembrance and recognition of strengths, abilities, and inherent gifts. The participants were able to identify and draw upon these inner resources to challenge and overcome adversities and traumas. To the participants, it is a practice that fosters closeness to culture and strengthens confidence and pride in cultural identity. Scarpino (2007) notes resilience is a life-long process, and that it is essential to centre the strengths, abilities, and achievements of Indigenous women as they are often marginalized, undervalued, and can lead to harmful stereotypes and assumptions about Indigenous women's identity.

Beading is also a practice of resurgence that is tied to cultural and personal renewal where Indigenous knowledges, epistemologies, and ways of doing are reclaimed. The participant's stories highlighted how engaging with this practice supported the potential for resurgence and decolonization to become embedded within their everyday lives. Through beading, the Indigenous women reclaimed traditional and cultural ways of exploring and expressing their life and experience within the current context of colonization. Decolonization is a process unique to each person's specific experience of colonization and its impact on their life. Beading creates space for processes of decolonization to occur while promoting the preservation of Indigenous culture and identity.

Self-determination is a concept significant to reclaiming and sustaining Indigenous cultural identity. It is also a concept often centred within social work and concerns choice, autonomy, and "the power to define oneself and to determine one's identity" (Bastien, 2004, p. 63). Self-determination was enacted through beading by the participants when they began to adapt this practice into their ways of defining and asserting who they are, thereby challenging assumptions about Indigenous women's identity and experience. Beading also instilled a sense of agency, supporting the participants to draw upon beading as a resource for healing and survival and to support and sustain themselves and their families within a modern, urban, and colonial context.

Significant to social work practitioners are the therapeutic characteristics of beadwork practice that participants described such as mindfulness, grounding, awareness, insight, self-care, and wholistic, embodied connections. The Indigenous women saw these beading qualities as beneficial to healing their experiences of anxiety, depression, grief, loss, and trauma. As social workers, these experiences are often the focus of our helping relationships with clients. Beading is a healing practice that Indigenous clients can incorporate into their lives and carry with them outside the boundaries of a therapeutic or helping relationship. I believe it is also important to recognize that there are existing teachers and traditional ways of helping and healing already in place within Indigenous communities, and that they must be sustained so that Indigenous people and communities may continue to thrive. Linklater (2014) cautions against the dangers of cultural appropriation and infringing upon the already established roles of Indigenous community helpers and suggests it is more appropriate for practitioners to foster connections and collaborations with these helpers, or advocate for their inclusion in our work within our agencies.

Social workers might also consider the potential and power of beadwork to inspire social action in Indigenous people and communities. Beading has been used by Indigenous women to express the impact of oppression, patriarchy, colonization, and violence on their lives, families, and communities and to advocate for social change (Anderson, 2016; Farrell Racette, 2017). Advocacy through beadwork is visual, meaningful, succinct, and not limited by language. It is also impactful—consider beaded poppies, beaded red dresses, or beaded orange t-shirts pinned to a lapel. They immediately draw attention and initiate conversations and opportunities to educate others on our experiences and our ancestor's experiences. As social workers, I think its important to be aware of this potential when we are supporting our Indigenous clients in finding their voice so that we might recognize when beading might be a fit with their ways of being and asserting themselves. It is not necessarily our role to teach and share beading knowledge. Our role is to take notice, uphold and uplift those voices when they come to our attention, and help our clients make the right connections so that they might use beadwork to evoke change, whether that is on a personal or collective level.

Beading methodology is also significant to social work research. It is a methodology that responds to the historical marginalization and oppression of Indigenous knowledges and ways of researching. It is a decolonizing methodology that promotes resurgence in the use of traditional Indigenous ways of knowing, being, and doing within research. Utilized within this research, it centres and upholds Indigenous women's voices, their lived experience, and their beading knowledges within the research process, bringing them out of the margins and into the forefront. It is my hope that this research will inspire Indigenous researchers, social work researchers, and especially Indigenous social work researchers to continue to reclaim beading methodology within their research. I believe there are many questions that might be explored through this decolonized approach to knowledge, not only within social work, but across a variety of research disciplines. Beading has the quality of being distinct and unique. A beading methodology also holds this quality and how it is undertaken will depend largely upon the knowledge, experience, and relationship the researcher holds with beadwork and the questions they seek to understand through this practice.

FINAL THREADS

The practice of beading is more than simply creative expression or art; it is a practice that "becomes a part of your life" (Ray, 2016, p. 364), situating it outside of this realm into a distinct Indigenous women's way of knowing, being, and doing that has important implications for Indigenous women's identity and healing. Through this practice, we may know and connect to ourselves, our world, and our ancestors in a much deeper way. Métis artist and historian Sherry Farrell Racette (2008) offers some insight into the practice of beading: "Through the small actions of our needles, and the careful stitches we make, we create and recreate our world; and through the fine strand of thread and fabric we connect ourselves to our grandmothers" (p. 78). Through this practice, the generational transmission of knowledges that are needed to sustain our identities as Indigenous women may be stitched back together.

I am also reminded about the critical importance of context order to fully appreciate and understand Indigenous women's identity and beadwork. Identity is not simple, but rich and multi-faceted, much like beadwork. What we see on the surface does not reflect its full depth and complexity, much like identity. If we only focus on the aesthetical and tangible, we diminish its value and the knowledge held within. This is why context is so critical. Bead by bead, we retell our stories and keep these critical contextual pieces alive within our collective memories. Within beadwork, each individual bead makes up a small part within its larger overall pattern, just as each beadwork story is a small piece of the larger story of Indigenous women's struggles and journeys to reclaim cultural identity and ways of knowing in response to the legacy of colonization. Beadwork is a symbol of Indigenous cultural survival and resilience. My hope is that this research will validate the experience of reconnecting with Indigenous identity through beadwork for others, and that it might also encourage Indigenous students to utilize artistic storytelling methodologies such as beadwork within their thesis work. If Indigenous people continue to thrive through this practice, and this practice continues to thrive through us, we will be able to stitch and create new narratives of Indigenous experience and resiliency into the fabric of our collective consciousness.

REFERENCES

Anderson, S. (2016). Stitching through silence: Walking with our sisters, honoring the missing and murdered Aboriginal women in Canada. *Textile*, 14(1), 84–97.

Archibald, L., & Dewar, J. (2010). Creative arts, culture and healing: Building an evidence base. *Pimatisiwin: A Journal of Aboriginal and Indigenous Community Health*, 8(3), 1–25. https://journalindigenouswellbeing.co.nz/media/2018/12/1_Archibald.pdf

Bastien, B. (2004). *Blackfoot ways of knowing: The worldview of the Siksikaitsitapi.* Calgary: University of Calgary Press.

Belcourt, C. (2010). *Beadwork: First peoples' beading history and techniques.* Owen Sound: Ningwakwe Learning Press.

Bourgeois, C. (2018). She beads like a Cocom but designs like a young person: An exploration of beading as Anishnaabe epistemology. In M. Macaulay & M. Noodin (Eds.), *Papers of the Forty-Seventh Algonquian Conference* (pp. 43–56).

East Lansing: Michigan State University Press.

Coholic, D., Cote-Meek, S., & Recollet, D. (2012). Exploring the acceptability and perceived benefits of arts-based group methods for Aboriginal women living in an urban community within northeastern Ontario. *Canadian Social Work Review*, 29(2), 149–168.

Farrell Racette, S. (2008). My grandmothers loved to trade: The Indigenization of European trade goods in historic and contemporary Canada. *Journal of Museum Ethnography*, (20), 69–81.

Farrell Racette, S. (2017). Tuft life: Stitching sovereignty in contemporary Indigenous art. *Art Journal*, 76(2), 114–123. https://doi.org/10.1080/00043249.2017.1367198

Gray, M. J. (2017). *Beads: Symbols of Indigenous cultural resilience and value* [Master's thesis, University of Toronto]. Tspace. https://tspace.library.utoronto.ca/bitstream/1807/82564/3/Gray_Malinda_J_201711_MA_thesis.pdf

Hanson, C., & Griffiths, H. F. (2016). Tanning, spinning, and gathering together: Intergenerational Indigenous learning in textile arts. *Engaging with Indigenous Communities*, 2(1), 225–245. https://doi.org/10.15402/esj.v2i1.208

Hill, M. (2003). Aspects of traditional beadwork. In L. Leblanc (Ed.), *A compendium of the Anishnabek: An overview of the historical Anishnabek with special reference to the peoples of the Three Fires Confederacy* (pp. 473–479). M'Chigeeng, ON: Kenjgewin Teg Educational Institute.

Linklater, R. (2014). *Decolonizing trauma work: Indigenous stories and strategies*. Winnipeg: Fernwood Publishing.

Ray, L. (2016). Beading becomes a part of your life: Transforming the academy through the use of beading as a method of inquiry. *International Review of Qualitative Research*, 9(3), 363–378. https://www.jstor.org/stable/26372213

Robertson, C. (2017). Land and beaded identity: Shaping art histories of Indigenous women of the flatland. *RACAR: Revue d'Art Canadienne/Canadian Art Review*, 42(2), 13–29. https://doi.org/10.7202/1042943ar

Prete, T. (2019). Beadworking as an Indigenous research paradigm. *Art Research International*, 4(1), 28–57. https://doi.org/10.18432/ari29419

Scarpino, G. (2007). Resilience and urban Aboriginal women. *Native Social Work Journal*, 6, 33-55.

Scofield, G., & Briley, A. (2011). *Wapikwaniy: A beginner's guide to Métis floral beadwork*. Saskatoon: Gabriel Dumont Institute

Reconstituting Indigenous Identities through Portraiture and Storytelling

Reclaiming Representation for Indigenous Women and Two-Spirit People

Juliet Mackie

INTRODUCTION

My name is Juliet Mackie, and I am a Métis painter, beader, and graduate student with Cree, Gwich'in, and English ancestry. I am a PhD candidate at Concordia University, located in Tiohtià:ke/Montreal on the unceded lands of the Kanien'kehá:ka Nation. In this chapter, I will discuss my research project *Reconstituting Indigenous Identities through Portraiture and Storytelling: Reclaiming Representation for Indigenous Women and Two-Spirit People*. In this research, I meet with Indigenous women and Two-Spirit participants to explore cultural belonging, representation, and identity. Based on this storytelling process, I will paint portraits of participants that are identity-affirming and honour how they choose to represent themselves. I embrace Indigenous research methodologies as the foundation of this study to centre decolonizing practices and Indigenous traditional knowledges. I centre women and Two-Spirit people in this project as a response to the issue of missing and murdered Indigenous women, girls, transgender, and Two-Spirit people (MMIWGT2S) in order to contribute to reclaiming "power and place" through conversations about representation, identity, and strengthening cultural belonging (National Inquiry into Missing and Murdered Indigenous Women and Girls [NIMMIWG], 2019).

I am an Indigenous woman and citizen of the Métis Nation of British Columbia. My Cree name is *nika acahk*, which means "star that leads the way." I locate myself in this chapter to ground myself culturally, which is a practice that invites reflexivity and ethical accountability into my research (Archibald, 2008; Kovach, 2009; Parkes, 2015). I share my family story to provide insight of how I came to this area of study and to acknowledge the importance of cultural belonging in my own life. I also explore how my experiences as an artist and student inform my research approach and process.

My Métis family has community connections to Fort Chipewyan, Alberta, and Red River, Manitoba; our family names are Flett, Wylie, and Hardesty. Generations back, my Métis "foremothers" married men who came to Canada from the Orkney Islands to work for the Hudson's Bay Company. My mother is Catherine Richardson, her mother is Greta Oak, her mother is Evelyn Wylie, her mother is Emily Anna Maria Flett, and her mother is Jannie Hardesty. I look to the matriarchs in my family to shape my own sense of cultural belonging and draw knowledge from their experiences.

My great-grandmother, Evelyn, was the matriarch of my Métis family during my childhood. She was raised in Fort Chipewyan by her mother, Emily Anna Maria Flett, and father, William Wylie Jr. She lived in "the bush" for most of her life and attended Anglican Day School in Fort Chipewyan as a child. She drove a dogsled team, hunted caribou, snared rabbit, crafted birchbark baskets, sewed clothes, beaded moccasins, and spoke Cree; however, she never identified as Métis. The term Métis wasn't available as a designation at that time. Métis people were still referred to as "Halfbreeds" (Campbell, 1995). Even when it came into use, she rejected the term. When my mother was growing up, it was a joke in their family that they were all Métis except for Evelyn.

My grandmother Greta (born in 1937) and her two sisters were raised seasonally between Fort Chipewyan and a trapline at Hill Island Lake, Northwest Territories. She has fond memories of riding the dogsled with her sisters while her mother checked her traps, eating bannock and moose meat prepared by her mother, and watching the northern lights move across the night sky. During Greta's teenage years, her family lived in Uranium City, Saskatchewan, located on the shores of Lake Athabasca. Her Swedish father Alvar Oak worked as a prospector, mine manager, and held a uranium claim. Without having been warned of the dangers, Evelyn lined her flower garden with radioactive uranium ore rocks. Today, my family experiences health conditions such as cancer, autoimmune disease, allergies to metals, as well as bone and joint issues, all of which are results of the environmental extractivism that disproportionately affects Indigenous communities in Canada (Palmater, 2019; Simpson, 2017).

Greta describes her upbringing as traditional and often expresses love for the time when her family lived off the land. In 1942, Evelyn moved her daughters to Edmonton as a strategy to escape the Indian residential school system. Greta recalls that her mother moved their family to Edmonton to avoid the Indian agent. Being born to a Swedish father allotted Greta and her sisters "white dad privilege," which had spared them from the Indian agent's previous visits, but Evelyn feared that her girls might be taken while Alvar was away trapping. Evelyn considered Edmonton a safer option where her family could attempt to assimilate into the dominant culture.

This was not the case and in Edmonton my family experienced racism. They were often addressed with derogatory terms and faced discrimination and poverty. In the late 1950s, my grandmother moved to Vancouver to study pharmacy at the University of British Columbia (UBC). She was the first woman in our family to obtain a university degree. At UBC, she met my grandfather Edward Richardson. They married, had their daughters Cathy and Judy, and moved to Vancouver Island. During these years, Greta did not speak publicly about her Indigeneity, due to the ever present anti-Indigenous racism in society. She chose to raise her daughters without identifying the family as Métis, even though she engaged in many Métis cultural practices, including sewing with moose hide, making birchbark baskets, picking berries, baking bannock, and visiting with her Métis family at Fort Chipewyan. She lived a cultural life without naming the Métis practices overtly.

The decision to remain quiet about one's Métis identity was a common theme for the Métis people who lived apart from Métis communities (Dumont, 1996; Carrière, 2007; Richardson, 2016). Because of this history, the women in my family (my grandmother, mother, and aunt) went through processes of healing from the shame, racism, and discrimination they experienced. They found a variety of ways to embrace, connect, and embody their cultural pride. This process looked different for each of them and reflected how they chose to exist as Métis women, mothers, community members, and cultural beings. My grandmother Greta describes this process in a story she wrote in the late nineties. She wrote:

> I went home to Fort Chipewyan, where I was born, to visit my relatives. We camped on the shore of Lake Athabasca and all my anger, hatred, fear, and bitterness began to wash away. I was home. I learned how to make a birchbark basket and roast fish over the campfire. I finally had a feeling of belonging. Today, at the age of sixty-one, I've finally admitted to the world that I am Métis and proud of it. All my shame and blame have been transformed into pride and love for all my relations. I know who I am, I know where I come from, I know why I am here. (Oak, 1998)

I was raised within my culture. My mother made sure that her children were brought up within an environment of cultural pride, kinship, visiting, songs, stories, and food. I am also bi-cultural and honour my father's heritage as well. My paternal ancestors are from England and Scotland. My grandfather George Mackie was a child evacuee from London to Vernon, British Columbia, during World War II. After the war he returned to England, but later immigrated to Canada with my grandmother Gillian. They raised their five children on Vancouver Island. Despite always knowing who I am and where I come from, there were still times when I experienced shame and discomfort expressing my Métis identity in settings that I deemed to be culturally unsafe.

My own journey of discovering, remembering, and embracing who I am as an Indigenous woman has motivated my research into cultural identity and belonging. In recent years, as I took steps to strengthen my own identity, I became curious about how other Indigenous women experience cultural belonging. Inspired by my initial experiences, this study explores representation for Indigenous women and Two-Spirit people, and asks what cultural belonging can look like, or feel like, or sound like for individuals.

Arts-based methodologies are culturally congruent with many Indigenous worldviews, and I explore portrait painting and storytelling processes as I conduct this research (Farrell Racette, 2023). I will explore if and how holistic, positive, and affirming artistic representation leads to strengthened cultural belonging. Grounded in Indigenous methodologies, this research project aims to serve the community of Indigenous women and Two-Spirit people who are exploring their identities. I concentrate on the ways people work to create and experience enhanced cultural belonging within the context of Canada's ongoing colonial violence. This project centres the concept of dignity and asks, *How can Indigenous women and Two-Spirit people feel dignified and culturally proud? Can positive representation assist in that process?*

CONTEXT, OBJECTIVES & QUESTIONS

Inspired by a larger social movement of decolonization, this research examines the role of portraiture in strengthening a sense of belonging for personal and intergenerational healing (NIMMIWG, 2019). Due to Canada's history of colonial violence, Indigenous Peoples have been deprived of our lands, languages, families, and cultures (Carrière, 2007; Smith, 2012; Simpson, 2016). The experience of Indigenous cultural disconnection is sometimes referred to the *soul wound* or as *fire illness*, in the Métis context (Duran, 2006; Richardson, 2016). In Canada, First Nations and Métis people experience a suicide rate three times higher than non-Indigenous people, due in part to contextual issues, such as ongoing oppression, systemic barriers, an absence of justice in the legal system and racism in social services. Inuit communities experience a suicide rate that is nine times higher than non-Indigenous people (Kirmayer et al., 2007; Inuit Tapiriit Kanatami, 2016). In Inuit Nunangat and regions with large Indigenous populations, suicide is the leading cause of death for children and youth (Oliver et al., 2012; Peters et al., 2013). Many social services are delivered by non-Indigenous professionals and use strategies that are not Indigenous-centred (Oliver et al., 2012; Peters et al., 2013). This may further increase disconnection from culture, as it decentres Indigenous healing knowledges. Having strengthened connections to culture, community, and Indigenous languages, are associated with lower suicide rates (Lelonde & Chandler, 2009; National Inuit Scuicide Prevention Strategy, 2016). These statistics demonstrate the ongoing suffering within Indigenous communities and highlight the importance of kinship and connection.

It is not only the acts of racialized violence that cause pain, but also the ongoing lack of care in colonial society that denies appropriate social responses and support when this violence occurs (Richardson & Wade, 2008). Structural and interpersonal racism gives Indigenous Peoples the message that we are not wanted in mainstream Canadian society. There is a dire need for Indigenous communities to be supported in our efforts to (re)claim and (re)connect with our cultures and traditional practices. Motivated by the ongoing resistance to colonial violence, this research aims to offer Indigenous participants a space to explore identity and to strengthen cultural belonging in order to enhance overall well-being.

In Canada, many Indigenous women, girls, transgender, and Two-Spirit relatives have been violated through violence, in a context of relative impunity for perpetrators (NIMMIWG, 2019). Erased from the social landscape, Indigenous women must fight for "power and place" within Canadian society (Bear, 2014; NIMMIWG, 2019). This research aims to support Indigenous women and Two-Spirit participants as they reclaim representation and their personal narratives. By creating space for ourselves through portraiture and storytelling, we aim to strengthen, honour, and celebrate our identities, stories, and cultural backgrounds.

Mississauga Nishnaabeg scholar Leanne Betasamosake Simpson writes, "White supremacy, capitalism, and heteropatriarchy have targeted and continue to murder, disappear, attack, criminalize, and devalue our bodies, minds, and spirits" (Simpson, 2016, p. 21). There are many paths for healing after colonial violence. Through my research, I hope to expand knowledge about the potential of portraiture for cultural and self-reclamation. I aim to provide a space in which Indigenous women and Two-Spirit participants may enhance their self-worth, their presence, and their voices.

In this research, I focus on the stories of Indigenous women and Two-Spirit within a context of identity, cultural (re)connection, and healing. I also create ethical visual representations of participants through portraiture, based on our conversations about belonging. I aim to contribute to research on the importance of positive and consensual representation of Indigenous women; challenge the history of racism, sexualization, and stereotyping within western representations of Indigenous women in society, art, media, and museums. I additionally celebrate traditional Indigenous knowledges through embracing decolonizing methodologies and artistic creation in order to contribute to the reclamation of power and place for Indigenous women in Canada.

My study asks the following questions: *Can positive, affirming representations in portraiture be used to strengthen the sense of the cultural self, dignity, and identity for Indigenous women and Two-Spirit people? Can seeing oneself represented in a dignified and culturally centred manner precipitate healing and strengthening for Indigenous women and Two-Spirit people? How can reflexive storytelling enhance cultural belonging and create new (self) knowledge as well as research knowledge?* Through sharing stories and exploring past experiences with belonging, I hope to find answers to some of these questions as well as discover new questions that I am sure will arise through this process.

KINSHIP-BASED RESEARCH PROCESSES

This research will consist of conversational "interviews" with participants on the topics of identity, cultural belonging, representation, and kinship.

To enhance comfort, and move away from a rigid academic interview, these conversations are held in a "kitchen table" style; often over a cup of tea in the participant's home (Colley, 2018; Farrell Racette, 2022; Mattes, 2019). These conversations include a few predetermined guiding questions but are flexible and follow the lead of the participant. Questions might be: *What is your culture(s)? Have you always felt like a cultural person? What activities, places, stories, people make you feel embraced by your culture? Was there ever a time when you did not feel a strong cultural connection? Growing up, what representation of Indigenous women (in film, media, culture, etc.) did you see? How did these representations make you feel about yourself? How do you see yourself today and how do you want others to see you?* Based on these stories of belonging and identity, I will paint a portrait of each participant. Portraits will offer a representation that is consensual, affirming, holistic, and reflexive. After offering a time of reflection, I will meet with participants again to discuss their portraits, and if the process of being represented created pathways to strengthened belonging or well-being. In this project, the purpose of painting portraits is to facilitate conversations about the "preferred representation" of each participant.

As part of my PhD Candidacy exam at Concordia University, I reviewed literature on topics relating to my research such as identity formation, colonial history, MMIWGT2S, representation of Indigenous women, Indigenous feminism(s), and the historical uses of portrait painting. Of these topics, I identified three themes that are most relevant to my research: *decolonization, cultural belonging,* and *reframing narratives* pertaining to Indigenous women. I will outline in the following section why these themes are foundational to this research.

Decolonization

Māori scholar Linda Tuhiwai Smith writes about how the history of Indigenous Peoples in research has been "inextricably linked to European imperialism and colonialism" (Smith, 2012). As such, Indigenous Peoples and Indigenous epistemologies were excluded from the construction of western knowledge (Kovach, 2009; Smith, 2012; Wilson, 2008). Due to this history, Indigenous scholars have begun incorporating frameworks of decolonization, self-determination, and social justice into their research. When using a decolonizing framework, scholars deconstruct the "profoundly exploitative nature" of western research (Smith, 2012). Indigenous and non-Indigenous scholars have addressed the colonial history of academic institutions by proposing methods of decolonizing research (Simpson, 2017; Smith, 2012; Tuck & Yang, 2012; Wilson, 2008). Decolonizing methodologies respect and centre Indigenous epistemologies, traditional knowledges, and worldviews, which are necessary within academia for Indigenous students to thrive.

Decolonizing literature offers Indigenous scholars and researchers many methodological approaches that are grounded in Indigenous cultural practices, worldviews, or traditions. These methodologies are important as they reject the harmful history of western research that is embedded in colonialism (Kovach, 2009; Smith, 2012). The Pope's 2022 visit to Canada drew attention to policies such as the *Doctrine of Discovery*, which reveal the broader context of ethnocide and assimilation that aimed to destroy Indigenous cultures and knowledge (Eneas, 2022; Jamieson, 2022; White, 2022). Created specifically to challenge this colonial history, decolonizing methodologies offer culturally embedded approaches for research. In my research I explore different Indigenous methodologies to build a foundation of cultural safety for my project.

Decolonizing methodologies incorporate theories that are based in cultural knowledge that have been practiced for countless years within Indigenous communities, such as storytelling, arts-based practices, or practices that are grounded in kinship (Archibald, 2008; Farrell Racette, 2022; Igloliorte, 2017). Decolonizing methodologies centre Indigenous ways of knowing and being, worldviews, pedagogies, as well as truth-telling and placing events accurately in historical context (Smith, 2012). Through embracing decolonizing methodologies, I join many Indigenous researchers who weave community practices into their work to celebrate the new knowledge being created (Wilson, 2008). Although Indigenous scholars have identified many different methodological approaches, they are united in the understanding that decolonizing methodologies are centred within Indigenous worldviews.

Cultural Belonging

As outlined earlier in this chapter, the literature on Indigenous suffering demonstrates how Canada's colonial history has caused devastating cultural loss and fragmented identities for Indigenous Peoples in Canada and across Turtle Island (Carrière, 2007; Evans-Campbell, 2008; Richardson, 2016). This has meant that as Indigenous Peoples, we do not always have a strong cultural identity or connection to our communities (Battiste, 2008; Carrière, 2007). Forced disconnection from family, ceremony, language, and land has resulted in disproportionate rates of suffering among Indigenous communities. For many Indigenous communities, this violent history has resulted in what is known as intergenerational trauma.

Some Indigenous scholars attest that historical trauma can be applied to all Indigenous Peoples who continue to survive ongoing colonial violence (Evans-Campbell, 2008; Fast & Collin-Vézina, 2010; NIMMIWG, 2019). Although not all Indigenous Peoples experience colonialism in the same way, violence and suffering have contributed to the marginalization of Indigenous Peoples and resistance has become a part of our daily reality (Richardson & Wade, 2008; Wade, 1995). Systemic violence serves to disempower and silence Indigenous Peoples and the strength of our presence within mainstream society (Richardson & Wade, 2008). As a result, Indigenous bodies, sovereignty, and processes of "individual and collective self" have become politicized (Coulthard, 2014, p. 131; Simpson, 2016). Clearly, there is a need for more pathways to achieve strengthened cultural connection for many Indigenous Peoples.

When discussing intergenerational trauma, it is important also to acknowledge intergenerational healing. Māori psychotherapist and artist Donny Riki emphasizes that when, as Indigenous Peoples, we take action to create healing in our own lives, we are offering healing to our ancestors and our future generations (Riki, 2023). For instance, three generations of women in my family have used beadwork as a tool for healing and as an act of resistance against colonial violence. After this traditional practice was "lost" in my family though forced assimilation and cultural genocide, my grandmother Greta taught herself to bead moccasins from a book on Métis beadwork. In 2019, I learned how to make beaded earrings at a workshop in Montreal. Since then, beading has become a foundational pillar of my life. I bead almost every day. I started my business Little Moon Creations in 2020, and since then have made well over a thousand pairs of beaded earrings. In 2022, I taught my grandmother how to make beaded earrings, and in return she taught me how to make moccasins. My grandmother then taught my mother how to bead. Through this web of intergenerational learning and healing, the women in my family have reclaimed beadwork as an act of decolonization, which connects us to the matriarchs in our family.

Reframing Narratives and Decolonial Mapping

In my research and artistic practice, I am interested in the notion of *remapping* (Goeman, 2013). Indigenous authors, scholars, and artists remap colonial narratives when they reconsider and reimagine histories, stereotypes, perceptions, or geographies in their work (Goeman, 2013; Robertson, 2017; Simpson, 2017). Whether they are virtual or physical geographies, remapping is the reclamation of space for Indigenous Peoples. Seneca scholar Dr. Mishuana Goeman describes remapping as "the labour Native authors and the communities they write within and about undertake, in the simultaneously metaphoric and material capacities of map making, to generate new possibilities" (Goeman, 2013, p. 3). Through Canada's ongoing colonialism, Indigenous women have been the target of violence (NIMMIWG, 2019). Through misrepresentation and racist stereotypes, Indigenous women and Two-Spirit people are sexualized and infantilized, which leads to further acts of violence (Bear, 2014). Due to this history, Indigenous feminist scholars have acknowledged the centuries of resistance and identified the urgent need to reframe representations of Indigenous women in Canadian society (Green, 2007; Simpson, 2016). This reframing can be achieved through creating accurate and holistic representations of Indigenous women in media, film, literature, and visual art.

My dissertation will be guided by the scholarship on Indigenous feminism(s) and representation of Indigenous women, in order to use portraiture to remap existing colonial narratives. My intention is to offer alternative representations that redress a history of racist and inaccurate portrayals of Indigenous women. I look to Indigenous art historians whose scholarship problematizes the colonial nature of art history, while uplifting Indigenous art and artists (Igloliorte, 2010; McGeough, 2012). After considering this history, I am interested in creating consensual and identity-affirming representations through this project.

METHODOLOGICAL APPROACHES

As I begin to navigate the research creation of my degree, I acknowledge my position as both an "insider" and an "outsider" (Kwame, 2017; Smith, 2012). I am an insider because I am an Indigenous person who is part of a culture, community, and kinship network. I am an outsider because of my position within academia as a researcher. Due to the colonial nature of academic institutions, research can be hostile for Indigenous community members (Smith, 2012). Thus, it is important to approach this role carefully and respectfully. As I detail in the next section of this chapter, I look to Indigenous methodologies in my research, such as Kitchen Table, storytelling, and artistic practices. I do this to ensure that my research remains ethical, respectful, reflexive, and critical. I also look to my academic community: I am grateful for the support and guidance of my supervisors Dr. Heather Igloliorte and Jason Lewis.

Métis Kitchen Table Methodology

Métis Scholar, artist, and curator Dr. Sherry Farrell Racette theorized *Métis Kitchen Logic*, in which the kitchen table relates to the Cree notion of *pa washakapik*, "which means to sit together in a circle, but on a deeper level infers 'being open to learning together' and also carries the suggestion that the circle has unlimited capacity to open and include" (Farrell Racette, 2023, p. 87). Métis Kitchen Table Methodology embodies visiting, kinship, storytelling, and traditional practices such as beadwork, food, or music. In this setting, feelings of comfort, community, and warmth are created. "We can reclaim and reimagine the kitchen table as a sovereign place," Farrell Racette writes, "where women, men, and children work, dream, and create. Where we grow knowledge, gather strength, and clean up after ourselves" (2023, p. 15). When applied to a research setting, this methodology allows community learning in the comfort of a culturally safe environment. In practice, this theory allows flexibility, time spent together, and does not require formality. Farrell Racette compares this methodological process to an unofficial talking circle, where deep listening, critical reflection, and growth are embraced (2023). While Kitchen Table practices have been used in multiple contexts, and have been described as safe environments for dialogue, Farrell Racette theorizes this methodology within a Métis cultural context. I will set my conversations with participants within this context to invite comfort and cultural safety into our meetings.

Storywork

Cree and Saulteaux scholar Dr. Margaret Kovach emphasizes the importance of storytelling, stating that "stories remind us of who we are and of our belonging. Stories hold within them knowledges while simultaneously signifying relationships" (Kovach, 2009, p. 95). In my research, I embrace storytelling as a framework that will allow a human connection and reject a western hierarchy between the researcher and research participant. Stó:lō scholar Jo-ann Archibald (Q'um Q'um Xiiem) theorized the story-based methodological practice of *storywork*, which she applies to the field of education and curriculum building. Archibald identified respect, responsibility, reverence, reciprocity, holism, interrelatedness, and synergy as the seven principles of storywork (Archibald, 2008). Grounding my research in these principles invites Indigenous epistemology to an academic setting. Kovach puts forth the notion that when we share stories with each other, we are exchanging and gathering knowledge as part of a process that is centred in nêhiyaw (Cree) epistemology. The academic concept of an *interview* does not honour the holistic nature of sharing stories (Kovach, 2009). I look to *storywork* to exemplify Indigenous knowledge and remove the exclusionary academic jargon of western theories. Fundamental to my research creation, storytelling is a process filled with interconnection, teachings, and resonance for each individual in a meaning-making process.

Remapping through Portraiture

In this project, portrait painting is a critical component of my methodological approach. Through this process, I expect to develop deeper analysis of the function of painting in relation to identity formation. Among my inspirations is art educator Rose Barron, who writes that "thousands of contemporary artists use their artwork to try to better our society…in our complex society, many voices go unheard, people go unseen, and unjustified. The messages created through art become information, remembrance, resolution, and stories untold" (Barron, 2006, p. 11). I expect that the act of painting Indigenous women and Two-Spirit people will offer new and different insights into remapping, or reimagining, narratives of Indigenous identity and value in Canadian society (Goeman, 2008).

This will be a large focus of my doctoral dissertation, and as a result, I hope to be able to theorize a methodology based on portrait painting. I utilize portrait painting in my art practice and research to explore if and how identity can be strengthened through creating visual representations of Indigenous participants, followed by conversations about this experience. American artist Kristen G. Congdon states, "Many female artists and traditional communities view art and life as connected... For many artists and various cultural communities, art is more about storytelling, tradition, identity, autobiography, and the ordinary turned into something extraordinary than it is about the end product" (Congdon, 1996, pp. 14, 15). My dissertation will examine how these experiences of co-creation and engagement through portraiture can enhance the sense of "cultural self" and self-appreciation for the participants in my study.

KINSHIP, PARTICIPATION, AND BELONGING

In this research, there are eight women and Two-Spirit participants, all with connections to the Montreal urban Indigenous community. Participants vary in age and have differing experiences in relation to cultural connection. Some participants have been raised within their cultures or in their Indigenous communities. Other participants have been raised outside of their traditional homelands but with an understanding of who they are. I will be interviewing Métis, First Nations, and Inuit participants who are already part of my community in Montreal. My research project is grounded in kinship. Due to the nature of my research, it is crucial for there to be trust, familiarity, and mutual respect between the participants and myself. I look again to Kovach, who writes, "Having a pre-existing and ongoing relationship with participants is an accepted characteristic of research according to tribal paradigms" (Kovach, 2009, p. 15). I am interested in practicing *purposeful* sampling in my qualitative research (Palinkas et al., 2015). An example of this practice is described by Kovach: "When choosing participants, it is suggested within qualitative studies that research participants be chosen for what they can bring to the study as opposed to random sampling" (Kovach, 2009, p. 51). In my attempt to choose participants purposefully, I have identified this recruitment method as embodying the Indigenous worldview and methodologies that I look to in my research.

The use of language in this project is important. The effects of colonialism on identity are nuanced, and it would be extremely limiting to categorize participants in ways that diminish the multi-faceted nature of their lives and experiences. For example, some participants may have status but do not experience strong cultural belonging. There are also non-status women who have strong ties to their communities and homelands, who may have lost their status through the patriarchal policies of the *Indian Act* or adoption. When selecting and situating participants into this research project, I will work to capture the complex and holistic nature of how we express our identities as Indigenous Peoples. I will build my research project to meet and embrace participants wherever they locate themselves in relation to cultural connection. I will not select participants based on if and how well they fit into a category.

Instead, I am interested in exploring how Indigenous Peoples resist the imposition of meaning of who they are from outside, while holding space for self-analysis and self-representation (Fforde et al., 2013; Goffman, 1963). As an artist and researcher, I want to expand knowledge about the potential of portraiture for cultural and self reclamation, as well as decolonization and enhancing Indigenous voices in Canada. In addition to creating new knowledge, I aim to provide a space in which Indigenous women and

Two-Spirit participants may strengthen their self-worth, their presence, and their voice. I will consult with the participants at each step, integrating their reflections and feedback to ensure that this process remains culturally safe, ethical, and respectful at all times.

AFTERWORD

In her recent book chapter, "Kitchen Tables and Beads: Space and Gesture in Contemplative and Creative Research," Farrell Racette describes the Cree expression *tawow*, which is often translated as "welcome," but literally means "there is room for you here." (2022, pp. 87-88). I experienced this notion of tawow when I began exploring decolonizing methodologies, and it is what brought me to this area of study. I had difficulties positioning myself within academia's often rigid and prescriptive structure. I only felt that I belonged once I found a program that allowed me to build my academic education around my lived experiences, family stories, art practice, and Métis worldview, rather than around the existing formal structure of academic life. My advice for any Indigenous graduate student is to remember that your traditional knowledge can be more valuable than what you will find in a university setting. Universities are colonial institutions that were designed to keep you out, and although academia is uncomfortable at times, you deserve to be here. Find your university's Indigenous student centre and familiarize yourself with all the support available. There are many ways to uphold traditional knowledge and contribute to processes of decolonization. If an academic path is not for you, that is also valid.

REFERENCES

Archibald, J. (2008). *Indigenous storywork: Educating the heart, mind, body, and spirit.* Vancouver: UBC Press.

Barron, R. (2006). *Exploring identity through self-portraiture* [Master's thesis, Georgia State University]. ScholarWorks. https://doi.org/10.57709/1062144

Battiste, M. (2008). Research ethics for protecting Indigenous knowledge and heritage: Institutional and researcher responsibilities. In N. K. Denzin,

Y. S. Lincoln, & L. T. Smith (Eds.), *Handbook of critical and Indigenous methodologies*. Thousand Oaks, CA: Sage Publishing.

Bear, T. (2014). Walking with our sisters: An art installation centered in ceremony. *Aboriginal Policy Studies*, 3(1&2), pp. 223–230.

Campbell, M. (1995). *Stories of the road allowance people*. Saskatoon: Gabriel Dumont Institute.

Carriere, J. (2007). Promising practices for maintaining identity in First Nations adoption. *First Peoples Child and Family Review*, 3(1), 46-64.

Congdon, K. G. (1996). Art history, traditional art and artistic practices. In G. Collins & R. Sandell (Eds.), *Gender issues in art education: Content, contexts, and strategies* (pp.10–19). Virginia: The National Art Education Association.

Coulthard, G. S. (2014). The plunge into the chasm of the past: Fanon, self-recognition, and decolonization. In *Red skin, white masks: Rejecting the colonial politics of recognition* (pp. 131–150). Minneapolis: University of Minnesota Press.

Colley, B. (2018). *Power in the telling: Grand Ronde, Warm Springs, and intertribal relations in the casino era*. Seattle: University of Washington Press.

Datta, R. (2018). Traditional storytelling: An effective Indigenous research methodology and its implications for environmental research. *AlterNatives: An International Journal of Indigenous People*, 14(1), 335-344.

Dumont, M. (1994). The red and white [poem]. In C. Camper (Ed.), *Miscegenation blues: Voices of mixed race women* (p. 196). Toronto: Sister Vision.

Duran, E. (2006). *Healing the soul wound: Counseling with American Indians and other Native peoples*. Teachers College Press.

Eneas, B. (2022, May 12). The Doctrine of Discovery: Its effects are still being felt, but only the Pope can rescind it. *CBC News*. https://www.cbc.ca/news/canada/saskatchewan/doctrine-of-discovery-calls-to-rescind-can-it-happen-1.6450029

Evans-Campbell, T. (2008). Historical trauma in American Indian/Native Alaska communities: A multi-level framework for exploring impacts on individuals, families and communities. *Journal of Interpersonal Violence*, 23, 316–338.

Farrell Racette, S. (2023). Kitchen tables and beads: Space and gesture in contemplative and creative research. In H. Igloliorte and C. Taunton (Eds.), *The Routledge companion of Indigenous art histories in the United States and Canada* (pp. 81–88). New York: Routledge.

Fast, E., & Collin-Vézina, D. (2010). Historical trauma, race-based trauma and resilience of Indigenous peoples: A literature review. *First Peoples Child & Family Review*, 5(1), 126–136. https://doi.org/10.7202/1069069ar

Fforde, C. Bamblett, L., Lovett, R., Gorringe, S., & Fogarty, B. (2013). Discourse, deficit, identity: Aboriginality, the race paradigm and the language of representation in contemporary Australia. *Media International Australia,* 149(1), 162–173. https://doi.org/10.1177/1329878X1314900117

Goeman, M. (2008). (Re)mapping Indigenous presence on the land in Native women's literature. *American Quarterly,* 60(2), 295–302. http://www.jstor.org/stable/40068538

Goeman, M. (2013). *Mark my words: Native women mapping our nations.* Minneapolis: University of Minnesota.

Goffman, E. (1963). *Stigma: Notes on the management of spoiled identity.* Englewood Cliffs, NJ: Prentice-Hall.

Green, J. (2007). *Making Space for Indigenous Feminism.* Black Point, NS: Fernwood Publishing.

Igloliorte, H. (2017). Curating Inuit Qaujimajatuqangit: Inuit knowledge in the qallunaat art museum. *Art Journal,* 76(2), 100–113. https://doi.org/10.1080/00043249.2017.1367196

Igloliorte, H. (2010). The Inuit of our imagination. Gerald McMaster (Ed.), *Inuit Modern* (41–49). Toronto: Douglas and McIntrye Press.

Inuit Tapiriit Kanatami (2016). *National Inuit suicide prevention strategy.* Ottawa: Inuit Tapiriit Kanatami. https://www.itk.ca/download/12091/

Jamieson, C. (2022, August 2). Pope Francis's visit to Canada was full of tensions—both from what was said and what wasn't. *The Conversation.* https://theconversation.com/pope-franciss-visit-to-canada-was-full-of-tensions-both-from-what-was-said-and-what-wasnt-186886

Kirmayer, L. J., Brass, G.M., Holton, T., Paul, K., Simpson, C., & Tait, C. (2007). *Suicide among Aboriginal people in Canada.* Ottawa: Aboriginal Healing Foundation.

Kovach, M. (2009). *Indigenous methodologies: Characteristics, conversations and contexts.* Toronto: University of Toronto Press.

Kwame, A. (2017). Reflexivity and the insider/outsider discourse in Indigenous research: My personal experience. *AlterNatives: An International Journal of Indigenous Peoples,* 13(4), 218–225. https://doi.org/10.1177/1177180117729851

Lalonde, C. E., & Chandler, M. J. (2009). Cultural continuity as a moderator of suicide risk among Canada's First Nations. In L. Kirmayer & G. Valaskakis (Eds.), *Healing traditions: The mental health of Aboriginal peoples in Canada.* Vancouver: UBC Press.

Mattes, C. (2022). Frontrunners as an exploration of Indigenous littoral curation. In H. Igloliorte and C. Taunton (Eds.), *The Routledge companion of Indigenous art histories in the United States and Canada* (pp. 176–185). New York: Routledge.

McGeough, M. (2012). Indigenous curatorial practices and methodologies. *Wicazo Sa Review,* 27(1), 13–20. https://doi.org/10.1353/wic.2012.0004

National Inquiry into Missing and Murdered Indigenous Women and Girls (Canada). (2019). *Reclaiming power and place: The final report of the National Inquiry into Missing and Murdered Indigenous Women and Girls.* Retrieved from https://www.mmiwg-ffada.ca/final-report/

Oak, G. (1998). *A Métis story.* [Unpublished memoir].

Oliver, L. N., Peters, P. A., & Kohen, D. E. (2012). Mortality rates among children and teenagers living in Inuit Nunangat, 1994 to 2008. Statistics Canada, Catalogue no. 82-003-xpe, *Health Reports,* 23(3): 17–22.

Palmater, P. (2019). The radical politics of Indigenous resistance and survival. In R. Kinna & U. Gordon (Eds.), *Routledge handbook of radical politics* (pp. 134–162). London: Routledge.

Palinkas, L. A., Horwitz, S. M., Green, C. A., Wisdom, J. P., Duan, N., & Hoagwood, K. (2015). Purposeful sampling for qualitative data collection and analysis in mixed method implementation research. *Administration and Policy in Mental Health,* 42, 533–544. https://doi.org/10.1007/s10488-013-0528-y

Parkes, A. (2015). Reflexivity as autoethnography in Indigenous research. In L. Bryant (Ed.), *Critical and creative research methodologies in social work* (pp. 93–106). London: Ashgate Publishing.

Peters, P. A., Oliver, L. N., & Kohen, D. E. (2013). Mortality among children and youth in high-percentage First Nations identity areas, 2000–2002 and 2005–2007. *Rural and Remote Health,* 13(3), 105–115. https://search.informit.org/doi/epdf/10.3316/informit.305152188921993

Richardson, C. L. (2016). *Belonging Métis.* Vernon: JCharlton Publishing.

Richardson, C., & Wade, A. (2008). Taking resistance seriously: A response-based approach to social work in cases of violence against Indigenous women. In S. Strega & Sohki Aski Esquao [J. Carrière] (Eds.), *Walking this path together: Anti-racist and anti-oppressive child welfare practice.* Winnipeg: Fernwood Publishing.

Riki, D. (2023, May 5). *First Nations response-based practice conference* [speech]. Conference, Curtin University, Perth, Australia.

Robertson, C. (2017). Land and beaded identity: Shaping art histories of Indigenous women of the flatland. *racar: Revue d'Art Canadienne/Canadian Art Review,* 42(2), 13–29. https://doi.org/10.7202/1042943ar

Simpson, L. B. (2016). Indigenous resurgence and co-resistance. *Critical Ethnic Studies,* 2(2), 19–34. https://doi.org/10.5749/jcritethnstud.2.2.0019

Simpson, L. B. (2017). *As we have always done: Indigenous freedom through radical resistance.* University of Minnesota Press.

Smith, L. T. (2012). *Decolonizing methodologies: Research and Indigenous peoples* (2nd ed.). London: Zed Books.

Tuck, E., & Yang, K. W. (2012). Decolonization is not a metaphor. *Decolonization: Indigeneity, Education & Society*, 1(1), 1–40.

Wade, A. (1995). Resistance knowledges: Therapy with Aboriginal persons who have been subjected to violence. In P. H. Stephenson, S. J. Elliott, L. T. Foster, & J. Harris (Eds.), *A persistent spirit: Towards understanding Aboriginal health in BC* (pp. 167–206). Vancouver: UBC Press.

White, P. (2022, August 3). Why Pope Francis faces calls to revoke the Doctrine of Discovery. *Globe and Mail*. https://www.theglobeandmail.com/canada/article-pope-visit-doctrine-of-discovery/

Wilson, S. (2008). *Research is ceremony: Indigenous research methods*. Halifax: Fernwood Publishing.

PART THREE

Indigenous Bodies
and
Meaning Making

Dancing My Way Home
Cultural Reclamation through the Embodiment of the Michif Language

Victoria May

ABSTRACT

*We danced for those that can't dance, those that are no
longer with us, and for those to come.
We danced to show that we are still here, we are the unbroken link that
the colonial project attempted to break and failed to do.*

This chapter describes a research-creation process focusing on Michif language embodiment through dance. This blended research-creation approach is grounded in Keeoukaywin, the Visiting Way methodology (Gaudet, 2019), and nêhiyaw kiskêyihtamowin (Plains Cree Knowledges) of relational ethics involving an Indigenous research paradigm of truth-telling, holism, reciprocity, relational accountability, conversational method, and storywork. The process of cultural reclamation offers possibilities to the many generations responding to colonial violence and resisting by going underground (Richardson, 2004), a period referred to as the "Michif underground years." It is one of many projects happening inside and outside the homeland that will help repair the fragmentation brought on by historical and ongoing colonial violence on our Michif peoples. **Keywords:** *Michif, Red River Métis, dance, embodiment, language, research-creation, performance, video, identity, reconnection*

TRIGGER & CONTENT WARNING

Some content in this thesis may refer directly and indirectly to:

- Colonization, white supremacy
- Trauma/intergenerational trauma
- Death and dying
- Physical/sexual violence
- Child abuse
- Emotional abuse
- Slurs, stereotypes, racism, ableism
- Suicide and self-harm

SELF-LOCATION IN THE RESEARCH

Taanshi, I am a Red River Métis/Michif woman, researcher, choreographer, artmaker, dancer, and mother. I identify with my maternal family and community in Prince Albert, Saskatchewan, and am a member of the Manitoba Métis Federation. I am part of a generation of Michif that were raised outside of the Métis homeland and away from the community. My mother was Roberta, and my grandmother Irene Victoria, after whom I was named. My Métis family names are Vermette, Delorme, Sayer, Laliberté, Frobisher, Pepin, Davis, Gaudry, and Villebrun; my paternal side is settler.

My grandmother Irene is from the Delorme and Vermette family lines. Her mother (my great-grandmother) was Sarah Jane Delorme, born in 1880 in Baie St. Paul, Manitoba. Her father was Jean-Baptiste Delorme (dit Bidou, born 1831 in Norway House, Manitoba), and Sarah's mother was Marguerite Pepin (born 1834 in St. Boniface, Manitoba). Bidou was a guard during the 1885 resistance; his father was Jean-Baptiste Delorme (born 1781), and his mother was unknown. Marguerite Pepin's parents were Antoine Pépin (born 1808 and died in 1858, killed by the Sioux) and Marguerite Davis (born in 1819 in Pembina, Manitoba). Marguerite's parents were Jean-Baptiste Davis (born 1784) and Josèphe M., only described as Saulteaux.

My great-grandfather Joseph Albert Vermette (born 1873), married to Sarah Delorme, would have been twelve years old during the 1885 resistance. His father, Joseph Vermette (dit José, born 1830 in St. Norbert, Manitoba), was a nephew of Gabriel Dumont. José was shot in the top of the head and was killed during the 1885 resistance during at the Battle of Coulée des Tourond (Barkwell, 2011). Jose was married to Marguerite Sayer (born 1837).

Marguerite's parents were Pierre Guillaume Sayer (born 1793), who was arrested for fur trading, pictured seated by supporter Louis Riel Sr. in this

FIGURE I. Pierre Guillaume Sayer and Louis Riel Sr. Public domain.

undated photo (Figure 1). Pierre Sayer was married to Josèphe Frobisher (born 1795). Josèphe's parents were Alexander Frobisher and Marguerite Crise/Cree. Pierre's parents were John Sayer (1750) and O Saulteuse/Saulteaux.

Joseph Vermette (José)'s parents were Joseph Vermette Toutpetit (born 1806 in St. Boniface) and Angelique Laliberté (born 1810 in St. Norbert). Joseph Vermette Toutpetit's parents were Joseph Vermette (born 1761) and Josephte Plouffe Villebrun. Angelique Laliberté's parents were Pierre Colin (dit Laliberté, born 1777) and Josephte Gaudry/Baudry.

These are my direct Métis ancestors on my maternal mother's side. There are many kinship ties and stories woven into all these people. I am unsure of my maternal grandfather's side beyond his full name, which is Albert Desormeaux. At the urging of my Vermette family that grew up close to a Desormeau(x) family from the same area, I have come to understand that quite likely my grandfather, Albert Desormeaux, is from the same community as my grandmother, Irene Vermette; however, as of this writing I haven't been able to confirm.

I only had my father, Edward Tew, in my life until I was approximately three years old, after which he and my mother lost contact and never met or corresponded again.

I am a light-skinned woman who grew up in an urban setting, with far more privilege than my cousins. Growing up in a family on welfare living in project housing, I faced classism, not racism. Despite issues of financial insecurity, my mother was extremely loving and supportive and facilitated my access to education, dance, the arts, and other life-enhancing opportunities. Within my family, I am the youngest of six children and was born to a different father than my siblings; there is a twenty-year age gap between my eldest brother and me. Though my mom was a single mother, I was always surrounded by family, being held and, from my earliest memories, cherished. My Nan Irene had nicknames for all of us. Mine was "Papoose," which is consistent with the rest of my Métis family. Oftentimes my cousins have a hard time recalling anyone's given names. Sadly, my brother Gerry and Nan Irene passed away within ten days of each other when I was a toddler. I acknowledge the privilege of growing up in Ottawa away from the stigma of being Métis, like that faced by my Saskatchewan-raised family. I bore the cost of not knowing who and where we were from and was temporarily distanced from our Métis family and identities after the passing of Nan Irene.

With what little my mother had, she nurtured my love of dance and was a large part of why I was able to continue in dance. Later, thanks to a crowdfunding initiative spearheaded by Elisabeth Arnold and my mother, I was supported with financial help from my community.

During the summer of 1989, the first trickle of funding was raised, and a seed was planted for the Young Performers Bursary. My dream of becoming a dancer became a reality. I attended the school of the Royal Winnipeg Ballet, moving away from my family "home" in Ottawa to Winnipeg, alone at fourteen, to study dance, and later dance professionally for the company.

My family's origins emerged from the Red River (St. Boniface), a place I called home for five years. It was in the Fox Farm/Nordale where our family lived for generations. My relatives played an important role in Canadian history when they resisted the invasion of Lii Canadas. In the Métis Resistance, my two second great-grandfathers, Jean-Baptise Delorme and Joseph Vermette, fought Lii Canadas. In April 1885, Joseph Vermette gave his life fighting for the Métis way of life and land during the Battle of Fish Creek, and he is buried in the Métis cemetery at Batoche, Saskatchewan. In 2019, during the annual Métis gathering of Batoche Days, my sister, daughter, cousins, and kin gathered to commemorate his life and subsequent sacrifice. We honoured him by jigging, by singing, and by listening to our stories on the land he fought and died for.

My career as a professional dancer, mid-career choreographer, and teacher has spanned nearly thirty years. I danced with the Royal Winnipeg Ballet and spent twelve years performing as a ballet and contemporary dancer in Sweden and Denmark. In 2007, I moved to Montreal.

Alongside my artistic practice, I am currently pursuing my PhD in the Individualized Program (INDI) at Concordia University, a multidisciplinary research program.

INTRODUCTION

n the following section I will briefly introduce the Red River Métis people, the Michif language, and an outline as to how the thesis is laid out.

The Red River Métis people are a post-contact Indigenous people that emerged during the eighteenth-century fur trade in the Red River Settlement (Bakker & Papen, 2003). Michif has three "varieties" that emerged from the Red River Valley (Souter, 2018): Southern Michif, French Michif, and Michif-Cree. The variation I identify with is now known as Southern Michif.

While there are 600,000 Métis people in Canada, only a handful can converse in Michif, and fewer than 100 use it as their main language at home (Statistics Canada, 2017). The language is now considered critically extinct (Mazzoli, 2019). Michif is the only language on the planet intertwining two grammatical systems: gendered nouns and adjectives in French with verbs in nêhiyawêwin (Plains Cree) using inanimate and animate forms (Bakker, 1997; Bakker & Papen, 2003). Learning Michif is a fundamental step in the process of decolonization and strengthening for the Métis. Historically, Métis culture and language were prohibited by the Canadian state as part of their violent colonial project, leading to linguistic near extinction (Campbell, 2010; Richardson, 2016; Teillet, 2019). Despite these challenges, I believe it is my responsibility as a Métis person to learn, protect, and preserve this birthright.

The Michif language has not yet been standardized in writing and is spelled phonetically.

Traditionally, Michif has been passed down orally (Burnouf et al., 2007; Louis Riel Institute, 2013). These factors make it even more important to decolonize language learning itself through processes that also allow space for the trauma that came through the suppression of our language and birthright. For example, it has been difficult for Métis Elders to speak Michif after being tormented and punished for communicating in their language (Logan, 2015). Métis scholar Judy Iseke (2013) states: "Michif language revitalization will continue to support communities and individuals in meeting the challenges of life and in regenerating speakers of Michif language in younger generations if some of these many forms are drawn upon as community strengths and are encouraged in younger generations" (p. 109).

My MA research is comprised of the creation of four distinct works: two dance performances, and two video installations, all focused on learning Michif through oral acquisition and dance. This research-creation series is a unique contribution to, and departure from, academic sources, which fail to grasp the holistic and embodied potential of language acquisition.

This document is laid out in the following sections: thesis statement and research summary; literature review; methodologies; and outcome, findings, and making meaning. Brief descriptions of the four supporting artistic works, *Michif x 40*, *Michif x 40 –live*, *Echoes of Plexus*, and *Assimilation is an ill-fitting suit*, are the building blocks of the main artistic work *Kiwapamitinaawaaw*.

THESIS STATEMENT AND RESEARCH SUMMARY

Thesis statement: "Reclaiming and decolonizing
Métis identity through embodiment of the Michif
language using dance and oral acquisition."

Like many, I am the first of seven generations of Métis people to have not heard the Michif language in my mother's womb (*Bill C-91*, 2019). I begin with the question of how embodying Michif through dance might make up for this layer of loss? I hope this project will contribute to the body of knowledge around Michif revitalization by showcasing the Michif language, embodying it through dance and oral acquisition, and beginning to repair the fragmentation brought on by historic and ongoing colonial violence. It is my aspiration that this project will be personally healing, but also will be an entry point for other Michif that wish to have diverse entry points into language learning. Gathering stories, learning cultural practices, and creating a performance with dance and music to mirror back to my community how reclaiming our language demonstrates the agency of this generation of the Métis Nation is all part of my healing journey.

LITERATURE REVIEW

Métis writer, playwright, grandmother, and Elder Maria Campbell speaks about the importance of words, knowing their meaning in relation to our identity, where we come from, our culture, "or the way we lived" (Campbell, 2022). Campbell speaks about a "bundle," specifically a word bundle. Each word is like each object; it has a story, comes from somewhere, and is connected to language (2022). Every item you would find in a backpack would have a story attached to it relating to where it came from and one's relationship to it.

For me, embodying the Michif language means to both express and manifest Michif in and through movement. The movement connects and transforms, adding a layer to my "bundle." Linking object and craft-making to relationality and embodiment, Alutiiq choreographer Tanya Lukin Linklater writes: "I've directed contemporary dancers in 'movement investigations' that deconstruct the principles of traditional dances in order to construct new dances. I've also performed works that engage with Alutiiq language and song, and become an embodied investigation of the language, deconstructed, from my perspective as a non-speaker" (Linklater, 2016). By transforming my bundle, and manifesting something entirely new for myself, I create another layer comprised of language and dance, each connected by words (language) and steps (choreography).

Thinking in the language becomes an essential part of the learning process. One begins to see the world from the perspective of the language one is trying to learn. Indigenous languages are relational (Chiblow & Meighan, 2022). In relation to Michif language learning, thinking in the language is important when strengthening one's identity as a Michif person. Michif speaker and Elder Brousse Flammand (2019) speaks of "thinking in Michif." He says that the Michif language was gifted to us, the Michif people, by Creator: "This language did not die, but because ke-puknigwataaw—the language was released onto earth. The Spirit World created the Michif peoples like it created all other nations and languages. Language is central to nationhood" (Flammand, 2019). Here, a parallel process involves remembering, understanding, learning, and expressing through movement. I am thinking in dance in ways akin to "thinking in Michif" (2019).

Indigenous language speakers from across Turtle Island have echoed these sentiments. Harry Oosahwee, a Cherokee speaker and teacher from Tahlequah, Oklahoma, speaks about the importance of being able to not only speak one's language but to think in it as well:

> If you don't think in that language, I mean, you can't honestly say you're that particular group of people, you know. I can say I'm white cuz I speak that language. I understand with the concepts that they have and when I say the concept maybe not, but I understand well enough to get by. Now, if a person is able to speak Cherokee, they see a whole new concept, ideology, worldview that doesn't exist in a white man's world, in a white man's English. (Wilbur & Keene, 2019, 18:09)

This connection to identity through language is also voiced by Kanien'ké:ha:ka Elder Sedalia Kawennotas Fazio, who shared a story in one of my graduate courses, saying when we lose the language, we no longer exist as a people. Our culture and worldview and who we are as a people live in our language (personal communication, October 7, 2020). My research is related to reclaiming language and how language is central to a person's health in all body, mind, and spirit. This speaks to how we are our language in Michif: *Li Michif niya* means both "I am Michif" and means "I am my language" (Graham Andrews, personal communication, March 16, 2020).

I chose to focus on the oral recordings of the language to learn by way of repeating the cadence and rhythm of the Michif words and sentences. The Gabriel Dumont Institute has an online Michif Dictionary, which also has audio recordings of words and sentences. Bakker and Fleury (2004) state:

> Like any living language, Michif is first and foremost, an oral language. The sounds, words and sentences in this section are the important items... The texts are made available just to support the oral texts in this section. It is much more important to learn to understand—and speak—the language than to learn to write it.

Algonquian Linguistic Atlas (2005), an open-source, online linguistic atlas of the Algonquian languages that uses recordings of Elders along with written translation, is described by its project director, Marie-Odile Junker, as "a fertile ground for knowledge transfer and mutual inspiration, with all parties working in a collaborative spirit. Our ultimate goal is to make sure that the beautiful Algonquian languages and the cultures they embody will be heard and spoken by many more generations to come" (2005).

When we are connected to our language, we are connected to ourselves. We may learn Michif through the process of oral acquisition, bypassing as much as possible the written system and including different ways of embodiment to support a language learning process.

Relationality is key to connecting language and this includes connection to the individual to kin, both past and present, and to community. As such, Linklater states, "I see my role as the artist as embodying or activating a relational process. I am in relation to the dancer. We are in relation to the text. We are in relation to the ideas—the ideas of treaty, the land, women's work, women's leadership. I am in relation to the structure of the movement score" (2016, pp. 26–27).

I am not engaged in this process alone. Each time I dance with the Indigenous dance collective *Maquahatine* this relationality is echoed through sharing individual gifts to the collective space and the strength of layered knowledge and resurgence through knowledge transfer. Simpson (2011) writes about resurgence: "In order to dance a new world into existence, we need the support of our communities in collective action" (p. 68).

In discussing the importance of learning one's hereditary language, Simpson writes, "And I learned the route that the salmon would have gone in our language. And so that was one of the ways I was trying to connect my community back to that story and back to that river system through this performance" (Simpson, as cited in Mumford, 2016, p. 139). Similarly, I attempt to dance myself and others home by connecting to myself, to my kin, and to my ancestors and the knowledge that exists in the spaces and process of dance-making and sharing circles. Later in this chapter, I will describe my process of sharing my learning with others.

What is carried in utero? Research indicates that language development starts as early as in utero (Gervain, 2015). Language is one of the
foundations of one's health and well-being and is essential to being connected to ourselves and where we come from; it's connected to our culture and is how we interpret the world. Does water carry the memory
of language? During pregnancy, the womb is filled with amniotic fluid
or water, reflecting that women are considered water carriers, carriers of
life (Anderson et al., 2013). As Michif speaker Graham Andrews (*Bill C-91*,
2019) shares, he is the first of seven generations to have not heard Michif
in his mother's womb.

As a Métis woman I can assert my identity and connection to my ancestors and culture by embodiment through dance, resisting assimilation and
learning the language through this process, thereby contributing to its continued preservation. Oosahwee said, "No language, no ideology, no philosophy, no worldview, just like everybody else, homogenized.... [Cherokee
word], or Cherokees, we have been so colonized that a majority of us have
become so assimilated, so acculturated, through the western concepts and
ideology that we have become desensitized to our own history, language,
and culture, that we deny our being and become one of them, the melting
pot of America" (Wilbur & Keene, 2019, 23:56). Dian Million (2009) writes
of the importance of language when asserting Indigenous resurgence:

> By exploring the early work of Maria Campbell, Lee Maracle, Ruby
> Slipperjack, and others, I suggest ways that Indigenous women partic-
> ipated in creating new language for communities to address the real
> multilayered facets of their histories and concerns by insisting on the
> inclusion of our lived experience, rich with emotional knowledges, of
> what pain and grief and hope meant or mean now in our pasts and
> futures. It is also to underline again the importance of felt experiences
> as community knowledges that interactively inform our positions as
> Native scholars, particularly as Native women scholars. Our felt schol-
> arship continues to be segregated as a "feminine" experience, as polemic,
> or at worst as not knowledge at all. (p. 54)

By stepping out of the western language acquisition mould and connecting the language to our way of life through the reclamation of our kinship ties and stories that tell about the way we lived and continue to live, Cindy Gaudet speaks about the importance of disrupting the colonial state, that is unyielding and individualistic (2019). As part of decolonizing language learning, Indigenous Knowledge Keepers, artists, and scholars have related the interconnectedness of language to our ways of life through stories and narrative, cultural resources and healing practices, cultural and pedagogic practices, social movements, organization of families and communities, cultural products like music, art, stories, poetry, media, and fashion. (Dei, 2011, as cited in Iseke, 2013, p. 109). Gaudet speaks about the attempted destruction of *keeyokewin* through colonialism (Gaudet, 2019). By exploring concepts of time through ancestral ways of knowing, that were shared from passing knowledge down between generations picking up the pieces from the attempted elimination of the Michif people.

I am guided in the research-creation process by Marilyn Dumont's use of themes of time and resurgence in her poetry, specifically in *That Tongued Belonging* (2012). This resurgence and movement through time and space are also shared by Michi Saagiig Nishaabeg scholar Leanne Betasamosake Simpson: "My interpretation of this is that the present, then, is a colliding of the past and the future. Everyday embodiment is, therefore, a mechanism for ancient beginnings" (2017, p. 198).

By remembering and re-remembering through movement and memory, I feel my ancestors and am reminded of their presence each time I dance the solo *Kiwapamitinaawaaw*. Through the movements I have connected to the Michif words, I am able to recall and physically feel the connection to my family, those living and those that have passed and those to come, and to connect to myself (*Bill C-91*, 2019). Similarly, Linklater (2016) discusses relationality across generations, between objects, bodies, people, and across time: "I instruct her to look back and forward. By looking forward and behind, the dancer is acknowledging future and previous generations. I explain to Ziyian that time can operate simultaneously in Indigenous ways of being—that past, present, and future operate simultaneously" (p. 27).

The bundle of my Michif grandmother (and my relatives of that generation's time) was intact and contained their culture, including the Michif language and our ways of knowing. Re-establishing these broken links for some Michif is essential in reclaiming identity. The relationality between the generations is expressed through language and reasserted through a physical embodiment of words through dance. I connect to our culture by resisting the colonial state, by asserting a Métis worldview through learning language assisted through my dance bundle. To embody the Michif language, express and manifest Michif in movement, is to connect, as our languages do, and to transform and re-add our languages to our collective "bundle" by way of embodiment through dance.

METHODOLOGIES

Indigenous Methodologies

This blended research-creation approach is grounded in "*Keeoukaywin*," the Visiting Way methodology (Gaudet, 2019), and *nêhiyaw kiskêyihtamowin* (Plains Cree Knowledges) of relational ethics involving an Indigenous research paradigm of truth-telling, holism, reciprocity, relational accountability, conversational method, and storywork (Archibald, 2008; Cardinal & Hildebrandt, 2000; Kovach, 2009; Wilson, 2008). I am guided by the ethical principles of Métis research, including reciprocity, respect, diversity, safety, relevance, and centring Métis knowledge (National Aboriginal Health Organization [NAHO], 2018) and *Kaayash ki ishi Pimatishiiyaak*, Red River Cart Wheel Teachings (Dorion & Fleury, 2009). Kaayash ki ishi Pimatishiiyaak are Métis values of patience, tolerance, respect, love, kindness, strength, sharing, caring, courage, honesty, and Mother Earth, centred around Creator.

This work was an autoethnographic exploration with my own dance/embodiment as central to the research. Gathering specific choreographic material as a base for connecting the movement to language, the process of embodiment included rehearsing and refining these movement phrases and in connection to Million's Felt Theory of "emotion as an embodied knowledge" (Million, 2009, p. 71). To reinforce this language learning, I composed a dance language (Brandstetter, 2010) to embody Michif words and grammar.

Western contemporary dance and ballet are rooted in oppressive practices that favour performative and external validation (Green, 2001). It has been my personal experience that this pervasive, problematic, and abusive pedagogy left me as a student and professional dancer lacking self-awareness and agency. Therefore, I was open to both exploitation and abuse during my education and professional career. I've learned and decided that dance and artmaking are essential experiences that can provide rich opportunities for growth and exchange. I engaged in this work with a decolonized approach from a Métis perspective. By investigating and creating a research methodology, my hope was to offset the harmful history and current practices being employed, in my experience, by the contemporary Eurocentric dance community.

By following the Predatory vs. Consensual Allyship practices guide (Lickers, 2019), I aim to foster a research-creation environment that is anti-oppressive and anti-colonial while best practices are being observed. Key points I will draw from this guide and further extrapolate on, related to the specificities in dance and artmaking are:

1. "Relationship building for consent"
2. Nothing about us without us
3. Truth-telling
4. Cultural safety & harm reduction
5. Facilitating access
6. Reciprocity

FINDING CEREMONY
THROUGH MY ART PRACTICE

I am deliberately choosing to work with research-creation from the outset to ground and make meaning throughout the process. Since I have spent the last three decades involved in artistic inquiry, mainly as a dancer/interpreter, and more recently (for the previous seven years) as a choreographer, the research-creation process is intuitive, and I wish to use an Indigenous research-creation paradigm as a statement from the outset.

My practice in Indigenous research comes from having intimate knowl-edge of dance from all sides of the studio: this knowledge includes the practicalities of being a dancer, the diligence to listen, to interpret, to learn new things all the time, to be used to discomfort and thinking outside the box. My own creation methodology came by way of engaging in therapy, writing, thinking, and researching and has helped me discover and to learn to listen to myself by developing my artistic voice, which is growing louder by the day. This voice is supported by those ancestors that surround me, those who came before her, and those who will follow. I am heartened by knowing I am not alone in seeing the world this way, and, according to Shawn Wilson (2008), "Indigenous people think and behave in a manner that is unique to ourselves" (p. 20).

As I learn to understand myself better, I have come to realize that I'd lived in a state of mild dissociation for many years. Otherwise, I couldn't have put myself through what I did for so long, as part of being a successful dancer is putting one's needs aside for the benefit of others, the choreog-raphers. I connect to how Wilson (2008) explains relational accountabil-ity through axiology, specifically in what I value as the creative process of making dance, rather than the outcome and methodology and how I con-nect this to my experience as a dancer. During my career working for other artists, dubious ways of gathering material were employed, with question-able ethical and moral standards under the guise of artistic excellence. I wish to diverge from the types of unethical methods to which I was sub-jected as a dancer during my performing career.

It is my hope that learning the Michif language will give me a chance to learn stories and songs in the language and will provide me with a richer sense of belonging. At times I have been impatient due to feeling discon-nected, though I understand that the reconnection process will all unfold in good time. Like my dance process, this is one of becoming. It is about time, about listening, and about the pathway and direction being revealed when the time is right. According to Wilson (2008), "research is about unanswered questions" (p. 6). To date, my understanding of Indigenous research, both from Kovach (2009) and Wilson (2008), includes the desire to work within the following parameters:

- holism
- accountability
- understanding that process outweighs the product (it's *how* we get there, not *where* we get to that is important)
- suspension of disbelief
- relations and how to care for one another
- doing no harm
- trust
- sharing knowledge with those that are trusted and part of the circle
- understanding that knowledge isn't proprietary
- understanding that Indigenous research moves away from commodifying our ideas, ideas that come from a dream world
- honouring each other
- creating balance and therefore strength from placing value in the gifts and talents each individual has been given (the community depends on directing each person towards their role)

It's about connection:
to each other
to ourselves
to the environment that surrounds us
to the four-legged
to the ones that swim and fly
to the cosmos
to the ancestors.

When listening and reading works about Indigenous research by Indigenous scholars, I have realized that most of it is not new to me. Rather, it confirms and validates what I know on an intuitive, creative, and embodied level. I have been searching for and working towards these parameters my whole career, more recently with a sense of agency in these later years. I began in a place of little agency, as a dance student, and then a dancer to teacher and then a dancer who commissioned work and eventually became a choreographer. For me, the shift in these roles was accompanied by new responsibilities and power. I came to understand that those who held power during my career were oftentimes acting irresponsibly with little accountability shown.

Once I became the person responsible, both in the creative process and in the role of the choreographer, I consciously examined what was important to me. I decided to place less stress on importance of the artwork and focus more on the people making the art. During the making of *Absorbed in Silence* (2017), I consciously decided to allow each dancer to do whatever they wanted or needed in any way I could accommodate up until the day of the show. I tried to keep the stakes very low for them, to remain authentic. I wanted to listen to where the process was taking us. It took a massive amount of willpower not to freak out when it felt like the dancers were being "flaky" (i.e., human). "Trust the process," "carry on," and "hope for the best outcome" were mantras I repeated to myself.

Humans are complicated and messy. We have good and bad days, sometimes all at the same time. I always felt it important to make space for what the dancers had going on. I sensed it was better to stop the creative flow for the time it took to hear about what someone just went through, acknowledge it, and move forward together, rather than ignoring it and telling them to "leave it at the door." Ignoring hides things and allows problems to fester. I preferred to work intuitively, feeling the creative process and the decisions I was making.

Relationality was paramount throughout the research processes with which I have been engaging, especially in the role of a choreographer. Wilson (2001) awakened me to the realization of what ceremony could mean to a person that has reclaimed her identity, like me. As a dancer, we take a morning dance class, day in and day out. It's where, on a superficial level (muscles and bones kind of way), we warm up, practise, and refine movement patterns. As a Métis person who was not raised with ceremony,[5] I have found my own way of place making and meaning making through the practice of dance class.

---

5 Ceremony such as moon ceremony or sunrise ceremony, for example.

Dance class is a practice and is more than bones and muscles. It's also where we reflect, where we process what happened over days, weeks, or years and prepare for what is to come. It's about connecting to each other and to ourselves, and getting in synch with a room of ten to 100 or more of your colleagues, depending on the size of your company. It's where you hold yourself accountable through the articulation of your right ankle or where you realized last night during a performance that someone dropped you too hard and you feel it in your lower spine. It's where you find your balance first on two legs and then on one, to find out, in your body, where you are at in your day. As dancers we ask ourselves: More floor time? More abs? More release? It is checking in first with yourself and then with those around you under the guidance and direction of the teacher and musician.

Together, a symphony of bodies and spirits: a glance of a knowing eye to the girl you were with onstage last night when you blanked out, and she whispered you through that section in front of an audience of 1,300 people; as you turn at the barre to the other side (always towards the barre, never away[6]) and your hand brushes the hand of the guy that dropped you. *Sigh*.

Knowing you will have to pull them aside during the day and go through that section to figure out what happened and how you can, together, make it work, and if it doesn't, who you can call on to spot that lift and make sure at least you don't get dropped again. It's all the little details and checking in that are part of class. After ninety minutes of listening to the same music, and doing the same movements together, you synch with each other and yourself and are ready for the day's work.

This ceremony happens day in and out throughout the course of a dancer's life. It's both mind-numbing at times, painful at others, and joyously the thing you would never want to go without. It's complex, necessary, and important.

---

6 In classical ballet we take a daily ballet class, which begins by holding the ballet barre with one hand for balance, and to change sides we turn towards the barre, never away from the barre. The ballet barre represents our audience, and one rarely turns their back on the audience—one of many learned ballet class protocols in classical ballet technique.

BEGINNINGS

Prior to the creation of *Kiwapamitinaawaaw*, my choreographic work was presented annually through the support of Rafik Sabbagh and Festival Quartiers Danses, with performances at Place des Arts in Montreal. This opportunity to create four dance works over a four-year period from 2015 to 2018 greatly influenced my creative process: *Or*, solo (2015), *This is nothing new*, solo (2016), *Absorbed in Silence*, sextet (2017), and *8 wishbones*, duet (2019).

This first solo, *Or*, was about identity, a trauma in dance and a recent car accident, and the need to heal from both aspects through artmaking (see Figure 2). Kintsugi is the Japanese art of repairing broken pottery using a paste of precious metals, often gold. Or is also the French word for gold. Objects that undergo Kintsugi are celebrated for their beauty and history of imperfections and are more valuable than before they were broken. Influenced by an unconventional recording of Schubert's Winterreise, *Or* shows transformation, reparation, and eventual resolution that arrived by processing the experiences of life events. During my research, I read from a diary I had been writing in 2015:

June 19th
As a stranger I arrived, as a stranger,
I depart. May favoured me with many
a bunch of flowers The girl spoke of
love
Her mother of
marriage Now the
world is so
gloomy The road
shrouded in snow
(Schubert, 1828)

June 21st
I cannot choose the time to begin
my journey I must find my own

way
In this darkness
(Schubert, 1828)

I was born Irene but became Victoria for reasons unknown to me. My inner self, at times, seemed as unfamiliar as a new land, with a foreign language, challenges, and customs. How easily I am distracted by my outer life, and at times my inner self is unknown, immature, and defensive.

It's as though the moment it all went wrong brought forth this emotional sickness that had been hiding inside and brought it to the surface. It's as though 2 significant life crashes happened 25 years apart and seem to be being dealt with simultaneously.

I hope that through these words to become whole, and my feelings significant.

June 23rd
It's like Vicki inside was calling for a break—this can't continue as it is. I don't feel safe in my home, I need to feel safe in my home.

Don't let your guard down. Protect your heart from feeling disappointment and sadness, true sadness.

June 24th
My defence system has a personality of its own. I thought at times it was a cobra, but I remain unconvinced.

I changed; yes, I've become the person I really am. Not pretty and sweet all the time, nor kind. Someone else entirely.

June 25th
Missing out, I am so afraid of
missing out. When life gives you
lemons, make lemonade. Just don't
pretend its fucking orange juice.

June 27th

Nothing wrong with bringing up the past, the creepy crawlies, the fragments, the whispers and secrets, the double meanings and pieces of myself that become whole again.

Albeit with cracks.

FIGURE 2. *Or.* Photo by Rasmus Sylvest, 2015.

OUTCOME, FINDINGS, AND MAKING MEANING

Learning Michif through Dance: Five Works

Each work is interconnected, nourishes the subsequent work, and is the building blocks of the solo *Kiwapamitinaawaaw*. Hawaiian educator Dr. Peter Hanohano said,

> Data and analysis are like a circular fishing net. You could try to examine each of the knots in the net to see what holds it together, but it's the strings between the knots that have to work in conjunction in order for the net to function. So, any analysis must examine all of the relationships between particular events or knots of data as a whole before it will make any sense. (Hanohano, quoted in Wilson, 2008, p. 120)

The connections between all the works and relationality are what build a full picture of the process and outcome, in particular for people that are not well versed in historical and contemporary Métis realties.

- Piece 1a: Single-channel video, *Michif x 40* (2020)
- Piece 1b: *Michif x 40—live* (2022)
- Piece 2: *Echoes of Plexus* (2020)
- Piece 3: *Assimilation is an ill-fitting suit* (2020)
- Piece 4: *Kiwapamitinaawaaw* (2022)

Piece 1a: *Michif x 40*—a single-channel video (2020)

Michif x 40 is a single-channel twenty-minute video documenting my journey of learning Michif through dance, influenced by the work of performance artists Faye Mullen, who engages with their audience in a live-streamed, live-edited video process, and Ignacio Pérez Pérez, who engages with his audience in performative activism via Instagram. I practised learning Michif through dance choreography, one step and sentence at a time. I then filmed, edited, and disseminated each word and sentence via Instagram as capsules of my learning journey. Working with a screen in this

FIGURE 3. Screenshots of each word shared on Instagram in *Michif x 40*. Photos by
Victoria May, 2020.

FIGURE 4. Screenshots of each word shared on Instagram in *Michif x 40*. Photos by Victoria May, 2020.

way, as a recourse to share what I was doing, build community, and counter my feelings of isolation in 2020, I set out to live-stream recorded capsules over a period of six months at the height of the lockdown and pandemic. There is validity in the Insta-moment, and capturing micro-moments and sharing them immediately can be a powerful tool for reclamation and, in my case, decolonization through taking back the Michif language from the oppressor and publishing in real-time the reclamation through an embodied research process.

Piece 1b: *Michif x 40—live* (2022)

Michif x 40—live is a twenty-minute solo with the projected video of *Michif x 40*. In front of a live audience, I attempt to learn the choreography in real-time, while simultaneously watching, remembering, re-remembering, and re-enacting all of these processes. The focus is on relationality of myself to me onscreen, demonstrating the staging of dialogue between teacher and learner when learning the language.

FIGURE 5. Screenshots of *Michif x 40—live*. Photos by Victoria May, 2022.

Piece 2: *Echoes of Plexus* (2020)—a single-channel video

Echoes of Plexus is a twelve-minute single-channel video that explores the connection between land, place, and parts of the body related to language. My landscape is my body; my language is dance. Michif is connected to the land; it is my point of orientation and the birthplace of who I am and from where I emerged.

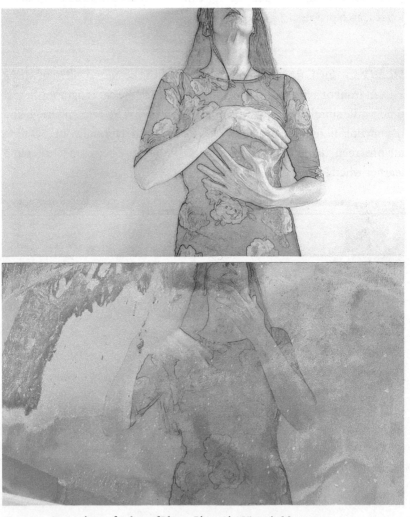

FIGURE 6. Screenshots of *Echoes of Plexus*. Photos by Victoria May, 2020.

Echoes of plexus *(transcript from video)*

Where does language lie?

Where do the words sit?

Where do all those in-between words, where do they come from? And when they're taken from us, where do they go?

"When the language is gone, the culture is gone, and its people cease to exist. Cause without the language, we're just ghosts." (Kawennotas Sedalia Fazio, personal communication, 2020)

But what if it's still there, somewhere... Between the cartilage and the muscles and the bones and the blood and the heart and the lungs.

What if it's still there under the layers? Waiting.

Never fully extinguished.

In absence of hearing your mother, telling you, ki sha ki hik.

How can one truly know how to love if you've never heard it in your words? You can cause you can feel it.

It's in the body.

The body is connected through tissue and fascia.

It's like a map, it's like a road map leading us to who we are, to who we are meant to be.

"To who we are meant to be, and each of us is exactly where we are meant to be on this journey." (Amelia Tekwatonti McGregor, personal communication, 2020)

So, I'm learning to trust.

Trust in the bones, that have carried me and the heart that has pumped my blood for 45 years

and allowed me to feel

the nerves that run from the stem of my brain through my spine to the tips of my fingers and the tips of my toes and carry messages of the vices of my ancestors speaking to me in our words in our language.

In absence of knowing in my mind

but knowing in my heart that it will come together in time

and that by being and "becoming Indigenous to place" (Kimmerer, 2015), wherever that place may be, is a step in reconnecting to who I am and to those words that I so desperately need to feel and connect to.

The ebb and flow of the waters thanks to grandmother moon (Amelia
    Tekwatonti McGregor, personal communication, 2020).
Becoming Indigenous to place.
Me in Tio'tia:ke, where the rivers split, or also called where the people
    split (Fran Beauvais, personal communication, 2020).
Like grandmother moon keeps the rivers flowing and, like an oral lan-
    guage is passed from an ear to a mouth, it stays alive. Being put on
    paper, it stagnates like a pool of water and dies.
The solar plexus, the place where the nerves meet and split off, like
    Tio'tia:ke.
Where the people carefully moved so that land would be able to heal.
    Such as a language, gathering, exchanging, moving, and living. Not
    one sole monolith.
These words are now gone. Echoes from the plexus What lies in my
    rivers?
Resisting assimilation, what echoes of my language are still there, wait-
    ing to be heard? Land…
Becoming Indigenous to place

    these
    same
    sounds
    once
    forbidde
    n
    are now pronounced
    and the echoes of a
    language that would
    have spared us grief
    (not to mention,
    alienation)
    had our parents
    communicated to us will
    continue to grow

like moss on
our backs and
no matter
which way we
turn to the light
it will
always
exist on
our cold
side and
ache
like a phantom limb
(Dumont, 2012, pp. 1–2, reprinted with permission)

Piece 3: *Assimilation is an ill-fitting suit* (2020)—projection

Assimilation is an ill-fitting suit is a nine-minute projection that is an autoethnographic exploration of processing various states surrounding Métis identity. In this too-large or ill-fitting chroma key suit, I could be anyone and no one, anyone could "be me." The chroma key element of projecting anything onto this suit in post-production was relatable to my identity as I had been living the better part of my life as a "Canadian" person without really knowing why this didn't fit, but feeling it didn't. This ill-fitting borrowed suit that could, from the outside, be anything to anyone, represented that layer of artifice. The work is a slow reveal, removing a layer in the video and getting dressed into what I wear for the solo *Kiwapamitinaawaaw*. I chose, in post-production, to transform the chroma key green to a pixelated grey colour.

This work was created as a performative action in response to a recorded speech in Parliament made on behalf of the Métis people by Graham Andrews. The text was about the importance of Indigenous languages, giving an example of how the Michif language is an essential part of Indigenous identity. I first videoed myself improvising a movement sequence in response to the audio of Andrews' text. The impulse I chose was to interpret his words through the pacing and cadence of his words. The second part was to place this video recording of my improvised movement structure on a video-screen monitor on the floor in front of me and re-filmed myself learning and following the movement on the monitor in real-time with the text. This proved challenging due to the chroma key mask, and the improvised choreography that included standing on angles

FIGURE 7. Screenshots of *Assimilation is an ill-fitting suit*. Photos by Victoria May, 2020.

that made it impossible to stay in time—pretending or assimilating as best as possible, with a layer on top. This layer masking the ability to see the "real" choreography, one gets lost but keeps going. The result that is left is not the "real" version but the one with the layer.

Piece 4: *Kiwapamitinaawaaw* (2022)

Kiwapamitinaawaaw is a fifteen-minute contemporary dance solo performance. It is a love letter to my ancestors about embodying Michif and the dances that guided me home. Embodying Michif is a way to connect, help me remember, and orient myself in reclaiming this part of my culture. This work is a hybrid performance of video, text, dance, and music woven together to give a picture of my process. As I struggle, the words fall from my head through my body like a waterfall, and I have difficulty locking them into my memory. As I stumble and forget, I choose to embody the words of Michif through the familiar world of dance I already know.

After thirty years of interpreting the visions of other dance makers, their dreams are imprinted on my body, memory and spirit. I acknowledge these transformative processes I experienced through every work I danced; every step is still embedded in me. These steps are my markers, and I have transformed them into a hybrid of my own dance language. My landscape is my body; my language is dance. *Kiwapamitinaawaaw* is a work for those who came before me, my ancestors, and those who will follow.

CHALLENGES

This work and process have provided me with a platform to learn and process Michif and many other parts of Métis culture, including but not limited to jigging, learning songs, beadwork, traditional moosehide tanning, making a drum, sewing a pair of dancer's moccasins, in addition to learning through storywork (Archibald, 2008). Importantly, it has allowed me to heal by presenting my story. Dance provided this healing layer of embodiment to facilitate language learning while approaching complex subjects of loss, trauma, and the effects of displacement, assimilation, and genocide due to colonial practices of the Canadian government. I could face my truth and connect to my family, community, and culture to share my story and that of others through the dance and the process of making.

GOING FORWARD

Our recent history as Métis peoples is built of survivance (survival as resistance as coined by Gerald Vizenor, 2008) of generations of Métis that were dispossessed, first of land, then opportunity and identity. I deeply respect those who carry deep knowledge of Métis ways of knowing. This knowledge is carried by those that grew up in community, some with language, some on the land—these ways of knowing need to be acknowledged and distinguished from mine. I believe my role, as a reconnecting Métis person, is as someone that has created a scaffolded and layered learning process, piecing together what has embodied knowledge and what is learned. This is a way to make a vessel for future generations to carry forward our shared history and contemporary reality as a people. *Kiwapamitinaawaaw* envisions our future through an embodied existence and is another step towards this future beyond that of survivance into resurgence.

REFERENCES

Algonquian Linguistic Atlas. (2005). *About the atlas*. Retrieved September 9, 2020, from https://www.atlas-ling.ca/

Anderson, K., Clow, B., & Haworth-Brockman, M. (2013). Carriers of water: Aboriginal women's experiences, relationships, and reflections. *Journal of Cleaner Production, 60*, 11–17. https://doi.org/10.1016/j.jclepro.2011.10.023

Archibald, J. (2008). *Indigenous storywork: Educating the heart, mind, body, and spirit*. Vancouver: UBC Press.

Bakker, P. (1997). *A language of our own: The genesis of Michif, the mixed Cree-French language of the Canadian Métis*. Oxford University Press.

Bakker, P., & Fleury, N. (2004). Learn Michif by listening [website]. Gabriel Dumont Institute of Native Studies and Applied Research Virtual Museum of Métis History and Culture. Retrieved from https://www.metismuseum.ca/browse/index.php/13147

Bakker, P., & Papen, R. A. (2003). *Michif and other languages of the Canadian Métis*. Gabriel Dumont Institute of Native Studies and Applied Research

Virtual Museum of Métis History and Culture. Retrieved from https://www.metismuseum.ca/media/document.php/00735

Barkwell, L. J. (2011). *Veterans and families of the 1885 Northwest Resistance.* Saskatoon: Gabriel Dumont Institute. Retrieved April 18, 2023, from https://www.metismuseum.ca/media/document.php/149693

Brandstetter, G. (2010). Political body spaces in the performances of William Forsythe. In M. Hallensleben (Ed.), *Performative body spaces: Corporeal topographies in literature, theatre, dance, and the visual arts* (Critical Studies, vol. 33), 57–74. https://doi.org/10.1163/9789042031944_005

Burnouf, L., Fleury, N., & Lavallée, G. (2007). *The Michif resource guide: Lii Michif Niiyanaan, aan Michif biikishwanaan.* Gabriel Dumont Institute. Retrieved from https://www.metismuseum.ca/media/document.php/149703

Campbell, M. (2010). *Stories of the road allowance people* (Rev. ed.). Saskatoon: Gabriel Dumont Institute.

Campbell, M. (2022, May 3–6). *Closing keynote* [speech]. Let's Get Together Métis Studies Symposium [Symposium]. Mawachihitotaak 2022 Conference, Winnipeg, Manitoba. https://www.mawachihitotaak.com/mawachihitotaak-2022

Canada, Parliament, Senate. Standing Committee on Canadian Heritage. (2019). *Bill C-91, An Act respecting Indigenous languages.* 42nd Parl., 1st sess. Evidence (Graham Andrews)

Cardinal, H., & Hildebrandt, W. (2000). *Treaty Elders of Saskatchewan: Our dream is that our peoples will one day be clearly recognized as nations.* Calgary: University of Calgary Press.

Chiblow, S., & Meighan, P. J. (2022). Language is land, land is language: The importance of Indigenous languages. *Human Geography*, 15(2), 206–210. https://doi.org/10.1177/19427786211022899

Dorion, L., & Fleury, N. (2009). *The giving tree: A retelling of a traditional Métis story.* Saskatoon: Gabriel Dumont Institute.

Dumont, M. (2012). *That tongued belonging.* Kegedonce Press.

Flammand, B. (2019). The genesis of the Michif peoples. *Thinking in Michif.* Retrieved June 5, 2022, from https://thinkinginmichif.family.blog/the-genesis-of-the-michif-peoples/

Gervain, J. (2015). Plasticity in early language acquisition: The effects of prenatal and early childhood experience. *Current Opinion in Neurobiology*, 35, 13–20. https://doi.org/10.1016/j.conb.2015.05.004

Gaudet, J. C. (2019). Keeoukaywin: The visiting way—fostering an Indigenous research methodology. *Aboriginal Policy Studies*, 7(2), 47–64. https://doi.org/10.5663/aps.v7i2.29336

Green, J. (2001). Socially constructed bodies in American dance classrooms. *Research in Dance Education*, 2(2), 155–173. https://doi.org/10.1080/14647890120100782

Herman, N. (1987). *Why psychotherapy?* London: Free Association Books.

Iseke, J. (2013). Negotiating Métis culture in Michif: Disrupting Indigenous language shift. *Decolonization: Indigeneity, Education & Society*, 2(2), 92–116. https://ourelderstories.com/wp-content/uploads/2019/03/Iseke-Negotiating-Metis-culture.pdf

Kimmerer, R. W. (2015). *Braiding sweetgrass: Indigenous wisdom, scientific knowledge, and the teachings of plants.* Milkweed Editions.

Kovach, M. (2009). *Indigenous methodologies: Characteristics, conversations and contexts.* Toronto: University of Toronto Press.

Lickers, A. (2020, February 3–7). *Indigenous solidarity: Best practices* [Lecture]. First Voices Week [Event]. Wake Up! Re-Storying the Land, Concordia University, Montreal, Quebec. https://www.concordia.ca/students/otsenhakta/events/first-voices-week.html

Linklater, T. L. (2016). Slow scrape (2012–2015). *Dance Research Journal*, 48(1), 24–28. https://doi.org/10.1017/S0149767716000061

Logan, T. (2015). Settler colonialism in Canada and the Métis. *Journal of Genocide Research*, 17(4), 433–452. https://doi.org/10.1080/14623528.2015.1096589

Louis Riel Institute. (2003). *Speaking Michif French Resource Manual.* Winnipeg: Louis Riel Institute. https://www.louisrielinstitute.ca/metis-languages-learning-resources

May, V. (2015, September 16). *Or* [Solo choreography]. Quartiers Danses [Festival], Place des Arts, Montreal.

May, V. (2016, September 14). *This is nothing new* [Solo choreography]. Quartiers Danses [Festival], Place des Arts, Montreal.

May, V. (2017, September 15). *Absorbed in Silence* [Sextet choreography]. Quartiers Danses [Festival], Place des Arts, Montreal.

May, V. (2019, September 14). *8 wishbones* [Duet choreography]. Quartiers Danses [Festival], Place des Arts, Montreal.

May, V. (2020, August 14). *Kiwapamitinaawaaw* [Solo choreography]. Contemporary Native Art Biennial [Exhibition], Centre de Création O Vertigo, Montreal.

May, V. (2020). *Michif x 40* [Video]. Instagram.

May, V. (2020). *Echoes of Plexus.*

May, V. (2020). *Assimilation is an ill-fitting suit.*

May, V. (2022). *Michif x 40* [Live performance, video].

Mazzoli, M. (2019). *Michif loss and resistance in four Metis communities: Kahkiyaw mashchineenaan, "All of us are disappearing as in a plague."* Zeitschrift für

Kanada- Studien, 39, 96–117. http://www.kanada-studien.org/wp-content/uploads/2021/02/zks_2019_5_Mazzoli.pdf

Million, D. (2009). Felt theory: An Indigenous feminist approach to affect and history. *Wicazo Sa Review*, 24(2), 53–76. https://doi.org/10.1353/WIC.0.0043

Mumford, M. (2016). Naadmaagewin…The art of working together in our communities. *Dance Research Journal*, 48(1), 127–151. https://www.jstor.org/stable/48629483

National Aboriginal Health Organization. (2018). *Principles of ethical Métis research*. Métis Centre. https://achh.ca/wp-content/uploads/2018/07/Guide_Ethics_NAHOMetisCentre.pdf

Richardson, C. (2004). *Becoming Métis: The relationship between the sense of Métis self and cultural stories* [Doctoral dissertation, University of Victoria]. Dspace. https://dspace.library.uvic.ca/server/api/core/bitstreams/1942fd9f-47e4-4f27-9ccf-d598279f4208/content

Richardson, C. L. (2016). *Belonging Métis*. JCharlton Publishing.

Simpson, L. (2011). *Dancing on our turtle's back: Stories of Nishnaabeg re-creation, resurgence and a new emergence*. Winnipeg: Arbeiter Ring Publishing.

Simpson, L. B. (2017). *As we have always done: Indigenous freedom through radical resistance*. Minneapolis: University of Minnesota Press.

Smith, L. T. (2012). *Decolonizing methodologies: Research and indigenous peoples* (2nd ed.). London: Zed Books.

Souter, H. (2018). *Ti parii chiiñ? (Are you ready?): Preparing adult learners and proficient speakers for the challenge of Michif reclamation* [Master's thesis, University of Victoria].

Statistics Canada. (2017, February 8). Census profile, 2016 census. https://www12.statcan.gc.ca/census-recensement/2016/dp-pd/prof/index.cfm

Teillet, J. (2019). *The north-west is our mother: The story of Louis Riel's people, the Métis Nation*. Patrick Crean Editions/Harper Collins.

Vizenor, G. 2008. Aesthetics of survivance. In G. Vizenor (Ed.), *Survivance: Narratives of Native presence* (pp. 1–24). Lincoln: University of Nebraska Press.

Wilbur, M., & Keene, A. (Hosts). (2019, July 2). Can our ancestors hear us (No. 9) [Audio podcast episode]. In *All My Relations Podcast*. https://www.allmyrelationspodcast.com/podcast/episode/491847a3/ep-9-can-our-ancestors-hear-us

Wilson, S. (2001). What is an Indigenous research methodology? *Canadian Journal of Native Education*, 25(2), 175–179.

Wilson, S. (2008). *Research is ceremony: Indigenous research methods*. Halifax: Fernwood Publishing.

Researching through miyo ohpikinâwasowin (Good Child-Rearing)

A Framework for Knowledge Emergence and Transmission

Lindsay DuPré

ABSTRACT

This chapter offers a snapshot into my early thinking as a PhD student when I was first attempting to develop and articulate a conceptual framework to guide my research. I describe how I have come to understand my work as a researcher as being inseparable from my work as a mom and auntie, and argue that miyo ohpikinâwasowin (good child-rearing) is a powerful mechanism for seeking knowledge and upholding laws of wâhkôhtowin (extended kinship). I also argue that children should not only be seen as recipients of knowledge but as valued knowledge producers who collaborate with us every day to generate and transmit knowledge within Métis and Cree kinship systems. Throughout the chapter I weave together family experiences with references to academic scholarship, emphasizing attentiveness, care, play, and balance as central principles to my research approach. **Keywords:** *Indigenous research, Indigenous knowledge, wâhkôhtowin, ohpikinâwasowin, kinship, child-rearing, relationality, everyday resurgence*

⁄⁄⁄⁄⁄⁄⁄⁄⁄⁄ ⟍⟍⟍⟍⟍⟍⟍⟍

The day I found out I was becoming a mom I also became a researcher. I had previously completed a master's degree at the University of Toronto and had been involved in a few scholarly and community-based research projects before; however, it wasn't until I started understanding the world as a parent that I began to recognize research as an inseparable part of my life. As my academic uncle and Cree scholar Shawn Wilson points out, "If research hasn't changed you as a person, then you haven't done it right" (2008). I would add to this and suggest that if parenting hasn't changed you as a researcher, then you aren't doing it within an Indigenous paradigm. Attending to the deep entanglement of these two roles has helped me develop a conceptual framework to guide my PhD research based on miyo ohpikinâwasowin (good child-rearing).

For you to better understand this conceptual framework, it is important to first tell you a bit about myself and my family. I am a Métis scholar, community organizer, mom, and auntie, but I was born and raised in Ontario on Haudenosaunee, Anishinaabe, and Wendat territories. My Métis family is Red River Métis, originally from Manitoba and most recently lived in Roblin, Manitoba. Our family names include DuPré, Pruden, Norquay, Miller, Monkman, Morwick, Setter, Spence, and Nestichio Batt. My grandfather Bob or "Duke" DuPré moved to southern Ontario with his parents and brothers when he was a teenager, which at that point had also become home to some of my European settler family (the Croziers, Hendersons, and Robillards). He married my nana Theresa Robillard not long after moving there, and they had four children, the youngest being my dad, Gil DuPré. He grew up in Long Branch and then Mississauga, Ontario, which is where he met my mom Dawn (daughter to my grandparents Bill Crozier and Marie Henderson), and where my brother Cooper and I eventually were born.

My family hasn't spent much time in Manitoba since my grandfather moved away, but we have found ways to stay connected and to build new community relationships. One of these ways has been through lacrosse, a sport that originated with the Haudenosaunee and has great significance in relation to healing, spirituality, nationhood, and inter-tribal relations (Downey, 2018). My grandpa Bob would drive out to the rez at Six Nations of the Grand River and got to know the families who could make the best wood lacrosse sticks for his sons. From the stories I've heard, my dad and uncles were fantastic lacrosse and hockey players, and play was at the heart of how they built community relationships. My dad went on to coach my brother and his friends, which meant that for many years our family life revolved around lacrosse boxes and hockey rinks.

The fondest memories I have of my childhood are playing with my dad. Whether it was joining them in the box for lacrosse practices, goofing around in our basement on my mom's BINGO nights, developing football plays in the back yard, or letting us ride in the bed of his pickup, my dad gave us consistent experiences of attentiveness and care that were foundational to how I now think about parenting and research. Play was his way of teaching us how to live a good life and reminding us that we can connect with knowledge anywhere so long as we're paying attention. Perhaps most importantly we laughed a lot together and he taught me to conduct all of my actions and interactions in a spirit of kindness, honesty, and compassion—what I would later come to understand as core principles of Indigenous research (Wilson, 2007).

Although I grew up surrounded by people who loved to learn, I was the first person in my family to attend university, and so academic language wasn't a part of my childhood experiences. We didn't talk about data collection and analysis at the breakfast table or self-consciously articulate theoretical principles of decolonization (hooks, 1997) on our way home from school. Pursuing higher education was very much encouraged but more as a means to secure a good livelihood than as a pathway to find purpose in scholarship. Eventually I familiarized myself with academic discourse enough to be able to critique the ways that western epistemologies clash with Indigenous paradigms. However, I was missing a deeper level of understanding of Indigenous research that comes with parenting in a Métis and Cree kinship network.

COMING TO UNDERSTAND MY ROLE AS A PARENT

I became a mother despite being told that there was a chance I would never be able to carry my own children. I live with an invisible disability and multiple chronic health conditions that interfere with my ability to be pregnant. Despite these physical barriers, my son Kîsik found his way to me, choosing me and my partner Dallas to be his parents. He is a mover, talker, and feeler who has always asserted his presence even before having words to do so. He now has an extensive vocabulary and uses it to describe his experiences, dreams, and memories of visiting loved ones in different places. He is putting together how everyone in his life is connected and will proudly tell you, "I have a whole lot of kôhkums, and môshums, and aunties, and uncles, and cousins looking out for me, you know…"

Kîsik also loves doing experiments and figuring out how things work, coming to us with long lists of *why* and *how* questions to help him understand. Bedtime is an integral part of the day for us to connect and consider these questions. More than just a process of getting our son to sleep, it is a time for critical inquiry. After washing up, brushing teeth, and putting on jammies, Kîsik picks a few stuffy companions to join us in bed. We entertain last requests for drinks and bathroom breaks before searching for his "little blankie," a tattered (and sometimes smelly) knit blanket he returns to each night for comfort. Our routine includes alternating which parent takes the lead on bedtime and sometimes welcomes other family members to join in on telling stories. Between these stories we talk about what happened during the day and help each other make sense of the feelings and curiosities that came up. Eventually the yawning kicks in and we turn off the light, lying quietly until Kîsik falls asleep. This quiet time is an important part of my own meaning making where I can reflect on new knowledge that emerged through our family's engagement in visiting (Gaudet, 2019), conversations (Kovach, 2010), witnessing (Hunt, 2018), and storywork (Archibald, 2008).

Dallas and I do our best to love Kîsik each day in ways that respect his fierce determination and abounding curiosity, coming to understand ourselves as a family of co-researchers making sense of the world together. Dallas is a Fiddler from Waterhen Lake First Nation through his mother's side—where he and Kîsik are registered Treaty Indians—and a Bear from Big River First Nation on his father's side, both nêhiyaw (Plains Cree) communities in Saskatchewan. He grew up with a large extended family, including many strong women who worked hard to raise him to be a kind person with a firm grounding in nêhiyaw culture. Ceremony has always been an important part of Dallas's life, and we want the same for Kîsik. We prioritize time and resources to ensure that Kîsik can also grow up with a strong relationship to traditional knowledge.

The concept of miyo ohpikinâwasowin was first introduced to me by Kîsik's ocâpan Sid Fiddler, who Kîsik will learn to refer to as nicâpan (my great-grandparent). This term refers to both a great-grandparent and a great-grandchild, and so Sid also refers to Kîsik as nicâpan (my great-grandchild). The term is genderless and speaks to the unique generational connection between these two relations (Vowel, 2011). It reflects Indigenous worldviews about kinship where relations are not focused on hierarchy but about balanced relationships (Potskin, 2020).

This emphasis on relationality embedded in our family's languages is also evident in how my son will learn to refer to his grandmother Marlena Fiddler. Kîsik will eventually use the term nôhkum (my grandmother) when speaking to her, though for now he calls her kôhkum (your grandmother) because that's how he hears us referring to her. To be clear, I am by no means a language speaker—though I have dreams that Kîsik could be one day—but I do my best to learn from nêhiyawêwin and Michif when and where I can. Language is critical to knowing and preserving Indigenous philosophies (Daniels-Fiss, B. 2008; Nyota et al., 2007; Steinhauer-Hill, P. J., 2008) and so it will be important for me to put in the work to seek out language-based knowledge that can guide me in research and miyo ohpikinâwasowin.

By spending time with Sid and Marlena, as well as other relatives from both of our families and community teachers, I have come to understand miyo ohpikinâwasowin as an integral part of our knowledge systems. The philosophy behind this concept encompasses a respect for the sacredness of children given their special connection to the earth and their role in purifying the circle of creation (Tine, 2020). By recognizing children in this way, we value them not only as recipients of knowledge but as valued knowledge producers with "undomesticated minds that are exactly the same as the minds of our ancestors, uncolonized and vibrantly connected to the worlds around us" (Yunkaporta, 2020). This opens doors for new knowledge to emerge and possibilities for families to heal from the emotional and epistemological disconnection imposed through residential schools and the child welfare system (Dorion, 2010).

As Dallas and I grapple with how to apply traditional knowledge to enact miyo ohpikinâwasowin, we are often confronted with tensions of cisheteropatriarchy. Issues of sexism and misogyny are a reality in many Indigenous communities, and this has significantly impacted how child-rearing responsibilities are perceived and distributed within families. In *Life Stages and Native Women* (2011), Métis scholar Kim Anderson explains that historically there has been jurisdictional responsibilities tied to gender; however, there has always been flexibility when it comes to the work that needs to be done and who is available to do it. Anderson and Mohawk scholar Jennifer Brant (2021) aptly name that "the imposition of heteropatriarchal models of mothering was a colonial strategy, and it resulted in generational disruptions of home." They go on to discuss that these disruptions have involved sophisticated campaigns to push the gender binary, which has served as a significant attack on Indigenous maternal knowledges and parenting today. Recognizing this, Dallas and I do our best to sift through which knowledge is nourishing and which perspectives are tainted with dogmatic views on traditionalism. This isn't always so easy to decipher, but we do our best to remain open to understanding different viewpoints. We harvest the teachings that align with our values and leave the rest behind.

FOREGROUNDING FAMILY IN RESEARCH

I became pregnant with Kîsik when we were living in Toronto and I was working in the Office of the Dean at the Ontario Institute for Studies in Education, a part of the University of Toronto. I held the position of Indigenous Education Liaison, where I helped oversee Indigenous education initiatives across the Institute. This role introduced me to incredible Indigenous scholars and students, and completely changed the ways that I think about institutional efforts towards reconciliation and Indigenization. While in this role I also taught as a sessional instructor in York University's School of Social Work. These experiences offered me new language to participate in conversations about Indigenous pedagogy and research, and provoked my concerns regarding how Indigenous knowledge is (and isn't) being cared for in the academy. A number of the people I met in these institutions continue to be in my life and have brought care to my family in significant ways.

Soon after Kîsik was born Dallas started a graduate program in Toronto and I moved on to a limited-term position as an assistant teaching professor in the School of Public Health and Social Policy (PHSP) at the University of Victoria. Given that the school's programs are primarily delivered online, I was able to negotiate a remote work arrangement. In the final year of Dallas's master's degree, I also started my PhD in interdisciplinary graduate studies at the University of British Columbia Okanagan (UBCO). To complete my studies remotely I needed to advocate for the residency requirement to be waived, and I was successful. This meant that we were both graduate students at the same time now actually talking about data collection and analysis at the breakfast table and decolonization on our drives home from study/work sessions at our local coffee shop. We both had a lot to juggle during this time, but we got through it with a lot of support from my parents, nana, and grandma—and Kîsik.

The ability to work and study remotely has been a gamechanger for our family as it has allowed us to spend our time living and visiting in places where we have access to culture and community support. Digital technologies have significantly impacted how we have been able to work and learn, and have allowed us to remain socially connected to loved ones in different provinces. Upon Dallas finishing his degree, we moved to Saskatoon, Saskatchewan, Treaty 6 Territory and the Homeland of the Métis, where I continue to work on my studies with trips to UBCO a few times a year. I now hold citizenship with the Métis Nation of Saskatchewan and my doctoral theorizing continues to be heavily influenced by Métis thinkers I actively collaborate with here and across the country.

Carrying out my work and studies remotely has also given me opportunities to engage more in online university environments, which is the focus of my PhD research. My work aims to investigate how Indigenous knowledge transmission has changed in online university environments since the onset of the COVID-19 pandemic. I am interested in how the rapid shift to use digital technologies made Indigenous knowledge vulnerable to misuse and exploitation, but more importantly, how Indigenous people have found ways to protect and encourage knowledge to emerge safely online. My research objectives are heavily influenced by concerns that emerged from my past experiences and my desire to protect the integrity of our knowledge systems for my son and generations after him. I believe that threats of epistemicide must be taken seriously as the educational, institutional, and computer-based digital protocols that govern online environments are not epistemically neutral (Bhatt & MacKenzie, 2019; Prabhakaran et al., 2022; Traxler, 2019).

I chose to pursue this research in a PhD program at UBCO in order to work with Shawn Wilson as my supervisor. I have known Shawn for several years, and he has generously nurtured my passion for being a Métis researcher. We first got to know each other through co-editing the book *Research and Reconciliation* (Wilson et al., 2019) with our friend Andrea Breen. Since then, we have collaborated on other writing projects and presentations where we have been playing with ideas about Indigenous methodologies and academic kinship. Working together for my PhD has allowed us to get to know each other more closely as researchers and as kin. We go with the flow of our academic uncle and niece relationship, taking time and trusting the process of relationship building. As part of this, we continue to navigate the university's expectations of our supervisory relationship and intentionally consider whether these views align with our own expectations for how we want to carry out our responsibilities to one another.

Despite not being biologically related, Kîsik is also learning to respect Shawn as part of our extended family and refers to him affectionately as one of his grandfathers. Kîsik likes to ask him questions and finds ways to inspire playfulness in the same way he does with my dad. There is lots of laughing when our families get to visit and of course a healthy amount of teasing as well. There is also compassion when things are difficult and an understanding that we will show up for one another when we need it. This way of relating is strongly influenced by our Métis and Cree identities (Shawn is Opaskwayak Cree from northern Manitoba). Our communities have long-standing relationships with each other, including shared laws of wâhkôhtowin that outline our kinship responsibilities (Campbell, 2007; Flaminio, 2013; Gaudry, 2014; Napier & Whiskeyjack, 2021). Plains Cree scholar Matthew Wildcat (2018) breaks down wâhkôhtowin into three parts:

> First, it references the act of being related—to your human and other than human relatives. Second, it is a worldview based on the idea that all of existence is animate and full of spirit. Since everything has spirit it means we are connected to the rest of existence and live in a universe defined by relatedness. Third, there are proper ways to conduct and uphold your relationships with your relatives and other aspects of existence. (p. 14)

I'm hesitant to describe this philosophy here so briefly as I have heard (and share) concerns about the oversimplification of traditional knowledge—and of wâhkôhtowin specifically—in academic writing. However, I mention it here because it is central to my doctoral work and the ways Shawn and I have come to engage with knowledge together. By applying a kinship model to our supervisory relationship, we acknowledge this relatedness and hold ourselves accountable to our different roles and responsibilities. This directly supports the integrity of my research, helping ensure that my theorizing remains grounded specifically in Métis and Cree epistemology—a deliberate effort to push back against the homogenization of Indigenous intellectual traditions and expression (Battiste, 2013; Graveline, 1998; Smith, 2021).

DRAWING A CONCEPTUAL FRAMEWORK

Raising our children to live healthy and liberating lives is an expansive community-based research project where we seek to understand and pass on "the accumulated knowledge of our ancestors" (Ermine, 1995). This community-based research is carried out intergenerationally, with ohpikinâwasowin serving as a powerful mechanism for seeking knowledge and upholding laws of wâhkôtowin. In line with this, I believe that miyo ohpikinâwasowin can serve as a valuable conceptual framework to guide Métis and Cree research—not only for researchers who are parents but for everyone invested in the emergence and transmission of Indigenous knowledges.

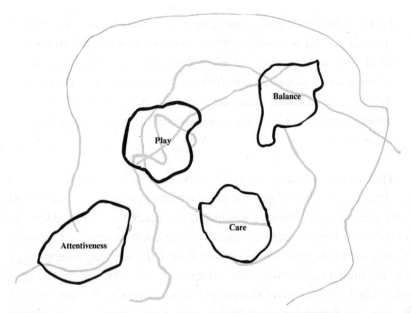

FIGURE 1. A miyo ohpikinâwasowin (good child-rearing) framework for research. Courtesy of the author.

Figure 1 represents a miyo ohpikinâwasowin (good child-rearing) framework for research developed in collaboration with my son and co-researcher Kîsik Fiddler. The original drawing was created by Kîsik when he was three years old on a day he was home sick from daycare. I had an Indigenous research methods class with Shawn that morning and connected via Zoom from my kitchen table. I set up a chair for Kîsik beside me with some markers and sticky notes, and let him know he was welcome to join if he wanted to. Most of the time he stayed on the couch across the room, focused on his toys and watching shows on his iPad, but every now and then he would come back to his spot at the table and listen. At one point he practiced his letters and numbers in the Zoom chat and later made silly faces at the camera. He was later invited to take a turn to say something during our closing circle for the day. Truthfully, I don't remember what his response was other than him proudly showing me the drawing he made while he was listening. I asked him if I could share it and he said yes.

Since that day I have been thinking a lot about children as knowledge producers and Indigenous research being a familial endeavour. Of course, there is risk of projecting our own ideas onto children's contributions and appropriating their knowledge, as well as some ethical uncertainty when it comes to consent in the collaboration process that needs to be carefully considered (as I am negotiating in my work); however, I am confident that if we pay close attention while maintaining balance, care, and elements of play that there are also great possibilities. In my example, I will probably never know what Kîsik actually absorbed from the class or what was going through his mind while he drew that picture. Maybe listening in on our conversations about Indigenous paradigms led him to channel pieces of ancestral knowledge—or maybe he was hungry and drew a pepperoni pizza. Regardless, his contributions that day were significant because I saw how his presence had an impact on the class and allowed for novel ideas to emerge. I also felt how relieving it was to bring my full self to that class and noticed how my own ways of listening and participating unfolded differently with him there.

Months after Kîsik created the original drawing I decided to digitize it and develop it into a conceptual framework that could help me visualize my research and put it into action. I recreated the drawing myself, doing my best to represent it as closely to the original as possible. There are four main shapes in the figure that represent four key principles of this approach: attentiveness, care, play, and balance. There are also lines positioned around the shapes and some that connect them together. The lines themselves can be interpreted as methods, where these research principles can be enacted through different methods of data collection and analysis, often simultaneously. You will notice that the *attentiveness* shape has a line that wraps around *play, care,* and *balance.* I have interpreted this to reflect the overarching importance of attentiveness in allowing a researcher to be present enough to enact these other principles and to identify knowledge when it does emerge. Attentiveness continues to be important in building a relationship to that knowledge through analysis. Additionally, I see the non-linear layout of the shapes and entangled lines between them as representing the non-linear and often circuitous nature of carrying out Indigenous research. Understanding does not flow in one clear direction and so miyo ohpikinâwasowin research requires an ability to trust the process. Finally, the imperfect edges of the lines are also meaningful in that they encourage humility and perseverance even when things do not unfold as anticipated.

Articulating miyo ohpikinâwasowin research as a conceptual framework for my PhD is a helpful endeavour in that it allows me to be clear about my assumptions about the world and how I will move forward in conducting research from that perspective. According to nêhiyaw and Saulteaux scholar Maggie Kovach,

> Explicit conceptual frameworks allow us the opportunity to be honest about our perspective as researchers and to illustrate how this perspective impacts the methods chosen . . . a conceptual framework is a plan that guides the researcher in developing a research question; contemplating epistemology, theory, and ethics; engaging with community; self-situating; considering existing knowledge; hearing story; choosing methods and analytical strategies; and presenting the research and arranging for reciprocity in disseminating the findings. (2021, pp. 44–45)

Kovach (2021) goes on to explain that the success of an Indigenous conceptual framework relies upon whether it encompasses four core foundations, including 1) Indigenous epistemology (knowledges); 2) ethics (axiology); 3) community; and 4) self (self-referent, experiential knowledge). I have attempted to speak to these core foundations through the information I have shared about coming to understand my role as a parent and researcher. My framework is unapologetically personal in an attempt to make Indigenous thought visible in my research actions according to my distinct cultural context.

Bringing my family into knowledge spaces with me—either physically or by reference—is an intentional epistemological, axiological, and methodological choice. It is an exercise of relational accountability (Wilson, 2008) and affirms everydayness at the family level as critical sites of resurgence and nationhood (Corntassel & Hardbarger, 2019; Simpson, 2017). Furthermore, this framework will serve as a catalyst for desire-based research (Tuck, 2009) where I will optimistically look to the past and future for wisdom on how to encourage Indigenous knowledge to emerge safely online. I have a long way to go in understanding how to appropriately apply miyo ohpikinâwasowin (good child-rearing) to my research and parenting—but I guess that is the point.

CLOSING NOTE

Since this chapter was originally accepted for publication the focus of my PhD project and my understanding of my research methodology has continued to evolve. I have moved on from describing my conceptual framework as a *miyo ohpikinâwasowin framework for research* to the concept of *Research from Home*, a similar idea that recognizes home as a place of research governed by wâhkôhtowin and ohpikinâwasowin. This shift came about through my comprehensive exam writing process where I was able to spend more time thinking through these ideas. Rather than changing the chapter completely to reflect developments in my thinking I have chosen to move ahead with publishing the bulk of the chapter in its original form with the original framework name. Keeping it this way pushes me to embrace the discomfort of putting imperfect or unfinished ideas out into the world (is any idea truly perfect or finished anyway?)—this seems particularly important for this book and its focus on honouring the ups and downs of the Indigenous graduate research journey.

REFERENCES

Archibald, J. (2008). *Indigenous storywork: Educating the heart, mind, body, and spirit.* Vancouver: UBC Press.

Anderson, K. (2011). *Life stages and Native women: Memory, teachings, and story medicine.* Winnipeg: University of Manitoba Press.

Battiste, M. (2013). *Decolonizing education: Nourishing the learning spirit.* UBC Press.

Bhatt, I., & MacKenzie, A. (2019). Just Google it! Digital literacy and the epistemology of ignorance. *Teaching in Higher Education*, 24(3), 302–317. https://doi.org/10.1080/13562517.2018.1547276

Brant, J., & Anderson, K. (2021). Indigenous mothering: New insights on giving life to the people. In A. O'Reilly (Ed.), *Maternal theory: Essential readings* (2nd ed., pp. 713–734). Coe Hill, ON: Demeter Press.

Campbell, M. (2007). We need to return to the principles of wahkotowin. *Eagle Feather News*, 10(11), 5.

Corntassel, J., & Hardbarger, T. (2019). Educate to perpetuate: Land-based pedagogies and community resurgence. *International Review of Education*, 65(1), 87–116. https://www.jstor.org/stable/45201094

Daniels-Fiss, B. (2008). Learning to be a Nêhiyaw (Cree) through language. *Diaspora, Indigenous, and minority education*, 2(3), 233-245.

Dorion, L. M. (2010). *Opikinawasowin: The life long process of growing Cree and Métis children* [Master's thesis, Athabasca University]. Virtual Museum of Metis History and Culture. https://www.metismuseum.ca/media/document.php/13768.Dorion_traditional_child_rearing_2010_GDI.pdf

Downey, A. (2018). *The creator's game: Lacrosse, identity, and Indigenous nationhood.* UBC Press.

Ermine, W. (1995). Aborginal epistemology. In M. Battiste & J. Barman (Eds.), *First Nations education in Canada: The circle unfolds* (pp. 101–112). Vancouver: UBC Press.

Flaminio, A. L. (2013). *Gladue through wahkotowin: Social history through Cree kinship lens in corrections and parole* [Doctoral dissertation, University of Saskatchewan]. Harvest. https://harvest.usask.ca/bitstreams/e4c8b150-6a91-4004-931d-c82ea112c1a9/download

Gaudet, J. C. (2019). Keeoukaywin: The visiting way—fostering an Indigenous research methodology. *Aboriginal Policy Studies*, 7(2), 47–64. https://doi.org/10.5663/aps.v7i2.29336

Gaudry, A. J. P. (2014). *Kaa-tipeyimishoyaahk—"We are those who own ourselves":*
A political history of Métis self-determination in the north-west, 1830–1870
[Doctoral dissertation, University of Victoria]. Dspace. https://dspace.library.
uvic.ca/bitstreams/7496faf4-053e-4e69-b5f4-86f838f20ae4/download

Graveline, F. J. (Ed.). (1998). *Circle works: Transforming Eurocentric consciousness.*
Winnipeg: Fernwood Publishing.

hooks, b. (1997). Homeplace: A site of resistance. In L. Mcdowell (Ed.), *Undoing*
place? A geographical reader (pp. 33–38). London: Routledge.

Hunt, S. (2018). Researching within relations of violence: Witnessing as methodology.
In D. McGregor, J. P. Restoule, & R. Johnston (Eds.), *Indigenous research: Theories,*
practices, and relationships (pp. 282–295). Toronto: Canadian Scholars' Press.

Kovach, M. (2010). Conversational method in Indigenous research. *First Peoples*
Child & Family Review, 5(1), 40–48. https://doi.org/10.7202/1069060ar

Kovach, M. (2021). *Indigenous methodologies: Characteristics, conversations and*
contexts (2nd ed.). University of Toronto Press.

Napier, K., & Whiskeyjack, L. (2021). wahkotowin: Reconnecting to the spirit of
nêhiyawêwin (Cree Language). *Engaged Scholar Journal,* 7(1), 1–24. https://doi.
org/10.15402/esj.v7i1.69979

Nyota, S., Mapara, J., & Centre for Advanced Studies of African Society. (2007).
Language as Indigenous knowledge. Centre for Advanced Studies of African
Society.

Potskin, J. (2020). *Indigenous youth in Australia and Canada: A modern narrative*
of settler/colonial relationships through Indigenous rap music [Doctoral
dissertation, University of Sydney]. Sydney eScholarship Repository. https://
ses.library.usyd.edu.au/bitstream/handle/2123/22963/rPOTSKIN_2020.pdf

Prabhakaran, V., Mitchell, M., Gebru, T., & Gabriel, I. (2022). A human rights-
based approach to responsible AI. arXiv, Cornell University. https://arxiv.org/
pdf/2210.02667.

Smith, L. T. (2021). *Decolonizing methodologies: Research and Indigenous peoples* (3rd
ed.). London: Zed Books.

Steinhauer-Hill, P. J. (2008). *Kihkipiw: A Cree way* [Doctoral thesis, University of
Alberta].

Tine, J. (2020). A research journey with Plains Cree Elders regarding their image of
the child. *Journal of Childhood Studies,* 45(3), 19–43. https://journals.uvic.ca/
index.php/jcs/issue/view/1485

Traxler, J. (2019). Only connect: Indigenous digital learning. *Interaction Design and*
Architecture(s), 41, 7–23. https://doi.org/10.55612/s-5002-041-001

Tuck, E. (2009). Suspending damage: A letter to communities. *Harvard Educational*
Review, 79(3), 409–428. https://doi.org/10.17763/haer.79.3.n0016675661t3n15

Vowel, C. (2011, October 24). Cree kinship terms. *Âpihtawikosisân*. https://apihtawikosisan.com/2011/10/cree-kinship-terms/

Wildcat, M. (2018). Wahkohtowin in action. *Constitutional Forum constitutionel*, 27(1), 13–24. https://www.ualberta.ca/wahkohtowin/media-library/data-lists-pdfs/wahkotowin-in-action.pdf

Wilson, S. (2007). Guest editorial: What is an Indigenist research paradigm? *Canadian Journal of Native Education*, 30(2), 193–195. https://doi.org/10.14288/cjne.v30i2.196422

Wilson, S. (2008). *Research is ceremony: Indigenous research methods*. Halifax: Fernwood Publishing.

Wilson, S., Breen, A. V., & DuPré, L. (Eds.). (2019). *Research and reconciliation: Unsettling way of knowing through Indigenous relationships*. Toronto: Canadian Scholars' Press.

Yunkaporta, T. (2020). *Sand talk: How Indigenous thinking can save the world*. New York: HarperOne.

Fat Bodies in Space
Explorations of an Alternate Narrative
N. Katie Webb

ABSTRACT

For far too long "obesity" and health care have been inextricably linked, both forming and maintaining distinct narratives responsible for the "fear of fat" North American societies have embraced. Largely unrecognized, fatphobia now permeates individual and social consciousness and creates considerable harm broadly and within health care practice and policy. The following chapter is derived from my graduate thesis research, *Fat Bodies in Space: Explorations of an Alternate Narrative*, completed during the springs of 2020 and 2021. *Fat Bodies in Space* was a qualitative study that took place on the unceded ləkʷəŋən territories between 2020 and 2021. This research work aimed to unsettle western, binary views of weight and bodies, make visible the implications fatphobia has on all bodies, and contribute to a more socially just, intersectional system of care. Grounded in critical race, queer, and decolonial perspectives, the personal and systemic impacts of fatphobia in health care are addressed through the collection of stories from five self-described fat individuals navigating health care in Victoria, British Columbia. Literature review as research, storywork (Archibald,

2008), narrative, and autoethnographic methods were utilized. Findings suggest a long-standing relationship between anti-Black racism, systemic inequities, social discourse, and the treatment of fat individuals within health care systems. **Keywords:** *fatphobia, weight, fat consciousness, health care, decolonialism, storywork, inequity, anti-fatness*

FATPHOBIA & HEALTH CARE:
A BRIEF SUMMARY OF PERSPECTIVES

For far too long the "obesity narrative" and health care have been inextricably linked. Dominant systems and narratives have built the wave of fat consciousness and contributed to the formation and perpetuation of fatphobia. North Americans have embraced the "fear of fat" while also embracing social stereotypes, misconceptions, and perceived "truths" about fat bodies. In this context, fat people are seen as unhealthy, lazy, sloppy, non-compliant, unintelligent, unsuccessful, and lacking self-control. Fatphobia *developed* through these dominant perceptions and is expressed through fear, aversion, hatred, or repulsion towards fat, or fat bodies, and has come to permeate individual and social consciousness, policy, and practice. Fatphobia does not just produce discomfort or embarrassment. People are dying. Fat people are dying because they are only being seen as fat (Canadian Press, 2018). Fatphobia has become interwoven with North American social and political systems and beliefs. Fatphobia has grown throughout the fabric of health care, influencing individual and systemic motivations, decisions, and actions. Anti-fatness has become more than discourse, has many histories, and has broad-reaching implications.

"Fat" touches everyone in some way, whether it's the experience of living in it or living to avoid it. The stories being told about fat, as one fat activist stated, "no one is getting it right…from the food industry to the media to the health policy experts themselves" (West, 2017, p. 1). Health care and western society's approaches to fatness have only succeeded in creating a space that stigmatizes fat and fat people without offering realistic help or support.

The following chapter, through reflection and critical analysis, centres and summarizes the learning from my graduate thesis work. When approaching this research, it was my intention to trace and make visible the stories being told by, and about, fat and fat bodies. As an Indigenous graduate student researcher, I was guided by the desire to challenge dominant discourse and to create space for stories and re-storying (White & Epston, 1990). I saw fatness as a series of underdiscussed issues placing undue burden upon myself and the communities I am both part of and support. I also approached the thesis process as an opportunity to impress upon the social work profession the necessity for inclusion and critical discussion of fatphobia in social justice work. It was my intention to unravel and unsettle fatphobia and its impacts within our current western-colonial society. With this work, I hope to contribute to the growing body of works making visible the connections between anti-fatness to anti-Black racism and the systemic inequities fat bodies are facing in North America.

HEALTH, CARE & THE DOMINANT DISCOURSE

Examining fatphobia within health care provided an entry point to the extensive and broad-reaching inequities fatphobia compounds for those often already existing at the margins of society. Considering fatphobia and health care within a social justice framework further highlighted the impacts and barriers facing everyone living in North America. Fat and fatphobia aside, the pathologization of bodies within medical systems has contributed to increased risk of burden and harm due to stigmatization, discrimination, blame, and avoidance (Campos, 2004).

The dominant and pathologizing narratives about fat bodies at present, medical and otherwise, work within binaries. Western society upholds the thin body as the ideal and stigmatize fatness as a temporary condition or disease. Stigma is an already present and studied force in health care with past and current research examining stigma's overall impacts on health and wellness. For fat bodies, stigma contributes to broadly drawn conclusions about health, lifestyle, or intelligence. Care rendered often includes weight loss as a prescription for common non-weight-related ailments

and care focused on perceived behaviours instead of causation (Fikkan &
Rothblum, 2012; Friedman, 2012; Rothblum & Solovay, 2009; Burgard referenced in Rothblum & Solovay, 2009). Physicians and policy makers are
often missing the mark for the current and future health of fat Canadians,
focusing public health efforts in obesity discourse and touting "obesity epidemic" narratives.

The polarization of fatness continues to overlook and contribute to the
growing list of harms and barriers produced by fatphobia itself. In doing
so, current fat narratives additionally erase the racial and religious under-
pinnings of anti-fatness and the connection to anti-Blackness. Western
fatness discourses have been characterized as a trend developed in more
recent time periods. It is often purported that fatness did not exist within
early history, prior to times stricken by war and scarcity, nor did the medicalization of fatness, which in most narratives is less than 100 years old.
Within "obesity" or medical discourse, fat is seen as a relatively new phenomenon, grown at the outset of the Second World War. It was believed
that waist bands began to expand during this period because of greater
food availability and a drastic reduction in society's overall physical activity (Eknoyan, 2006).

Sabrina Strings (2019), author of *Fearing the Black Body: The Racial
Origins of Fat Phobia*, traces the origins of fatphobia to the trans-Atlantic
slave trade and Protestantism, grounding the birth of fatphobia in racism
and western white supremacy. She found thinness as the preferred ideal
within North American since the early nineteenth century, predating the
medicalization of fat bodies by, at minimum, 100 years. Strings brings
attention to this piece of history not to give value to the early glorifica-
tion of thinness, but to create recognition for the ways in which fatphobia
grew from a racist, protestant, regulatory ideals, aimed at upholding white
supremacy and objectifying and demoralizing the Black body (2019).

Mainstream movements have begun to adapt ideas from fat acceptance
without truly adopting the systemic and racialized lens and intention that
come with fatphobia and fat acceptance history. Seen with many pivotal
movements still underway today, visibility and representation are not
enough. The assimilative nature of social representation is failing to be

recognized. Representation does not equate to acceptance, especially not fat acceptance. Movements, activisms, and research at present fail to centre Black, Indigenous, and people of colour (BIPOC) individuals and their voices. Fat-positive movements and activisms have forgotten their political upbringing. Fat acceptance, unlike body positivity, grew in response to the medicalization of obesity and was "forged in a political and social climate marked by...influential social justice movements such as African American civil rights, gay liberation and feminist movements" (Afful & Ricciardelli, 2015, p. 454). Fat activisms were already developing within Black and queer spaces in North America going back to protests against fat bias in the 1960s (Strings, 2019). Historically, fat acceptance and activism have been criticized for encouraging unhealthiness, when, in fact, it is quite the opposite: fat acceptance and activisms work in tandem to create space for fat bodies to thrive outside of social constructs and perceived normativity (Hayden, 2015) while simultaneously calling for change and equal rights within society.

Many of the dominant narratives explored in this study perpetuate fat binaries, pathologization of bodies, and lack an intersectional perspective. Fatness discourse is often categorized in few ways, as "celebrating" fatness or with the aim to disregard, dehumanize, or regulate the fat body (Eknoyan, 2006). Notions of good and bad bodies have long supported the disembodiment and marginalization of the "non-normative" including fat bodies, resulting in specific and tangible effects to the overall emotional, mental, and physical health and well-being of those inhabiting fat bodies. Each day in Canada, the rising tide of anti-fat stigma and fatphobia looms through social spaces and government policy, building greater risk for fat citizens at an alarming rate.

SOCIAL REGULATION, COMMODIFICATION & THE "OBESITY" EPIDEMIC

The health care lens within the fat context also amplifies connections between the regulation of bodies and the ability to capitalize on and profit from the "non-normative," on a person's wanting to change themselves in pursuit of the normative. Pharmaceuticals, specialty foods, diet, weight loss, and beauty industries have become increasingly aware that fatness is an area of mega-investment and mega-profit (Campos, 2004; Kirby, 2012). Burgeoning "wars" or "fights against obesity" indicate that many industries are waking up to the potential profit produced by self-hatred. Evidence suggests that fatphobia supports the turn of profit, growing any industry that stands in the fight against obesity (Kirby, 2012), allowing bodies to become markers of profit or commodities. Commodification, when considered in context, has created a shift in health care, forcing public services into for-profit enterprises (Lown, 2007). Concrete and demonstrative examples of commodification feature daily within health care spaces, such as government implemented doctor's office policies preventing patients from discussing more than one issue per visit. Such policies only further a "revolving door model of care" (Silva, 2015), which seeks to maximize the number of patients, increase government revenues while providing minimal pay to physicians. This notion supports universality and standardization by excluding time and space for the whole patient, individuality, context and needs. Patients take off work to access clinics multiple times (Silva, 2015), or they ignore symptoms, avoid early screening options, and have reported feeling abandoned by health care systems (Lown, 2007). Diagnosis and treatment within this model is done by exclusion and can take years, "open[ing] the floodgates for endless tests and procedures" (Lown, 2007, p. 42). Standardizing care balances economic necessity but fails to acknowledge the barriers being built for both patients and physician. For example, supporters of insurance privatization and user fees disregard barriers to access for individuals living in lower socio-economic conditions; universal measures of health are actively excluding those that fall out of a perceived category of normal, and/or those who are differently abled (Campos, 2004). Neoliberalism in alliance with capitalism has had a commodifying effect on North American health care and the individuals' accessing services. Commodification of health and care invariably becomes the commodification and regulation of bodies, evidenced, and experienced heavily by those who have been marginalized, such as the fat community.

Fat studies scholars argue that "obesity" discourse is both reflective of and complicit in the reproduction of neoliberal governmentality. Neoliberal governmentality refers to techniques and strategies of government, or the ruling class, that encourage citizens to think and act in particular ways (Guthman, 2009). During the 1970s, French political philosopher Michel Foucault's gaze into neoliberalism made visible the enmeshment of state responsibility and the market, with the emphasis placed on individual empowerment, responsibility, and self-regulation within the pursuit of health and wealth (Harjunen, 2017). Governmentality on one hand acts within neoliberalism to limit government intervention or "control," but on the other hand it seeks to control market conditions that promote and are conducive to the regulating of choices for individual citizens (Guthman, 2009). Indigenous scholar Dian Million (2013) better understands neoliberalism and its effects as "that which reaches beyond economics to become a way of life, a form of governance, not to be construed as an ideology but rather as a 'way of doing things' as a principle and method for the rationalization of the exercise of government" (p. 33). The "obesity epidemic" narrative is one such rationalization, one of governing bodies lording power over while simultaneously profiting on fat bodies.

FAT BODIES IN SPACE

Centring narrative and story in my thesis research was crucial to holding space for the stories of each participant, all fat individuals navigating health care locally in Victoria, British Columbia. *Fat Bodies in Space* was grounded in the notion that fatphobia permeates social and health care spaces, having real impacts on the wellness of all individuals. Though fat folks are mainly centred in conversations of fatphobia, others are impacted through the promotion of anorexia, bulimia, and the stigmatization of weight and size. By centring the *Fat Bodies in Space* study on health care, I hoped to demonstrate that fat, too, is a social justice issue demanding recognition within health and social care sectors. My intention is that the results may better inform education, practice, and policy within these sectors and contribute to offsetting the inequities being navigated in these spaces.

THE RESEARCH

To recruit participants, a convenience sampling method (Naderifar et al., 2016) was implemented utilizing my personal participation and access to fat support and activism groups on Facebook. This type of sampling is helpful for student researchers, often who are working within their own limitations, financially or otherwise. Inclusion criteria indicated individuals of any gender over the age of eighteen who identified as fat and were living and navigating health care locally on Vancouver Island. Following three weeks of online recruitment, sixteen individuals volunteered for the study. Individuals who wished to participate replied to the Facebook post indicating interest in the project and were contacted privately to offer more in-depth project information and determine eligibility. Maintaining a local sample saw twelve early volunteers excluded due to their location. The exclusion criteria were minimal and based mainly on logistical requirements, eliminating only those unwilling to provide consent or anyone residing outside of Vancouver Island. In alignment with these parameters, all participants lived on Vancouver Island, apart from one, who had grown up here but recently relocated. Each participant had relatively consistent access or need for access to health care over their lifetime and at present.

The final study sample included four participants, all identified and recruited from the previously mentioned Facebook groups. Participants primarily self-identified as female, one participant identified as trans. All participants were white-presenting, two indicated living with a disability, and one identified as a senior citizen. Though some participants self-identified or disclosed identifying information in various ways, I chose early on to refrain from collecting demographic related information during or after the interviews. With this research being grounded in Indigenous ways of being and doing and Indigenous research methodologies, I tried to consider demographics from a decolonial perspective. For example, I felt that requesting or asking about a participant's gender was less relational than simply providing space within the interviews for the individual to share who they were and what they believe to be pertinent. Participants were also encouraged to speak about their experiences across their lifespan, without confinement to a particular period. Not focusing on demographics aligned with my desire to contribute to decolonial research methods and acted to circumvent the impacts and connotations associated with classification and overarching terminology (i.e., Elder, young adult, school-aged). Using these terms and classifiers in research has left gaps for individuals who fit between or for whom there are no suitable categories. "Not fitting," or marginalization, increases exclusionary outcomes and barriers to supports (Driskill et al., 2011).

PARTICIPANTS & STORYWORK

The participants all engaged in an interview for which they received the questions ahead of time. All interview questions were open-ended, and participants were encouraged to share how and what they saw fit. As one participant put it, "So, I think I want to just tell you my beginning, my involvement in fat stuff…and…my experiences will come up, like my medical experience" (participant, personal communication, February 14, 2020). Methodologies discussing story or narrative and how to present this kind of information in one's thesis work described taking on the voice of the participant or writing a story *about* them (Iseke, 2013). Instead, I worked to maintain their voice and tone, and to reflect the exchange and time shared with the participant from my perspective. Four stories developed from the recordings and transcriptions, and participants were invited to be part of the iterative writing process. They were encouraged to offer feedback and request changes at any point in the process. The resulting stories were written as my own narration of those conversations interspersed with direct quotes to capture context and authentic flow. As stated, these sections were written with support of data collection (recordings, transcriptions, and notes) taken throughout the interviews and research process. The writing of participant stories took place prior to the main analysis, coding, and theming process and were used as well as the notes and data collected in identifying those codes and themes.

After storying the participants interviews and completing an initial analysis, I recognized, through ongoing self-reflection during this process, that I had effectively separated myself from my work. That, in the name of research, I had created separation between myself and the participants. It was at this point that I decided to include autoethnography. I recruited a community member to interview me following the same style, which was audio recorded, transcribed, and themed.

FINDINGS & IMPACTS

The first time I worked as a student researcher and was tasked with analyzing and theming interviews, I truly wasn't sure what I was doing. I developed a system that worked for me, grown from the teachings and mentorship from those who had held space for me as a new researcher. Through a manual process of narrative and thematic analysis, grounded in Indigenous ways of being and doing, I contributed a three-stage process of analysis. The first stage involves reading and familiarity with the participant's text and "voice." At the time of this thesis work, I approached my mentor on that project and asked them about including them and their articulation of this process in my work.

With permission and support, the analysis work of Cree/Métis researcher Dr. Lisa Borque-Bearskin informed this process. Dr. Borque-Bearskin (2019) suggests during the first reading of each transcript, view the document more wholistically to gain familiarity with each person's voice, the tones, and other elements of text. During the second read, a more in-depth approach is taken, considering phrases and terms that stand out or capture the participants' points of view in meaningful ways. The third reading examines the documents sentence by sentence, highlighting statements, topics, or ideas that step forward with significant meaning or hold commonality throughout other interviews. At each stage, I maintained separate notes, journaled thoughts, questions, and feelings that surfaced while completing the readings and logged prominent or repetitious phrases and words used during the stories. I used charts to track poignant quotes and to view participant ideas, visually, across all the interviews. Reading the transcripts together in this way provided an opportunity to build upon connections and ideas within and across the conversations and create ways to communicate findings to various types of learning style.

THEMES

One of the first themes, *fat consciousness*, was a term I felt brought meaning and dimension in contrast to other notions of weight consciousness. In the literature findings, weight consciousness had described how an individual's journey to their ideal size supposedly occurs through a process of mindful self-love. Other literature suggests weight consciousness regards a person's growing concern, awareness, and avoidance of increasing weight. What I came to refer to as *fat consciousness* in this context was articulated by the participants as the ongoing self-conscious discovery or awareness of their own fatness and growing awareness of external fat stigma. Fat consciousness also encapsulated the subsequent and changing decision-making processes they experienced following that discovery. In their stories, participants came to conscious awareness of their fatness and, over time, built understanding and ways of interacting with their fat identities. Bodies shift and change over time just as one's realizations or feelings about their body, fatness, or what it means changes over time. "Obesity" and medical perceptions of fatness seem to remain unchanged.

Fatphobia and diagnosis encapsulated the second theme. Among participants, there was a shared experience of "obesity" being centred across a variety of medical experiences. They all discussed in their own way the blatant, unproblematized acceptability of fatphobia within health care spaces. Participants provided examples of how "obesity" and fatphobia have come to define much of the dominant social and health care standards or belief systems. Both of these are not only dictating the inappropriate treatment fat individuals continue to receive but also the treatment many have become forced to live with. Participants reported significant issues brought to health care professionals were continually overlooked and ignored. Many of their practitioners were reported to have held a singular perspective of "obesity" and health. It was found that dominant narratives of obesity have contributed to the way doctors dismiss these and other fat patients, resulting in untreated issues or lack of prevention impacting health. Medical models have become reliant on *fat as a diagnosis*, placing the burden on the individual to, sometimes aggressively, advocate to be taken seriously.

The third theme, *compounding disbelief*, was characterized through pathologizing fatness and centring obesity in patient care, resulting in disbelief and mistreatment via unwelcome or harmful comments or suggestions like weight loss surgery or the latest fad diet, assumptions, and stereotyping. Participants' experiences of mistreatment left many "feeling invisible," receiving incorrect or unnecessary treatment or a denial of treatment entirely. The participants indicated that the *disbelief* of doctors has had major implications on their health and mental health. These effects are significant for those whose fatness existed alongside other intersections of identity ("racialization," "female-presenting," "trans," "disabled"). Participants were often viewed as a list of "obesity" risk factors. Each person who participated in this study, especially female-identifying members, talked about experiences of not being taken seriously from a young age, either because of, or despite, their weight.

The fourth theme demonstrated the *unintended consequences* of centring weight in most medical interactions and of patients not viewing their doctors as something they can turn to in a time of medical need. Compounding these consequences, participants also reported avoidant or resistant behaviours (Richardson & Wade, 2007; Wade, 1997). Negative experiences and a focus on weight or weight loss during a medical interaction, regardless of the reason for the interaction, had participants avoiding health care, taking matters into their own hands with at-home care, or needing to be pushed by a loved one to seek care when it was absolutely necessary. The stories and research reflect that "obese" patients are often encouraged to maintain poor eating habits (starvation), remain on conflicting treatments, or incur negative side effects, all to support weight loss. Fatphobia is largely acceptable in medical spaces where comments are made about fat bodies that would not be acceptable of a "slim" body. Acceptability and perpetuation of fatphobia in medical spaces was seen in this study and others to impede preventative care and increase patient avoidance (Drury & Louis, 2004). To provide care, practitioners ask that patients, who are already experiencing fear or anxiety, be in highly vulnerable positions. In one participant's case, it was a mammogram. "I once had a mammogram that had a shadow and so I had to go get an ultrasound... And the practitioner looked at me and said, 'How am I going to find anything in those breasts?' And there I am . . . like on my edge." The guilt, shame, or embarrassment grown out of a moment of fat shaming or fatphobic rhetoric might ensure the patient never returns and a lump or spot goes unexamined.

Disordered eating was another example of internalized socially and medically imposed narratives about bodies. Participant stories depicted struggles of living with but never addressing disordered eating, least of all with a doctor. Participants reported that doctors "triggered," "dismissed," or "congratulated" them when it came to admitting to an eating disorder. Less consideration was given to the connections participants had made between childhood experiences of fatphobia and their disordered eating patterns. The narratives reflected an undeniable relationship between how society views and treats fatness and fat bodies and the ways fat bodies and those around them come to see and treat themselves and each other. Those who had lost weight in "unhealthy ways" discussed the feelings and attitudes they encountered and the realization that "health and thinness [conflate] within the medical profession. It's there from the very beginning." In the face of this reality, many of the participants at one time or another, felt they were left without options for their health. Despite anti-fatness playing a consistent role in all five participants' medical journeys, there was also a unanimous and (nearly) unwavering narrative of self-advocacy. These individuals recognized along their process of fat consciousness and self-discovery that unequitable and discriminatory treatment in their health care was not only unacceptable, but it was also dangerous. Finding fat acceptance and learning how to self-advocate was their way of offsetting that danger.

The final theme, *reimagining care*, began to give voice to what fat bodies are seeking in health care, indicating two approaches. The first approach addresses and shifts the narrative practitioners incorporate in their understanding of "the care piece" in medical practice and education. One participant stated, "They've taken the care piece out of medical . . . It's no longer 'care,' its diagnostic and treatment. And I feel that . . . every human, fat or otherwise, suffers because of that." Participants indicated human centred care in medical practice must be prioritized to offset harm and patient avoidance. Participants stated that achieving human centred "good care" rested required "a good doctor." The "good doctor" was characterized by words and actions demonstrating respect, consideration of the patients' history, holistically, and centring weight differently in their office space and practice. Participants wanted the patient experience of being asked questions before the practitioner assumed. They also wanted to be believed and validated by the practitioner, non-fat-shaming office literature and posters, and attention to personal comforts and body differences. The tone of signage and pamphlets, size of gowns, sheets, chairs, and availability of large blood pressure cuffs were all indicative of a "good doctor," the type of physician who wouldn't generalize and gave enough time to better understand them as a whole patient.

Participants believed that patient centred care should be focused in the relational and conversational instead of instruction based. Being directive was sometimes seen as doctor's attempt to save time, but participants indicated that direction or medical advice out of context left them feeling unheard and forced to explain themselves, prompting further feelings of not being believed.

DISCUSSION

When it comes to individual health, there is no one that sits in the role of expert better than the patients themselves, fat patients included. While trans-disciplinary praxis and collaborative care aim to create more cohesive and wholistic approaches to health care based in improving outcomes (Canadian Medical Protective Association, 2007), these models fail to properly centre the patient as the expert in both diagnosis and treatment. Individual health care seekers are under-resourced and falling between the gaps in the system. Social workers and adjacent professions may be uniquely positioned to play a role in addressing these serious gaps.

Long ago, when beginning the thesis process, I believed that achieving good health care meant a focus on wholistic and patient-centred care. There is still necessity in making space for these elements, but the participants, my personal health care journey, and this process have validated the need for steps beyond patient-centred care. Patient-centred care aims to individualize medicine, include patients and their families as members of the care team, and encourage two-way communication and collaboration between physicians and patients (NEJM Catalyst, 2017). However, it has been found that simply implementing this model does little to address how practitioners are educated or how care systems are designed and managed. Findings examining outcomes of patient-centred care produce large gaps, indicating that physicians often lack financial incentive and time required to implement the models appropriately. As a result, revenue is lost as fewer patients are able to be seen (Budgen & Cantiello, 2017) and care becomes fractured and disconnected.

Much like the medical field, social work has demonstrated a failure to critically engage with fatness as a marginalized identity because it is typically viewed through the lens of "choice" or as a demonstration of "bad choice" (Cooper Stoll, 2019; McHugh & Kasardo, 2012; Puhl & Heuer, 2012; Sender & Sullivan, 2008). The "eat less-exercise more" myth sustains within many sectors, social work included, and is supported by the "obesity as disease" and 'war on obesity' narratives. Through research, policy, and practice, the war on 'obesity' has developed into a war against fat people" (Cooper Stoll, 2019). In this lens, Fatness is fundamentally "a social justice issue that continues to intersect with other systems of inequality like gender, race and class in very problematic ways" (Cooper Stoll, 2019, p. 12). Social work theory and practice has demonstrated that systems of oppression work in tandem to both produce and reproduce injustices and that identities must not be addressed as a unidimensional concept (Collins, 1990; Crenshaw, 1989).

As a profession concerned with addressing racism, inequity, disparity, and discrimination, social workers can no longer overlook the systemic marginalization of fat bodies in and outside of their practice. Fat acceptance seeks health, equity, and acceptance for all bodies. Fat acceptance is a growing social movement challenging the way professionals take up intersectional work and practice. Social spaces have begun to transform and reimagine notions of "normativity," supplanting diversity and perspectives that negate binary ways of being and doing. There is an absence of disputation to dominant body narratives reflected broadly within the fields of social work and medical practice.

FUTURE RESEARCH & RESEARCHERS

As a student with Indigenous and settler ancestry learning within an Indigenous social work program, I initially felt that my work must be grounded in or reflective of that part of who I am. As an uninvited visitor on these territories, I did not want to contribute to the imposition research has placed on Indigenous Peoples of Turtle Island. Further, Indigenous communities are expansive, and pan-Indigenizing has had harmful long-term effects. Examining fatness and fatphobia within Indigenous communities should be community-driven, land and nation specific, and culturally and environmentally relevant. First Peoples across North America continue to fight for land, food, and health sovereignty as a result of systemic racism and ongoing marginalization. From the colonial project and its oppressions, "obesity" has taken on different meanings in Indigenous stories locally and globally, necessitating community-implemented approaches. Fat acceptance and phobia cannot be discussed without centring the histories, narratives, and perspectives of each community and the work already being done to restore health and healing.

Fat acceptance and fat liberation movements have only increased visibility of the work Black and 2SLGBTQIA+ people have done for so long. By acknowledging the socially constructed nature of fatness and the racist history of fatphobia, all bodies have an opportunity to avoid being silenced by white, western, patriarchal, and misogynist standards infecting North American societies. As a fat person myself, this thesis process challenged my own internalized fatphobia, my perceptions and the ways in which I have contributed to a socially constructed world for fat people. When I chose this topic, I was fearful to tell others. I chose my words carefully when asked questions about my thesis and didn't always mention the "fat part." As I opened up, and the work took shape, I realized the grips fatphobia has had on so many in my life and how much work was already being done.

Though the *Fat Bodies in Space* study was small, and not at the point of generalizability, it held meaningful outcomes. Other researchers have suggested a study intent on bringing understanding to the nature of a phenomenon, in this case fatphobia, may use a relatively small sample size if the researcher acknowledges that even when similar themes are discussed by many participants in the study, generalizability cannot be claimed (Thorne, 2008). I believe, when positioned within the rapidly growing body of fat studies work and activisms, generalizability does not need to be claimed; it becomes evident. Conflating all fat people into the category of unhealthy or "obese" denies opportunity, limits options, and inhibits diagnosis and treatment processes. Current approaches to body size or health maintain a narrow, simplistic view that perpetuates avoidable harms and suffering upon all bodies. This study has shown that fat stigma and phobia are felt across a spectrum of communities, guiding many at an early age, fat or not, to dislike and change who they are. The fear of fat pervades our social norms, medical spaces, educational interactions, and political realms (Gordon, 2020). Perhaps the challenge then becomes not defining more ways to decrease "obesity," but ways to decrease fatphobia and weight bias in health care and broader societies. A shift in narrative may allow for a shift in fat consciousness contributing to anti-racist work in health care, improved policy change ad decision-making processes in health care, and improved health and well-being for bodies fat and otherwise.

Health, and researchers, come in all shapes and sizes. Anyone can write a thesis because a thesis can be anything you want it to be. It will be part of you, just like this work, the participants, and the impacts I've left behind will always be part of me. I encourage and support you as burgeoning researchers and scholars to find your passion, narrow your focus, and contribute to your field and your community in a way that feels meaningful, and of course, leaves an impression.

REFERENCES

Afful, A. A., & Ricciardelli, R. (2015). Shaping the online fat acceptance movement: Talking about body image and beauty standards. *Journal of Gender Studies*, 24(4), 453–472. https://doi.org/10.1080/09589236.2015.1028523

Archibald, J. (2008). *Indigenous storywork: Educating the heart, mind, body, and spirit*. Vancouver: UBC Press.

Borque-Bearskin, L. (2019). *Gifting Indigenous Wellness Knowledge* [PowerPoint Slides].

Budgen & Cantiello, (2017). Advantaged and disadvantages of the patient-cantered medical home: a critical analysis and lessons learned. *The Health Care Manager*, 26(4), 357–363.

Campos, P. (2004). *The obesity myth: Why America's obsession with weight is hazardous to your health*. New York: Penguin Group.

Canadian Medical Protective Association. (2007). *Collaborative care: A medical liability perspective*. Retrieved from https://www.cmpa-acpm.ca/en/advice publications/handbooks/collaborative-care-summary

Canadian Press. (2018, July 30). Woman uses obituary to advocate against fat shaming in the medical profession. *CBC News*. Retrieved from https://www. cbc.ca/news/canada/newfoundland-labrador/fat-shaming-medical-1.4766676

Cooper Stoll, (2019). Fat is a social justice issue, too. *Humanity and Society*, (43)4: 421–441. Retrieved from https://journals.sagepub.com/doi/10.1177/ 0160597619832051

Crenshaw, (1989). "Demarginalizing the Intersection of Race and Sex: A Black Feminist Critique of Antidiscrimination Doctrine, Feminist Theory and Antiracist Politics." The University of Chicago Legal Forum 140: 139–167.

Driskill, Q.-L., Finley, C., Gilley, B. J., & Morgenson, S. L. (Eds.). (2011). *Queer Indigenous studies: Critical interventions in theory, politics and literature* (3rd ed.). Tucson: University of Arizona Press.

Drury & Louis, (2004). "Exploring the Association between Body Weight, Stigma of Obesity, and Health Care Avoidance." Journal of the American Academy of Nurse Practitioners 14(12): 554–60.

Eknoyan, G. (2006). A history of obesity, or how what was good became ugly and then bad. *Advances in Chronic Kidney Disease*, 13(4), 421–427. https://doi. org/10.1053/j.ackd.2006.07.002

Fikkan, J.L. & Rothblum, E. D. (2012). Is fat a feminist issue? Exploring the gendered nature of weight bias. Feminist Forum, 66: 575–592. doi: 10.1007/ s11199-011-0022-5.

Friedman, M. (2012). Fat is a social work issue: Fat bodies, moral regulation and the history of social work. *Intersectionalities: A Global Journal of Social Work Analysis, Research, Polity and Practice* 1: 53–69.

Friedman, M. (2015). Mother blame, fat shame, and moral panic: "Obesity" and child welfare. *Fat Studies*, 4(1): 14–27, doi: 10.1080/21604851.2014.927209.

Guthman, J. (2009). Teaching the politics of obesity: insights into neoliberal embodiment & contemporary biopolitics. *Antipode*, 41(5): 1110–1133, doi: 10.1111/j.1467-8330.2009.00707.x

Guthman, J. & DePuis, M. (2006). Embodying neoliberalism: economy, culture, and the politics of fat. *Environment & Planning D: Society & Space*.

Harjunen, H. (2017). *Neoliberal bodies and the gendered fat body*. London: Routledge.

Hayden, F. (2015). Finally, a study that confirms what I knew all along: fat acceptance is good for our health. Independent. Retrieved from https://www.independent.co.uk/voices/finally-a-study-that-confirms-what-i-knew-all-along-fat-acceptance-is-good-for-our-health-10440615.html

Iseke, J. (2013). Indigenous storytelling as research. *International Review of Qualitative Research*, 6(4), 559–577. https://www.jstor.org/stable/10.1525/irqr.2013.6.4.559

Kirby, M. (2012, July 18). Investors in obesity industry are sure to make a big fat profit. *The Guardian*. Retrieved from https://www.theguardian.com/commentisfree/2012/jul/18/business-obesity-big-fat-profit

Lown, B. (2007). The commodification of health care. *PNHP 2007 Newsletter*. Physicians for a National Health Program. Retrieved from http://www.pnhp.org/publications/the_commodification_of_health_care.php

Million, D. (2013). *Therapeutic nations: Healing in an age of Indigenous human rights*. Tucson: University of Arizona Press.

Naderifar, C., Goli E, & Ghaljaie, F. (2016). Snowball Sampling: A purposeful method of sampling in qualitative research. Developing Medical Education, (14) 3: 533–554.

NAAFA Official. (2011, March 21). *Was it ever okay to be fat? With Dina Amlund* [Video file]. Retrieved from https://www.youtube.com/watch?v=bhR1e59voAI

"Naked Photos of Obese Patient". (July 15, 2015). Retrieved from https://vancouverisland.ctvnews.ca/doctor-who-emailed-naked-photos-of-obese-patient-suspended-fined-1.2482046

National Initiative for Eating Disorders, (2016). *Eating Disorders in Canada*. Retrieved from https://nied.ca/about-eating-disorders-in-canada

NEJM Catalyst (2017). *Patient-Centered Care? Explore the definition, benefits, and examples of patient-centred care*. Retrieved from https://catalyst.nejm.org/doi/full/10.1056/CAT.17.0559

Puhl, R.M. & Heuer, C.A. (2012). The stigma of obesity: A review and update. *Obesity Journal*, 17(5), 941–964. Retrieved from http://www.uconnruddcenter.org/resources/upload/docs/what/bias/WeightBiasStudy.pdf

Silva, S. (2015, September 22). Doctors' pay model needs to change to end "one issue per visit" policy: advocacy group. *Global News*. Retrieved from https://globalnews.ca/news/2232914/doctors-pay-model-needs-to-change-to-end-one-issue-per-visit-policy-advocacy-group/

Strings, S. (2019). *Fearing the Black body: Racial origins of fat phobia*. New York: New York University Press.

Thorne, S. (2008). Scaffolding a study in interpretive description in Beck CT, (Ed.), *Interpretive Description: Qualitative Research for Applied Practice*, (2nd ed.) (pp. 60–79) New York: Routledge

West, L. (2017) The Takeaway: The other f word: The politics of being fat. Retrieved from https://www.wnyc.org/story/other-f-word-politics-being-fatt

White, M., & Epston, D. (1990). *Narrative means to therapeutic ends.* New York: W. W. Norton & Company.

Conclusion

Jeannine Carrière and Catherine Richardson

It is with humility that we thank past and current Indigenous graduate students who contributed to this book of learning. We are grateful for their ancestors who prepared them for this work and ours who keep us focused on our families, communities, and nations. We thank our publishers for their assistance in making this manuscript available to those who are eager to learn about Indigenous ways of knowing and being.

This edition came together with diverse threads, ideas that we have "stitched together." One might say that "stitching" is one of our methodological practices, taking beautiful strands of learning to create a "textile of knowledge and acknowledgement." We acknowledge the stories and life experience that was shared and integrated into these chapters. These stories and ideas are situated in a context of Indigenous epistemology and worldview.

We began with an introductory chapter that laid out the land, the background, and context for the work. Our respective histories of supervision as social work educators are laid out in Chapter One, including our philosophy of mentoring and supporting students. Here, we focus on our particular commitment to supporting Indigenous students and navigating the racial-justice related challenges for these students within institutions that are still rather colonial in nature. This assessment relates to the existing hierarchies, funding mechanisms, educational barriers, and Eurocentric processes, standards of evaluation, and ineptitude in dealing with violence and harassment. Throughout our careers, we have tried to create decolonial "islands of safety" in which Indigenous students might thrive. These could be described as places of cultural safety, "aunty care,"[7] and revolutionary love. In such spaces educators take an interest in the whole person and their experience, not merely academic production. For a more intensive refresher on the multiple barriers for Indigenous people in Canada, the reader may refer to documents such as the *Report on the Royal Commission on Aboriginal Peoples* (1996), the Truth and Reconciliation Commission of Canada reports (2015, 2020, 2021), *Reclaiming Power and Place: The Final Report of the National Inquiry into Missing and Murdered Indigenous Women and Girls* (2019), and the Viens Commission (Government of Quebec, 2019). It is beyond the scope of this chapter to clarify ongoing forms of oppression in Canada. However, it is important to reiterate the dangers of one particular "arm" of the colonial project—the state child welfare system. While a few noticeable developments are noteworthy,[8] the child welfare sector in Canada, and in other former British colonies, remains violent and paramilitaristic (Fast et al., 2021; Richardson, 2016). It is not a system where Indigenous people find much dignity or care, parents particularly and mothers specifically. Indigenous children still undergo forced separation and displacement with removals from family and placements outside of Indigenous communities and culture. Part One of the book addresses some key issues for Indigenous children, youth, and families in this sector.

---

7   And in some cases "uncle care," although Schools of Social Work tend to be woman-dominated.

8   These notable developments include the Nisga'a (in British Columbia) accomplishment in 2000 of moving to child welfare sovereignty in "Nisga'a Final Agreement" (https://www2.gov.bc.ca/assets/download/ec6e13d4cbd542bc97976dc71778f037) in which the Nisga'a people will exercise their authority over child welfare services through their own tribal laws. As well, recent legislation in BC that grants similar authority to Indigenous communities and the transfer of files from the Ministry of Children and Family Development. These are ground-breaking social policy moves.

In Part One "Embedding Child Welfare Research into Indigenous Methodologies," Robert Mahikwa offers the reader a storytelling approach to understanding the experience of Inuit, Métis, and First Nations youth aging out of "care" in Canada. Here, processes of transition are treated through an Indigenous value system with reference to Medicine Wheel teachings. Mahikwa assesses the delivery and implementation of culturally informed supports. This writing relates to the fact that many child welfare systems across Canada have developed guidelines for intervening and interacting with Indigenous children and youth, and even with their parents and caregivers, but these tend to sit on the shelf while practice remains top-down and imposing. Meaningful cultural plans, with instructions for keeping children connected to everything that is meaningful for their growth and development, are seldom developed and implemented. Mahikwa offers approaches that could alleviate some of the current harms and dangers for children in state care. As well, he draws from his Anishinaabe cultural teachings and wisdom shared by Elders and Knowledge Keepers. His work displays a commitment to practice and the implementation of knowledge that supports the "aging out" experience for children in state child welfare systems.

Mahikwa's research provides an example of how research can be used for advocacy and positive social policy change, when implemented. Research can also be empowering for participants and Indigenous communities, largely due to the solidary that is shown—research as an act of care! Working with themes of interconnectedness and relationality, Mahikwa's study demonstrates an ethical approach that aims at making a positive difference in society (Smith, 2019). He concludes his chapter with a reminder to Indigenous researchers that Indigenous, culturally informed methodologies are legitimate, beautiful, and sacred and invites Indigenous students into the world of research, stating *"we need you and we are happy you have arrived"* (p. 40).

Indeed, the inclusion of more Indigenous researchers in universities will serve to contest less respectful research processes that tend to "other" the participants. Many academic researchers today still ignore OCAP principles (Ownership, Control, Access, and Possession) for engaging with

Indigenous people and communities or NAHO's Principles of Ethical Métis Research (explored in Chapter Three by Shelley LaFrance). Indigenous research, when done in alignment with the guidance of the numerous leaders and mentors in the field (Shawn Wilson, Linda Tuhiwai Smith, Michael Hart, Robina Thomas and Jacquie Green, Jeannine Carrière and Cathy Richardson), remains humble, collaborative, transparent, and accountable to Indigenous communities. Indigenous research contests the distance, the individualism, and elitist methods sometimes found in much of mainstream qualitative research. For example, in France today, ethical approvals are not needed as a prerequisite for human services research. There is a modernist assumption at work that the researcher is "expert" and that doing research that "does no harm" is not a priority. Mahikwa's chapter offers food for thought about ethical and caring approaches to research and knowledge creation with Indigenous Peoples, the original caretakers of Turtle Island, the land upon which settler society lives and breathes.

The book then continues its exploration of traditional teachings in Shelley LaFrance's chapter on Métis grandmother knowledge. LaFrance describes how contemporary child welfare practices could be enriched, and dignified, through incorporating the traditional grandmother/kokum teachings and respect-imbued approaches. LaFrance begins with a lament about the continual overrepresentation of Indigenous children in state child welfare despite the plethora of research advising against removal and disconnected practice. We are seeing, increasingly, young ones in care being targeted for sexual exploitation, or being recruited, lured, and kidnapped into various forms of slavery and exploitation. Group homes are sites for predators seeking to monetize Indigenous and disadvantaged youth in violent, criminal activities, including porn and forced prostitution. Stats Canada is gathering more evidence to show that much of the homeless population—those at risk for intense/dangerous drug use, violence, death, and/or suicide—are former children (or disappeared) in care (Dean, personal communication, 2023). Despite years of so-called "trauma-informed care," young people and their mothers are pathologized and conceived as being mentally ill through the lens of PTSD (post-traumatic stress disorder, listed as diagnosis 309.81 in the DSM5) and categorized as "problem people" in society (Strega et al., 2013). The "truck" of colonial mental health is pulled in to further marginalize, pathologize, and discredit Indigenous mothers (2013). Indigenous children are offered a "cradle-to-grave" pathway through multiple institutions, often ending up in prison or mental institutions. Through a method and methodology of storytelling and autoethnography, LaFrance highlights approaches that are important to, and typically neglected in, child welfare practice and that could potentially alleviate some of these social risks. LaFrance's chapter raises the question of why child protection work highlights and acts upon perceived human deficits rather than viewing protectiveness and safety through acts of survivance, resistance, and Indigenous forms of protectiveness. Parenting under siege and surveillance certainly requires a different skill set than middle-class, resourced family child-rearing. Grandmothers can be considered a group of humans who know a lot about resisting, protecting, loving, and enhancing safety, overtly and subversively.

LaFrance holds hope that child protection workers can be allies to Indigenous families—they can be what Patricia Hill Collins (1990) would call "insiders and outsiders" in their positionality. She believes that they, and the systems they work in, can disrupt colonial systems and use traditional, cultural knowledge to inform agency and community responses. I suspect this could include treating families with dignity, kindness, and life-enhancing action. As a case in point, since poverty is a real barrier to family well-being, one that underlies many child removals, social workers could conceptualize poverty as forced impoverishment of people seen as disposable in the colonial, capitalist system. As it stands, families are often blamed for challenges that are derived through systemic injustice and inequality. Social critics Ruth Wilson Gilmore and Kimberly Chiswell discuss the notion of "state abandonment," which certainly applies to Indigenous parents after child removal, and then later to the youth who transition into adulthood with few supports, as mentioned by Mahikwa. LaFrance cites Jean Teillet's words about the six times higher femicide rate for Indigenous women (many of whom are mothers) and how child protection practices often violate Indigenous rights generally, and Métis rights specifically, a lens through which Indigenous women should be granted safety and security. Métis and other Indigenous knowledges point to the upholding of women as sacred givers of life and that their violation is indeed a social and cultural crime even though violence is not depicted in this way in mainstream Canada.

In Canada, one of the broader issues relates to femicide. Perpetrators who harm Indigenous women tend to get away with it, sometimes with the complicity of the state or police.[9] Again, we point to documents such as *Reclaiming Power and Place* and the report on the Viens Commission for more evidence on the statement—that interpersonal violence against Indigenous women exists in a broader context where she is also targeted by epistemic, state, and systemic violence. LaFrance cites Renée Monchalin et al. (2019), who believes that women's knowledge could and should be used to support child welfare practice. Paradoxically, child welfare systems target mothers as the responsible parties for family insecurity (in the face of male violence—see Strega et al., 2013), in a system that is de-gendered and refers generally to parents and parenting over mothering and father-ing. In this context, little space is given to women's analysis or knowledges, and mothers are seen as alienating when trying to plan for safety for their children in the context of male-initiated domestic violence. LaFrance also refers to a Cree Medicine Wheel as a mechanism for intervention planning and promoting child, youth, and family well-being. One point of harsh reflection, in contextualizing LaFrance's work, is that child welfare tends to fail at stopping infanticide. Because they don't have the tools, or even the safety for its workers, the targets tend to be mothers who already feel de-stabilized and deflated rather than the large-scale drug dealers, violent biker gang members, homes with weapons, where the potential to do violence is optimal. One need only turn to any number of reports by the

---

9   The Viens Commission, for example, reports that police have sexually assaulted and mistreated Indigenous women in Quebec. There is similar evidence available in *Reclaiming Power and Place: The Final Report on the National Inquiry into Missing and Murdered Indigenous Women and Girls in Canada.* Many Canadian communities, such as Shawnigan Lake, BC, or Watson Lake, Yukon, have seen police suspended for sexually assaulting local women. Tom Barker's 2020 book *Agressors in Blue: Exposing Police Sexual Misconduct*, published by Pallgrave MacMillan, explores this issue.

British Columbia Representative's Office for Children and Youth, such as the case of Peter Lee or Allan Schoenborn, men who killed their children in the midst of ineffective child protection work. This chapter leaves readers with the question "Is reform possible or do child protection systems need to be dismantled?" The answer probably depends on who you ask and who is benefiting from the current ways. Clearly, the management of Indigenous Peoples, and their suffering, is one of Canada's most lucrative enterprises today.

While much of the contextual analysis here relates to Indigenous women who are mothers, the subsequent chapter by Tanille Johnston examines the role and possibilities when Indigenous Fathers are included in the process. Johnston laments that Indigenous Dads are not given enough support, consideration, and care in child welfare interventions. While in "on the ground" practice, cases of domestic violence may find that Indigenous Fathers need to be accountable when they harm women and their children, the broader view sees these men as also victims of colonialism and patriarchal violence. Johnston aims to present a balanced view on Indigenous men as victims, as well as protective carers. She elaborates on the dearth of services for Indigenous men in a greater context of colonial and state violence against Indigenous men. Programs with a holistic focus may not always been focused enough to promote violence cessation, to undo structural racism in Canada. More on this issue can be ascertained by looking at Brown et al.'s 2009 research on Aboriginal Fathers and why they are overlooked as resources in child protection work. Johnston leaves us considering how to support men while at the same time holding them accountable for harmful behaviour. We can also ponder the role of traditional Indigenous teachings around safety, dignity, and gender roles in the broader context of Canadian society, its laws, rights, and mechanisms for promoting respect and equality. Johnston uses a narrative analysis with Kwakwaka'wakw Fathers to breathe life into her perspectives. The book then moves into Part Two, a study of Indigenous arts-based knowledges and practices.

In Part Two, we experience a creative mixing of arts in research-creation and meaning making. mel lefebvre centres stories by urban Indigiqueers/trans/Two-Spirit people and Indigenous women on practices of decolonization, collective care, and self-care. They discuss how traditional tattooing involves a relationship to our ancestors, a mark filled with intention that Indigenous Peoples wear as expressions of who we were, are, and will be. They discuss self and cultural reclamation, bringing the Indigenous past into the present to bolster the future. lefebvre believes that unapologetic thriving means living our lives our way, coming forward to stand in authenticity. Traditional body markings can show the world who we are as Indigenous people and embolden us to take up our rightful places/spaces on the land, whether that be urban or rural. There is power in these markings. The traditional tattoo revival is growing, with a new generation of Indigenous traditional tattoo practitioners reawakening tattooing practices. lefebvre surmises that the markings are a reminder of how we need to carry ourselves. They help us celebrate our achievements as well as marking challenging moments. They are holistic medicine and methodology that encompass culture, belonging, identity, (re)connection, decolonization, sovereignty, empowerment, gender, transformation, and healing.

In ways similar to lefebvre's work, Shawna Bowler, the author of Chapter Six, explores the topic of urban Indigenous women's experiences of reconnecting with identity through beadwork practices rooted in tradition. Bowler uses the beaded flower medicine bag to depict a beading methodology. This approach can capture and represent the relearning of traditional culture knowledge, remembering, self-expression, and assertion and embodiment. One of her beautiful quotes says, "She becomes the embodiment of the strength, healing, and beauty held within her beadwork" (p. 138). Bowler is interested in how beadwork can be a way to assert self-determination within a social work framework, saying that "bead by bead, we retell our stories and keep these critical contextual pieces alive within our collective memories" (p. 142), exhibiting how beading is a practice of resiliency and resistance. We then move into Chapter Seven, which showcases another Indigenous beader's research journey, this time through the use of portraiture, storytelling, and Kitchen Table methodologies.

Juliet Mackie's chapter, entitled "Reconstituting Indigenous Identities through Portraiture and Storytelling," examines issues of representation for Indigenous women in Montreal. She has selected participants who have moved to Montreal from another place. What these women and Two-Spirit participants have in common is a history of seeing, and experiencing, negative stereotypes of Indigenous women, and Two-Spirit folk, in Canadian society. For example, when an Indigenous woman is killed, typically by a male perpetrator, that women is often cast as a "prostitute" in news reports. The reporting appears to titillate the public with allusions to dangerous places and shady stereotypes of dangerous places (like "the stroll" in Winnipeg) (*see* Razack, 2014). The wholeness of Indigenous women is deliberately omitted in favour of sensationalized, victim-blaming suggestion—surely it's her fault she is harmed if she frequents such places. Of course, such conceptualizations are racist and misogynist, and are documented by MediaSmarts: Canada's Centre for Digital Media Literacy. In an article entitled "Highway of Tears Revisited," journalist Adriana Rolston (2010) documents the media bias against Indigenous victims. Rolston analyzed the coverage of eighteen women who were disappeared on the "Highway of Tears" in northern British Columbia and pointed out many inaccuracies in the reporting, including the race of some of the disappeared. The Native Women's Association of Canada's Sisters in Spirit campaign each year seeks to acknowledge the fullness and wholeness of the disappeared Indigenous women. With a view to exploring self-concept, identity, and the ways in which Indigenous women might see themselves in a racist, colonial society, Mackie discusses self-representation with participants, then paints their portrait according to their specifications and preferences. She then asks the participants to spend time with the painting and reflect on the process of self-consideration and in light of questions such as, Who am I?, What is my culture?, and Can positive representations in portraiture strengthen the sense of the cultural self, dignity, and identity? Mackie develops a Métis/Indigenous portraiture methodology through which identity, belonging, and cultural affiliation can be explored in a research context. The book then moves into Part Three, entitled Indigenous Bodies and Meaning Making.

In Part Three, we find an account of Victoria May's research-creation project *Kiwapamitinaawaaw*. May is descended from a long line of prestigious Métis ancestors who defended Batoche against Canadian invasion in 1885. In Chapter Eight, May integrates Michif language with dance as a method of knowledge creation and embodiment. As both a classical (ballet) and contemporary dancer, her graduate research is comprised of two dance performances and two video installations that focus on learning Michif through oral acquisition. Her aim is to demonstrate the holistic and embodied potential of language learning. This thoughtful chapter takes the reader to a place where language clearly holds more meaning than mere communication. The Michif language in particular lights up a pathway into the Michif worldview, where words and phrases evoke the ancestors and resonate with the cultural synthesis that underscores Métis identity. May articulates her aspirations for her research: "I hope this project will contribute to the body of knowledge around Michif revitalization by showcasing the Michif language, embodying it through dance and oral acquisition, and beginning to repair the fragmentation brought on by historic and ongoing colonial violence" (p. 173). Language embodiment is one of the paths back to culture, alive with so many of the other aspects of Indigenous belonging and being. Another cultural transmission process can be found in Chapter Nine, "Researching through miyo ohpikinâwasowin (Good Child-Rearing)."

Here, Métis researcher Lindsay DuPré brings to light Métis mothering practices in miyo ohpikinâwasowin (good child-rearing). DuPré discusses key aspects of parenting from an Indigenous paradigm based on kindness, honesty, and compassion. Meaning making for DuPré revolves around kinship, including family visits, conversations, witnessing, and stories. As a mother/researcher, she writes that good child-rearing is central to her knowledge system and is rooted in the notion that children are sacred and connected to the earth and creation. As such, children's dignity and respect are upheld, in direct resistance to the systems that broke kinships such as the residential school system and colonialism. DuPré considers the inclusion of her family in her research as part of an Indigenous approach and, as such, "an exercise of relational accountability" (Wilson, 2018).

There are many forms of embodied accountability, and these may include respect for one's own body as the "material container" of spirit and life on Earth. N. Katie Webb's chapter "Fat Bodies in Space" seeks an alternative and better narrative about "bigness" and the body size of a woman. Women of stature have a significant place in Indigenous and tribal cultures. Thinness, while sometimes associated with a particular genetic constitution or committed athleticism, is revered in western culture while sizeable women tend to be "fat shamed." Webb documents these practices and seeks to contest stereotypes about size. The pressures of capitalist, colonial culture often put pressure on women to become thin, which are then manifested as dangerous conditions such as anorexia and bulimia. These practices exist within a larger mainstream pressure for women along the lines of a "beauty myth." Research shows that people who are considered "attractive" in these ways tend to receive more social status, including employment or romantic attention (Wolf, 1991). Webb also brings forth a problematic overgeneralization that says that largeness is always associated with pathology, such as diabetes or heart-disease. She asserts that more contextualization is needed when making meaning of these issues and that it is important to contest "hate talk" and medical fallacies that are not based in reality or science. This chapter promotes a "larger" view of beauty, health and the meaning around bodies and body size. Webb reminds us to contextualize the daily lives and daily stressors for Indigenous women in Turtle Island, including capitalist forces of violence, inequality, food insecurity as well as epigenetic responses to past harms, such as food deprivation and forced starvation in the prison camps for Indigenous children commonly called residential schools. This research problematizes "fatphobia" and "fat-shaming" and seeks to share more knowledge about the importance of Indigenous women, our bodies, our stature, beauty, and contribution to our people.

We then conclude the final stitching with a poem from Métis poet katherena vermette, from *river woman* (2018). katherena vermette originates from the homeland of the Red River Métis in Manitoba, where she writes her powerful stories and poetry. In "an other story" she reminds us that we as Indigenous Peoples have stories that need to be told. These are stories that stem from our blood memory and from the sacrifices that were made by our ancestors for us to remain on these lands. The colonial enterprise was designed to erase us; however, through our survival we have preserved some of our stories for those who are waiting to be born and take their rightful place to replace us when it's time.

All our relations,
Jeannine and Cathy

REFERENCES

Brown, D. W., Anda, R. F., Tiemeier, H., Felitti, V. J., Edwards, V. J., Croft, J. B., & Giles, W. H. (2009). Adverse childhood experiences and the risk of premature mortality. *American Journal of Preventive Medicine*, 37(5), 389–396. https://doi.org/10.1016/j.amepre.2009.06.021

Royal Commission on Aboriginal Peoples (Canada). (1996). *Report of the Royal Commission on Aboriginal Peoples*. Ottawa: Canada Communication Group—Publishing.

Barker, T. (2020). *Aggressors in blue: Exposing police sexual misconduct*. London: Pallgrave MacMillan.

Fast, E., lefebvre, m., Reid, C., Deer, B.W., Swiftwolfe, D., Clark, M., Boldo, V., Mackie, J., Mackie, R. (2021). Restoring our roots: Land-based community by and for Indigenous youth. *International Journal of Indigenous Health*, 16(2). https://doi.org/10.32799/ijih.v16i2.33932

Government of Quebec. (2019). Public Inquiry Commission on relations between Indigenous Peoples and certain public services in Québec: listening, reconciliation and progress (Viens Commission). https://www.cerp.gouv.qc.ca/fileadmin/Fichiers_clients/Rapport/Final_report.pdf

Monchalin, R., Smylie, J., Bourgeois, C., & Firestone, M. (2019). "I would prefer to have my health care provided over a cup of tea any day": Recommendations by urban Métis women to improve access to health and social services in Toronto for the Métis community. *AlterNative: An International Journal of Indigenous Peoples*, 15(3), 217–225. https://doi.org/10.1177/1177180119866515

National Inquiry into Missing and Murdered Indigenous Women and Girls (Canada). (2019). *Reclaiming power and place: The final report of the National Inquiry into Missing and Murdered Indigenous Women and Girls*. https://www.mmiwg-ffada.ca/final-report/.

Razack, S. (2014). Gendered racial violence and spatialized justice: The murder Pamela George. *Canadian Journal of Law and Society*, 15, 91–130. https://doi.org/10.1017/S0829320100006384

Richardson, C. (2016). Creating islands of safety for victims of violence: Critical systems approach. In I. McCarthy & G. Simon (Eds.), *Systemic therapy as transformative practice*. Farnhill, UK: Everything is Connected Press.

Rolston, A. (2010, June 1). Highway of Tears revisited. *Ryerson Review of Journalism*. https://rrj.ca/highway-of-tears-revisited/

Smith, L. T. (2019). Foreword. In J. Archibald, J. Lee-Morgan, & J. De Santolo (Eds.), *Decolonizing research: Indigenous storywork as methodology*. London: Zed Books.

Strega, S., Krane, J., Lapierre, S., Richardson, C., & Carlton, R. (2013). *Failure to protect: Moving beyond gendered responses*. Winnipeg: Fernwood Publishing.

Truth and Reconciliation Commission of Canada. (2015). *Honouring the truth, reconciling for the future: Summary of the final report of the Truth and Reconciliation Commission of Canada*. Winnipeg: Truth and Reconciliation Commission of Canada.

Truth and Reconciliation Commission of Canada. (2019).

Truth and Reconciliation Commission of Canada. (2020).

Vermette, K. (2018). *river woman*. Toronto: House of Anansi Press.

Wilson, S. (2018).

Wolf, N. (1991). *The beauty myth: How images of beauty are used against women*. New York: William Morrow & Co.

Epilogue

AN OTHER STORY

this country has an other story
one that is not his
or hers
or ours

it is written
in water
carved on earth
every stone
a song
that echoes
the erosion
hold one
to your ear
whispers
rise

this country has another story
and it is not his
or hers
or even ours

it is scrolled on wind
painted in blood
every bone
sings
hold them
to your heart
those buried voices
still
rise

—katherena vermette, *river woman*

Contributors

Shawna Bowler is a member of Tatanka Najin (Standing Buffalo Dakota Nation) and an urban Indigenous woman who comes from Red River Métis and European ancestry. She has spent her life living and working as a social worker within urban Winnipeg, on the ancestral lands of the Treaty One Territory and in the heartland of the Métis people.

Jeannine Carrière is Red River Métis from southern Manitoba. She has focused her academic scholarship on Indigenous child and family services. She is currently a professor in the School of Social Work at the University of Victoria.

Lindsay DuPré is a Métis scholar, community organizer, mom, and auntie who was born and raised in Ontario on Haudenosaunee, Anishinaabe, and Wendat territories with her Métis family originally from Red River in Manitoba.

Tanille Johnston, whose Bakwam name is Laqwalaogwa, is Ligwilda'xw from the We Wai Kai Nation belonging to the Cape Mudge Indian Band on Quadra Island, which is off the coast of Vancouver Island near Campbell River. Tanille has been a social worker for over ten years and completed a Master of Social Work with an Indigenous Specialization in December 2019.

Shelley LaFrance is Métis on her father's side with Cree and French ancestry from St. Boniface of the Red River Métis. Her Cree grandmothers came from Green Lake. Her social work practice and research explores how the lived experiences and teachings of Métis enhance social work practices for social workers and community members, as well as organizations and agencies that serve Métis children and families.

mel lefebvre is a Two-Spirit (2S) Red River Métis, nehiyaw, French, and Irish traditional tattoo practitioner. They are a mother, community worker, artist, and PhD student at Concordia University in Montreal.

Juliet Mackie is a member of the BC Métis Nation with Cree, Gwich'in, and English ancestry from the Cowichan Valley on Vancouver Island. She is a painter and beadwork artist with maternal roots in Fort Chipewyan and Red River. She holds a BFA in painting and is currently a PhD student in the Individualized Graduate Program at Concordia University.

Robert Mahikwa holds a Bachelor of Social Work and a Master of Indigenous Social Work from the University of Victoria. They also teach sessionally in the School of Social Work at UVic, as well as Indigenous Studies in the Centre for Indigenous Education and Community Connections at Camosun College. Robert is of mixed settler and Indigenous ancestry comprised of French-Canadian, American, Algonquin (Anishinaabe), Onondaga (Haudenosaunee), and Mi'kmaq peoples. Indigenous research methodologies, Indigenous social work, and Indigenous mentorship are key areas of interest in Robert's scholarly works.

Victoria May is Red River Métis (St. Boniface) who grew up in Prince Albert, Saskatchewan. Victoria is the great-granddaughter of two of the Métis men who fought against Lii Canadas, Jean-Baptiste Delorme and Joseph Vermette. In her research, Victoria seeks to revitalize the Michif language through dance and oral acquisition.

Catherine Richardson is a Métis professor and the director of the Concordia University First Peoples Studies Program. She is a registered clinical counsellor whose research focuses on Indigenous well-being, social service delivery, and recovery from interpersonal and systemic violence.

N. Katie Webb is a Two-Spirit person of Indigenous and settler ancestry and a second generation adoption survivor. Katie brings lived experience to their work, along with a commitment to social justice work and a drive to address systemic inequity and racism within health, education, and social sectors.